Rebellious Women

A Three Continents Book

REBELLIOUS WOMEN

The New Generation
of Female African Novelists

Odile Cazenave

LYNNE
RIENNER
PUBLISHERS

BOULDER
LONDON

Published in French as *Femmes rebelles: naissance d'un nouveau roman africain au féminin*. L'Harmattan, Paris, 1996. Translated by the author.

First published in the United States of America in 2000 by
Lynne Rienner Publishers, Inc.
1800 30th Street, Boulder, Colorado 80301
www.rienner.com

and in the United Kingdom by
Lynne Rienner Publishers, Inc.
3 Henrietta Street, Covent Garden, London WC2E 8LU

Paperback edition published in 2001

Library of Congress Cataloging-in-Publication Data
Cazenave, Odile M. (Odile Marie), 1961–
  [Femmes rebelles. English]
  Rebellious women : the new generation of female African novelists / Odile Cazenave.
      p. cm.
  Includes bibliographical references and index.
  ISBN 0-89410-884-0 (hc. : alk. paper)
  ISBN 0-89410-892-1 (pbk. : alk. paper)
  1. African fiction (French)—Africa, Sub-Saharan—History and criticism. 2. African fiction (French)—Women authors—History and criticism. I. Title.
PQ3984.C3913   2000
843—dc21   99-34821
                                                                CIP

British Cataloguing in Publication Data
A Cataloguing in Publication record for this book
is available from the British Library.

Printed and bound in the United States of America

        The paper used in this publication meets the requirements
  ∞   of the American National Standard for Permanence of
        Paper for Printed Library Materials Z39.48-1984.

      5 4 3 2

To the fond memory of my mother

Contents

Conclusion 239

Acknowledgments

When I wrote the original text, *Femmes rebelles: naissance d'un nouveau roman africain au féminin,* published in 1996 by L'Harmattan, I acknowledged a few people I want to thank again here: I am grateful to Thomas Hale for reading the first draft of *Femmes rebelles* and Mildred Mortimer for her critical suggestions on the ensuing versions. Ken Harrow, Irène d'Almeida, Patricia-Pia Celerier, Francesca Kazan, and Susan Andrade were very helpful with their comments at the meetings of the African Literature Association and African Studies Association. I also restate my gratitude to the Department of Romance Languages at the University of Tennessee for giving me time to concentrate on the French edition.

I would like to further acknowledge some of these colleagues and friends for encouraging me to publish this work in translation, especially Ken Harrow, Charlie Sugnet, and Susan Andrade. I am indebted to Susan for reading the entire manuscript and offering critical comments and useful suggestions. My thanks also go to Jean Hay, who put me in contact with Lynne Rienner Publishers. *Rebellious Women: The New Generation of Female African Novelists* is the result of their encouragement.

I would like to thank Gareth Gollrad for his assistance during the early stages of the translation. My thanks also go to Lynne Rienner's team, especially Bridget Julian and Shena Redmond for their support, and Diane Hess for her queries and patient reading. I would like to thank again the University of Tennessee–Knoxville and Wellesley College for their support and generosity.

Finally, I want to thank Alex, for being an attentive husband and father and for giving me the opportunity to work during what was normally family time, and Andreas, for being understanding of what it means to have an academic mother.

Odile Cazenave

Introduction

The French-language African novel of the 1980s and 1990s expresses general disillusionment with a postcolonial Africa marred by abusive regimes, widespread indecision and corruption, civil wars, intergenerational power struggles, the collapse of the economic system, and hardships within the educational systems. During these years, African women writers declared their growing presence on the literary scene and set out to unveil a different approach to postcolonial questions in their social criticism and their fictional writing, refusing to let themselves be confined by this predominant image of an aimless Africa.

Although certain critical works since the mid-1980s have analyzed the evolution of the African novel written in French, the role of women writers in this movement is still for the most part shrouded in silence. In *Littérature nègre* (1984), Jacques Chevrier classified different types of novels and different phases in the elaboration of novelistic forms in order to identify the tendencies of the contemporary novel. However, he dedicated only two pages to women writers. Although he agrees with André-Patrick Sahel that it is time for women to take charge and speak, he nonetheless concludes that "perhaps it is too soon to speak of a feminine writing" (1981, 153; my translation). In *Nouvelles écritures africaines* (1986), Séwanou Dabla conducted a survey of Francophone African literature from its beginnings in order to follow up with a definition of the characteristics of the novelists of the second generation, which he locates between 1966 and 1983. Dabla identifies the novelty of the "living and original testimony of 'women's words,' made by women themselves, that manage to offset the unilateral vision of African life given by literature" [témoignage vivant et original, des "paroles de femmes" qui viennent, de la part des intéressées elles-mêmes, contrebalancer la vision unilatérale que la littérature donnait de la vie africaine] (18).[1] However, like Chevrier, he did not devote much attention to individual women writers; in fact, he covered

1

only one, Werewere Liking, for her poem-novel *Elle sera de jaspe et de corail: Journal d'une misovire* (1983). These accounts might lead us to believe that women writers have produced nothing important up to this point, or at least nothing that exceeded the principles associated with the novels of the first generation of writers.

More recently, in *Threshholds of Change in African Literature: The Emergence of a Tradition* (1994), Kenneth Harrow examines the conditions presiding over the change from a testimonial literature (typically represented by Laye, *L'enfant noir* [1953]) to a literature of contradiction, ambiguity, and increasing antimimetism. Harrow retraces the evolution in the works of some key authors ("the ironic limits of revolt in Ouloguem," "a literature of oxymoron in Mudimbe," "a neutral point of transition in Soyinka," "a *métissage* in Lopes," etc.). In following this progression, Harrow first attempts to prove that a polyphonic tradition has always existed as heir to a group of different voices (tied not only to Western discourse—Christian, Marxist, colonialist, etc.—but also to Islamic tradition). This tradition has been characterized by the dual presence of the oral and the written word and of the realistic and the fantastic, all testifying to a certain cultural *métissage*. Second, through the "genealogical chart" of authors that he has drawn up, Harrow shows that African literature progressively detached itself from classical realism in order to form a subversive discourse that uses parody and dialogism to play on the nontransparency of reality and a hidden polemic.

Harrow's work includes an analysis of feminine writing; he recognizes the importance of revolt for Ama Ata Aidoo and places the revolutionary quality of Calixthe Beyala's writing on an equal footing with her male compatriots. Nevertheless, only Bessie Head has a whole chapter, "Change in the Margins," devoted to her work.[2] The title is in itself indicative of the peripheral status of women's writing.

In her introduction to *Contemporary African Literature and the Politics of Gender* (1994), Florence Stratton accurately observes that minimal attention is given to women writers in critical analyses of African literature and aptly attributes it to a refusal to consider the question of sex as a relevant analytical category.[3]

> In characterizing African literature, critics have ignored gender as a social and analytic category. Such characterizations operate to exclude women's literary expression as part of African literature. Hence what they define is the male literary tradition. . . . African women writers and their works have been rendered invisible in literary criticism. (1)

The meager critical space allotted to the woman's novel can be explained in part by the fact that its production is even more recent than the relatively new body of literature in which it figures. If we take the origin of the Francophone African novel to mean the beginning of its fully realized self-expression, it can be traced back to the 1980s. The first works appeared at the beginning of the 1970s and could be defined as testimonial literature even though the testimonial qualities of the narration and narrative voice were remarkably different as a result of the sexual difference of the protagonist. In "Private Selves and Public Spaces: Autobiography and the African Woman Writer," Carole Boyce Davies (1990) reflects on this subject and identifies particular aspects of autobiography written by women as opposed to men; one specific characteristic of women's autobiography resides in the fact that "she has long been constructed as publicly silenced" (109). Boyce Davies identifies three fundamental characteristics of feminine autobiography, namely that the very act of writing becomes a political action; that the story of the self becomes a part of the larger frame of familial or cultural history; and, consequently, that autobiography may end up erasing individual history. Notably, Boyce Davies emphasizes another paradox: "Whereas the man who speaks as 'representative of his people' . . . articulates both self and country, the woman's story is never seen as synonymous with the country's" (111). Thus feminine autobiography has been conceived and received differently.

In order to demonstrate this difference, several women critics have attempted to modify the perspective on this mode of writing and to break the silence regarding feminine literary production. Several works of particular importance are *Voix et visages de femmes dans les livres écrits par les femmes en Afrique francophone* (1989) by Madeleine Borgomano; the more recent *Francophone African Women Writers: Destroying the Emptiness of Silence* (1994b) by Irène d'Almeida; and, finally, Sonia Lee's anthology *Les romancières du continent noir* (1994).[4] As the title of her work implies, Borgomano creates both portrayals of and a classification of different types of female characters that appear in Francophone African literature. Her survey, which traverses several genres, includes women writers' works; yet it does not offer any detailed criticism of their different styles. At times it even minimizes the influence of several of these writers. Nevertheless, her work confirms the existence of a body of texts written by African women and the rise of a new feminine discourse. In her anthology of feminine works in Africa, Lee defines the aspects of this world of women, revealing its "paradoxes." In a selection of texts and passages by Francophone and Anglophone writers, she outlines the stages in the development of female writing: from marital conflict, a new self-awareness, and "coming to writing [venue à l'écriture]" to the appearance of "new writings" that show "women in their struggle" against the "instabilities [dérapages] of society." D'Almeida's analysis applies more specifically to the evolution of Francophone[5] African women novelists in their appropriation of speech and, consequently, of writing. She moves from an analysis of testimonial novels and novels of self-revelation to depicitons of the family and the problems that affect women in society.

As for my own work, I would like to call attention to what I have named a new generation of women writers and to examine why and in what sense one can speak of a new feminine novel. Here, my analysis picks up from Dabla and d'Almeida, focusing on the novel from the early 1980s to the mid-1990s by Francophone African women. I will begin by following Harrow's thesis, seeking to establish my own genealogy of women writers while also showing that they are heirs to previous forms in a development that leads to what Kristeva has termed a literature of subversion:[6]

> This is the place where literature opens us onto the possibility of multiple meanings—simultaneously surface, subtextual, supratextual, and metatextual—onto the planes of polysemy. (Harrow 1994, 347)

Within a decade, the voice of women writers became more openly rebellious, directly engaged, and markedly visible in both its themes and expression. Up to the early 1980s, the protagonist had spoken in a biographical or semiautobiographical mode: Speech bore witness to her difficulties, particularly the suffering she experienced as part of a couple, part of a polygamous social structure, and confronted with the issue of sterility.[7] The recording of feminine daily life has allowed women writers to single out various mechanisms of oppression that control women's status. From this point on, what was once considered the private domain passed into the public sphere.

In a second development, feminine speech has become more aggressive, more insistent, within an autorepresentative mode that has become more and more complex. This is the phase that will be the object of my study. More specifically, I examine the mechanism of rebellion that women writers have invented and implemented to replace the earlier works and their autobiographical character.

I believe that this process of rebellion has been infused within a larger systematic provocation, which is itself articulated in two different movements: first through a choice of female protagonists who are marginal in relation to their societies, through the exploration of cultural zones that until recently have been either taboo or dismissed as unimportant, and through reflection on the hidden mechanisms that explain the increasing instabilities of modern Africa; second, through a search for alternatives to sociopolitical questions about a stagnant postcolonial Africa and through the creation of a stable feminine/feminist voice that breaks with canonical masculine authority.

Far from constructing a marginal literature, African women writers have opened a space for discussion that figures prominently in the cultural debate in Francophone Africa. Nevertheless, it is by initially adopting a process of marginalization for their characters that they have managed to find this place in the center of the debate. Through an audacious exploration of forbidden areas such as sexuality, desire, passion, love—but also mother-daughter relations and the questioning of reproduction and obligatory maternity as the qualities defining womanhood—they guaranteed themselves access to areas of language that until only recently had been exclusively the domain of men. Beyond the study of this process, I want to demonstrate how women writers have sparked the development of a new political novel that speaks more directly to its male and female readers, that is visionary in the quality of the message delivered, and that bears the potential of changes that are promising.

At this point, it would be useful to recall briefly the general evolution of African literature in French and the appearance of new African styles of writing as well as the different elements that define "la prise d'écriture" by African women writers.

If we return to Dabla's survey of the African novel from its inception, this stage is characterized by the following elements:

1. the deliberately nostalgic reconstitution of "that Africa," of this world that is collapsing;
2. the rebuttal of colonialist principles affirming that blacks had never "invented anything, created anything, written anything, sculpted or painted anything, sung anything"; and finally
3. the revolt against colonialism, presented through cultural or generational conflict, or as an explicit condemnation, as appears in the novels of Mongo Beti or Sembène Ousmane (Dabla 1986, 13).

Dabla notes a certain stylistic sterility in addition to this thematic unity, a quasi-conformist copying of the French classical model that is followed by a period of silence (particularly in the work of Mongo Beti) and then by a second wind, a writing that is innovative in both style and thematics. This second generation of novelistic works can be defined as follows:

> If in the elaboration of their themes, each of them grants sustained attention to the present situation of the continent and the malaise of African consciences,—they also constitute a place where aesthetic mutations are highlighted in a sort of condensed form. (1986, 21)

These principles appear with force at the core of the works of writers such as Yambo Ouologuem, Valentin Mudimbe, Sony Labou Tansi, and Were-were Liking.

In a parallel movement, the critical works about this feminine writing can be divided into a succession of phases. Until 1980, critics of African literature, most of them male, declared (1) the near absence of African women on the literary scene and (2) the lack of homogeneity in the writing that existed. Several declared that it was high time for women to speak for themselves and to no longer let men do it for them, as their portrayals were not always faithful to reality. To this end, the analysis of Arlette Chemain-Degrange, *Emancipation féminine et roman africain* (1980) offers valuable testimony, as the portraits of the women that she examines almost all come from male writings at a time when any direct feminine voice was still almost entirely absent from the novel.

In fact, the first works by women are primarily reactions against the male representation of woman. This is noted by Bernard Mouralis (1994) in "Une parole autre, Aoua Keita, Mariama Bâ et Awa Thiam," in which he traces the steps of the African woman's appropriation of speech back to its sources. He stresses this point while reminding us that the types of representations of women by male writers confined woman to a sort of ideal role that in many instances was phantasmagorical or phantasmatic.[8] In this respect, both of the authors named in his study represent key moments in the realization of a female voice. Mouralis identifies Keita through her political militancy and her struggle to obtain recognition for woman's participation in political life, stressing African society's resistance to this type of participation.[9] Faced with the limits of recognition for Keita and more generally for a "literature focused on the question of women's political involvement" (Mouralis 1994, 24; my translation), the women writers that follow her return to a more neutral form of writing in the guise of seemingly autobiographical testimony. This is particularly the case in Mariama Bâ's *Une si longue lettre* (So long a letter). On this subject, Mouralis writes:

> The historical and political context is no doubt evoked by a certain number of signs that allow the reader to recognize the country—Senegal—and a period that roughly corresponds to the years from 1950 to 1970. However, in contrast to Aoua Keita, Mariama Bâ assigns only secondary importance to this aspect of the novel, because her primary goal is to describe what a woman's daily life might be for Ramatoulaye, Aïssatou, or her children. (24)

Before this and in an entirely more direct mode, Awa Thiam (1978) had spoken in order to address questions of sexuality and genital mutilation that previously had been ignored. Her *La parole aux négresses* attests to the vigor of her style. In this book based on collected conversations about women's experiences and life in a polygamous social order on the one hand and on genital mutilations on the other, Awa Thiam takes apart these two mechanisms that affect woman for the satisfaction of man alone.[10] As Mouralis concludes, "Awa Thiam's essay has made possible a freedom of tone and writing that one may find in numerous texts published thereafter. Indeed, *La parole aux négresses* broadens the referential field to domains that had too often been passed over in silence until then, either by conservatism or false virtue. It also shows that accounts of daily life play an essential role on women's writing" (1994, 27). Nonetheless, in the following years most women writers limited themselves to writing self-portraits and taking on questions concerning women in their immediate environment and their daily preoccupations. At the end of the 1970s and the beginning of the 1980s, most women writers evoked the difficulties of life within a couple and the difficulties of being a woman and of redefining her role in modern Africa. *Un chant écarlate (Scarlet Song)* (Bâ 1981 [1986]), *Lézou Marie ou les écueils de la vie* (Yaou 1982), *Vies de femmes* (Zanga Tsongo 1983), and *Une vie hypothéquée* (Adiaffi 1984) are all examples.

For the majority of these authors, the vital necessity of speaking out led them to privilege the autobiographical genre and, beyond that, allowed them to justify doing so. *De Tilène au plateau: Une enfance dakaroise* (1975) by Nafissatou Diallo is exemplary in this regard. The foreword is marked at one and the same time by a tone of humility, the avowal that what follows is the testimony of a simple life, and the denial of any extra-ordinary talent or creativity:

> I am not a heroine in a novel, just a simple woman of this country—a mother and a professional (midwife and child care specialist) whose home and job leave her little free time. I began to write several weeks ago. What would a woman who can imagine having neither an overflowing imagination nor any special talent for writing write about? About herself, of course. So, here are my childhood and adolescence as I remember them.
>
> *[Je ne suis pas héroïne de roman mais une femme toute simple de ce pays: une mère de famille et une professionnelle (sage-femme et puéricultrice) à qui sa maison et son métier laissent peu de loisir. . . . Depuis quelques semaines, je me suis mise à écrire. Sur quoi écrirait une femme qui ne prétend ni à une imagination débordante ni à un talent d'écrire singulier? Sur elle-même, bien sûr. Voici donc mon enfance et ma jeunesse telles que je me les rappelle.]*

For another example, one might think of *Une si longue lettre,* which opens in a similar fashion with Ramatoulaye's declaration of her need to write in order to fill the void caused by the death of her husband, Modou:

> Dear Aïssatou,
> I have received your letter. By way of reply, I am beginning this diary, my prop in my distress. Our long association has taught me that confiding in others allays the pain. (Bodé-Thomas 1989, 1)
>
> *[Aïssatou,*
> *J'ai reçu ton mot. En guise de réponse, j'ouvre ce cahier, point d'appui dans mon désarroi: notre longue pratique m'a enseigné que la confidence noie la douleur.]* (Bâ 1980, 7)

Some critics have argued that such devices betrayed a lack of mastery on the part of these women and that they served as a pretext for undertaking a literary project without making aesthetic choices and in the absence of a desire to effectively communicate with one's readers. In *Francophone African Women Writers: Destroying the Emptiness of Silence,* Irène d'Almeida (1994b) defends women writers' choice of these forms by pointing out their complicated structure and development. She demonstrates that these authors have used such forms to level the mechanisms of oppression that govern their status as women, as wives, as mothers and daughters, and to explore the interactions between individuals and their family and society. Considered from this angle, the first semiautobiographical works allowed these women to pass beyond the barriers of silence and the taboo against writing. In fact, they even go so far as to introduce critiques of their societies, and they do so in an indirect manner in order to avoid immediate suppression by publishers or male critics who may have seen only some dangerous audacity. Romuald-Blaise Fonkua, in "Ecritures romanesques féminines: L'art et la loi des pères" summarizes the essential qualities of early feminine writing:

> The will to speak for oneself is expressed in an autobiographical mode, or in the mode of a life story in the feminine. . . . An analysis of dedications, prefaces, openings of the novel, narrative points of view and other beginnings of contemporary texts enables us to bring forth a discourse out of the silence. (1994, 113; my translation)
> Feminine writing is first of all characterized by the creation of women's stories through which they propose to take control of speech in order to recount their lives. . . . It almost always turns around problems of matrimony and the body, love and the couple. (114).

Getting back to the critical assessment of the absence of women writers at the beginning of the 1980s, I should note that for the most part this criticism came from men. It would take at least several years to demonstrate the presence of women writers on the literary scene with the *Bibliography of African Women Writers and Journalists* (Berrian and Broek 1985). This study mentions 913 authors writing in European languages in different genres (fiction, poetry, theater, and journalism). However, the figures reveal a serious disparity between Anglophone and Francophone authors: The latter number only 75 out of the 913; 20 of these were from North Africa, and a third of the output came from only a handful of writers, such as Assia Djebar and Andrée Chédid).

The few studies on the topic of African women writers also deplored the absence of any specific recognizable method common to these few feminine voices. In *Women Writers in Black Africa* (1981), Lloyd Brown stresses precisely this phenomenon of the individuality of each woman writer and concludes that there must be an absence of any common ground among the feminists of the West.

> The point is not that African women necessarily share identical political objectives with each other or with Western feminists. What makes them of special interest to both non-African and African readers at this time is the fact that, despite the differences, they are engaged in a searching critical inquiry into the quality of women's lives, while raising pointed questions about the shortcomings of entrenched social attitudes. (185)

Later works of feminist criticism on black-African literature sought to prove the existence of an African feminism comprising its own specific traits and demanding appropriate critical tools for this purpose. In this respect, with her "Not Spinning on the Axis of Maleness" (1984) and "The Female Writer and Her Commitment" (1987), Molara Ogundipe-Leslie figures prominently as a pioneer in her exploration of the interdependence between women's status and notions of race, sex, class, and family traditions, including those factors resulting from male behavior. She insists in particular on what she defines as the triple task of the woman writer—being engaged as a woman, a writer, and a citizen—not only in one's own country but also in the context of the African continent and the Third World. Carole Boyce Davies and Anne Adams Graves's *Ngambika* (1986) can be considered a cornerstone of feminist criticism of African literature in this respect.

In her "Introduction to Feminist Consciousness and African Literary Criticism" (Boyce Davies and Adams Graves 1986), Boyce Davies focused more specifically on defining African feminism. Her definition functions on two levels: It covers not only African feminism but the canonical principles that should guide an appropriate feminist criticism of African literature. At the time, Boyce Davies wanted to demonstrate that a viable feminist criticism of African literature could exist in its own right and that this criticism was no longer condemned to operate within the norms dictated by traditional masculine Western literary criticism. Among other objectives, Boyce Davies proposed the development of the African canon in an effort to grant women's texts a status comparable to those written by men. She also proposed the examination (or reexamination) of stereotypical portrayals of women (the exhaltation of exotic beauty that typifies the principles of negritude, woman as an image of Mother Africa—either the prostitute and victim of the abuses of European civilization or the plain and fecund woman). Boyce Davies also offers an analysis of the writing and development of a feminine/feminist African aesthetic and, in this context, an examination of women in the oral tradition and an evaluation of the reasons for their exclusion from the literary canon. She thus challenges and encourages women's creativity at the same time. In a somewhat didactic manner, she suggests that women writers concentrate on "appropriate" portrayals of women, warning them of the risks of stereotypical feminine roles. She encourages them to produce feminine/feminist writing on maternity, on the trials of polygamous marriage, on the consequences of colonial heritage, and on the development of a distinct identity.

The first phase of feminine writing responded along these lines. The woman writer had to reestablish a true image of the African woman as seen from the inside, not through the eyes of African or European men. In 1986, Boyce Davies emphasized the relative scarcity of female Francophone production in relation to women's Anglophone literature and concluded by declaring her hope to see Francophone production increase significantly.[11] Then, in not even a decade, Francophone women authors saw their ranks increased by young authors whose writing was willful, combative, and full of a new energy that was typical of their generation. Those same writers no longer limit themselves to a single testimonial work, as Calixthe Beyala, Angèle Rawiri, and Véronique Tadjo demonstrate.

In all of these recent works, the initial principle of empathy and privileged communication in the articulation of the "I" has been retained and refined—by the use of polyphonic narrative voices, by the insertion of one or several designated narratees who may or may not be known by the narrator, by the use of either direct or delayed communication through a network of letters or epistolary fragments, by the creation of new myths or the exploration of old ones, and by renewed recourse to ritual.

In order to respond to the marginalization of women and of women's literature by male critics, women writers started to systematically favor certain kinds of female characters that are typically marginalized in African society. By taking this alternate route, they have created a privileged gaze and a greater space from which to freely express criticism of their society.

For primary texts, I will be using *Un chant écarlate* (1981; English translation, *Scarlet Song*, 1986) by Mariama Bâ; *L'appel des arènes* (1982) by Aminata Sow Fall; *Juletane* (1982; *Juletane*, 1987) by Myriam Warner-Vieyra; *G'amàrakano, au carrefour* (1983) and *Fureurs et cris de femmes* (1989) by Angèle Rawiri; *Le baobab fou* (1983; *The Abandoned Baobab*, 1991) by Ken Bugul; *Elle sera de jaspe et de coral: Journal d'un misovire* (1983) and *L'amour cent-vies* (1988) by Werewere Liking; *La voie du salut suivi du miroir de la vie* (1985) by Aminata Maïgaka; *Etrange héritage* (1985) by Gad Ami; *Sous la cendre, le feu* (1990) by Evelyne Mpoudi Ngolle; *La tache de sang* (1990) by Philomène Bassek; *A vol d'oiseau* (1986) and *Le royaume aveugle* (1990) by Véronique Tadjo; *Une vie de crabe* (1990) by Tanella Boni; and finally, *C'est le soleil qui m'a brûlée* (1987; *The Sun Hath Looked Upon Me*, 1996), *Tu t'appelleras Tanga* (1988; *Your Name Shall Be Tanga*, 1996), *Seul le diable le savait*

(1990), *Le Petit prince de Belleville* (1992; *Loukoum, the Little Prince of Belleville,* 1995), *Maman a un amant* (1993), and *Assèze l'Africaine* (1994) by Calixthe Beyala. Although this list is not exhaustive, it is a selection representative of thematic and narrative strategies used since the mid-1980s by the new generation of women writers. This generation is characterized by its youth as of 1994–1995—most of the women in question are in their thirties—and, perhaps as a consequence, by the forcefulness of its tone. I have also incorporated certain works from the early 1980s primarily because they contained some of the characteristics of the second generation's writing in nascent form. Clearly, through the diversity of their origins (Cameroon, the Ivory Coast, Gabon, Senegal) and beyond their own distinct cultural and religious backgrounds, these authors take Islamic law, the practice of polygamy, and the role of dowry into account when assessing woman's status in marriage, the family, and the community. However, these feminine voices all share the common trait of confirming both the African woman's self-appropriation of speech and writing and the new visibility of the feminine African novel and its determination in treating urgent social questions.

The first part of this work examines the different types of situations and female characters that recur in these texts and the nature and function of such choices. These female characters belong essentially to three different worlds (each the subject of Chapters 1, 2, and 3, respectively): the world of the foreigner (the imposed wife, the white wife, the Antillean wife, or the wife from any ethnic group different from the man's); the world of the female prostitute; and the world of the mad woman. The early works actually enact *une prise de parole* in a way that testifies to the frustrations and sufferings of African women in their public and private lives. These texts remain, apparently, at a level of personal testimony without daring to enter the stage of open rebellion whose unequivocally subversive messages might have provoked publishers to keep doors closed. These women writers made an effort to get their message across by strategically borrowing themes and characters employed by their male colleagues. The white man/white woman, the interracial couple, the prostitute and prostitution, are only a few examples. In both composition and the order of chapters, the organization of this first part of the book therefore relies on characters already present in African literature, such as the prostitute, and others that were created, such as the mad woman.

The character of the white woman is nothing new in African literature. However, the nature and function of this character differ significantly when treated by female as opposed to male writers. For the male writers, this character supports a political critique of colonialism—for instance, in Ousmane Sembène's *O pays, mon beau peuple!* (1957)—or of the current regime and elite classes, as in Mongo Beti's *Les deux mères de Guillaume*

Ismaël Dzewatama, futur cammionneur (1983) and its sequel, *La revanche de Guillaume Ismaël Dzewatama* (1984). In the texts of women writers, the foreigner or the imposed wife paradoxically becomes a symbolic vehicle for the difficulties facing young African women. Through her example and her unhappy experience of the new society she enters, the foreign woman becomes a mouthpiece for the dilemmas and torments that each woman in modern Africa must resolve, demonstrating the need for women to forge relations of solidarity that transcend racial and cultural differences. In addition, women writers start with the quintessential external gaze of the foreign woman and then proceed with a selection of characters from within their own communities, although they are often socially marginalized, as in the cases of the prostitute and the mad woman.

Here too, women writers subvert the literary nature and function of the prostitute; although the character exists within a long literary tradition, she takes on a new appearance. Of course, the female prostitute embodies a voice that is symbolic of woman's condition and her exploitation by man, but in a more radical fashion this voice equally emphasizes her exploitation by the family and even by her mother. Through the character of the prostitute, these authors put their finger on the commodifying nature of human relations in general, on each person's insidious slide toward some form of prostitution as a way of life and the dangers for women of staking anything on appearance.

The third category of woman and madness is the almost exclusive domain of women writers. We might think of Jean-Marie Pinto's *Mémoires d'Emilienne* (1991) as a kind of counterexample. However, its narration reveals that the madness attributed to Emilienne is in fact the product of some machination designed to silence the truth about the racist murder of an African friend that took place in her home. Emilienne stands wrongly accused of having perpetrated the crime during her breakdown. In this particular case, the female character confronts her madness and tames it by writing and recording her thoughts in a journal. Within a harsh accusation against stifling sociocultural practices, speech frees itself in order to express woman's frustration in its full amplitude.

Because these women are marginalized, or because they have marginalized themselves, they find themselves in a paradoxically privileged position that allows them to be introspective and to conduct an elaborate analysis of society. This position also affords them a fresh outlook not only on men but also on women, their parents, and their children. From this point, they grant themselves the means to move forward to a provocative exploration of areas that until now were either declared off limits or dismissed as trivial or marginal.

The second part of this work examines the various orientations of this exploration. I begin by defining the notion of taboos and interdictions. Chapter 4 analyzes the new angle along which parent-child relations have been reconceived, focusing especially on the approach to mother-daughter relations. These relations are examined in the light of theoretical works by Kathryn Allen Rabuzzi, Julia Kristeva, Elisabeth Badinter, and Luce Irigaray. Although Western in origin, these theoretical discourses are pertinent because of their search for keys to understanding universal divisions between the sexes and the importance placed on reproduction and the attribution of the role of mother to woman. The mother-daughter relation falls apart to the extent that it is fraught with tensions, discomforts, rivalries, and ambiguities. The rejection of motherhood, the absence of fathers, and the image of a responsible African fatherhood appear as recurring elements and integral parts of the new family unit: The African woman comes out in revolt against social and familial pressures, and in particular against the excessive power of the mother-in-law and the implicit obligation to bear children.

Chapter 5 examines the inscription of the female body in its diverse manifestations—as a suffering body, as a marketed body, and as a transformed body. The appearance of new semantic fields arising from the domains of sexuality and medicine is proof of women's appropriation of linguistic registers and areas that until only recently were still reserved for men. This chapter also studies new approaches to sexuality and desire that are found mainly in the texts of Beyala, Rawiri, and Tadjo. Because the portrayal of men is an element of considerable importance, I also look at how they are rendered by these same authors (Chapter 6). Women have begun to scrutinize men not only in the public sphere but in more crucial ways in the private sphere. As one would expect, they present the image of an oppressor, of unreliability, and of financial power, but also of man as a fragile being with all his weaknesses, limitations, and newly discovered aspirations, particularly that of establishing a dialogue with his sister. In this analysis, I use the critical works of Elisabeth Badinter: *L'un est l'autre* (1986) and *XY* (1992). The third and final section explores the question of feminine archetypes in writing and the inscription of difference in the light of works by Trinh Minh-ha, Lauretta Ngcobo, Florence Stratton, Hélène Cixous, and Luce Irigaray (Chapter 7). Taking Kristeva's (1980) *Pouvoirs de l'horreur: Essai sur l'abjection* as a point of departure, I focus on the prevalence of violence, abjection, suffering, and horror in women's texts, considering their impact and their therapeutic value within a writing that is cathartic in nature. I concentrate especially on identifying different moments of sadness, situations of violence and horror, that are inscribed upon the feminine body and that exist as integral parts of its environment.

The conclusion summarizes the gains of a new generation of women's writing and defines the contours of what I see as a new political novel in the feminine mode.[12]

Notes

1. In cases where only a French edition has been published, quotations will be given in English followed by the original passage in French.

2. See Ama Ata Aidoo, *No Sweetness Here* (Harlow: Longman, 1979); and Bessie Head, *When Rain Clouds Gather* (New York: Simon and Schuster, 1969) and *The Collector of Treasures* (Hanover, NH, and London: Heinemann, 1977).

3. Stratton cites the following works: *Manichean Aesthetics* (1983) by Jan Mohamed, *An Introduction to the African Novel* (1972) and *The Growth of the African Novel* (1979) by Eustace Palmer, *African Literature: A Critical View* (1977) by David Cook, and *Twelve African Writers* (1980) by Gerald Moore.

4. I should also mention as works of synthesis Elizabeth Mudimbe-Boyi, ed., *Post-Colonial Women's Writing, special issue, L'Esprit Créateur*, 33, no. 2 (Summer 1993b); Elizabeth Mudimbe-Boyi, ed., *Anglophone and Francophone Women's Writing*, special issue, *Callalloo*16 no. 1 (Winter 1993c); and *Nouvelles Ecritures Féminines* and *Femmes d'Ici et d'Ailleurs: Le Monde Post-Colonial*, special issues, *Notre Librairie* 117 and 118 (1994). These different issues specifically attempt to demonstrate, on the one hand, the existence of a prolific discourse about woman by women, and, on the other hand, the participation of these female writers in the postcolonial novel.

5. I will use the terms *Francophone literature (littérature francophone)* and *literature [written] in French (littérature d'expression française)* interchangeably in an effort to free the first term from the ambiguity of the concept of Francophonie and all of the political implications that the designation carries.

6. Harrow bases his characterization of a literature of subversion on Kristeva's definition: "If one grants that every signifying practice is a field of transpositions of various signifying systems (an inter-textuality), one then understands that its 'place' of enunciation and its 'denoted' object are never single, complete, and identical to themselves, but always plural, shattered, capable of being tabulated. In this way polysemy can be seen as the result of a semiotic polyvalence—an adherence to different systems" (Kristeva 1980, 60).

7. By a "semiautobiographical" narrative, I mean any narrative that is primarily autobiographical in character and in which the primary narrative voice, whether autodiagetic (in the first-person singular) or intradiagetic (when the narrating character gravitates around the protagonist) produces a self-portrait and/or is constituted as a witness to reality.

8. On this topic, Mouralis quotes Arlette Chemain-Degrange, who notes the following in *Émancipation féminine et roman africain* (1980): "The feminine image takes root in the fantasies of a man or in the collective unconscious that it reveals: one of aggression, a need for secularization, and difficulties with constructing a personality" (19).

9. In *Voix et visages de femmes* (1989), Madeleine Borgomano expresses the reserved silence that the author places on her private and sentimental life, revealing her complete modesty regarding her personal emotions (concerning her marriage and her divorce). Autobiography in the strict sense of the word gives way to "memoirs" on her political life as a woman and the opposition that she encountered in this role.

10. Although the author still raises the question of the validity of sexual operations, she also questions men's preference for circumcised women.

11. Boyce Davies simultaneously noted the irony in the fact that two of these critical studies dealt with the novels of Mariama Bâ and that in a sense the entire

study was framed in the context of the fame conferred to Bâ with the Noma Prize for *Une si longue lettre* (So long a letter).

12. I would like to offer several more clarifications of my methodological choices. I am clearly writing from an outsider's perspective insofar as I am a non-African. However, perhaps because I have seen myself as a foreigner in a different culture, I believe that I am quite sensitive to the difficulties of interpretation, to the force of unspoken implications, and to intracultural complicity. I believe that this viewpoint also gives me a certain strength and advantage in my desire to understand, to adapt to, and to empathize with another culture. I have tried to respect this attitude and to carry it into my literary work in refraining from any crude application of a Western critical apparatus, and in seeking the concepts that would facilitate my reading of the primary texts in African criticism and in criticism originating in countries of the Third World. This approach does not mean that I have renounced certain points of Western criticism; I have used them where they seemed applicable while justifying their relevance and making an effort to avoid any superfluous jargon.

PART ONE

*Women
in the Margins*

1

The Foreign Woman

I/i can be I or i, you and me both involved. We sometimes includes, other times excludes me. . . . You may stand on the other side of the hill once in a while, but you may also be me, while remaining what you are and what i am not.

— Trinh T. Minh-ha (*Woman, Native, Other*, 90)

It may seem surprising to begin a critical analysis of the new generation of African women writers with a chapter about non-African women, either white or Antillean, or about African women who are foreign to the ethnic community in question. This approach does not stem from a mistake or from what could be thought hasty judgment on my part. It is a conscious choice to proceed in a manner that can account for the chronological development in the selection of characters, which is itself related to the evolution of women's writing. There are abundant analyses that treat the question of madness in the works of Mariama Bâ and Myriam Warner-Vieyra; the question of the foreign woman brings a new perspective to the comparative study of African women writers.

The Foreign Spouse

Mireille, a White Woman
(Mariama Bâ's Un Chant Ecarlate [Scarlet Song])

The theme of the foreign woman or the white woman in the context of interracial marriage is nothing new in itself. Since the late 1950s, this theme has been treated by a number of male authors, for example, by Ousmane Sembène in *O pays, mon beau peuple!* (1957), by Rémy Medou Mvomo in *Mon amour en noir et blanc* (1971), and more recently by Mongo Beti in his two novels *Les deux mères de Guillaume Ismaël Dzewatama, futur camionneur* (1983) and *La revanche de Guillaume Ismaël Dzewatama* (1984). In *Rencontres essentielles* (1969), Thérèse Kuoh-Moukouri has also used a white female character, although she introduces the trope in a

19

new way with two female characters (one African, one French) vying for the same man's affections.

Mariama Bâ makes several innovations. In *Scarlet Song*, she clearly returns to the theme of interracial relations between a white woman and her black husband, the couple living in the husband's country.[1] The novel is typically organized around the opening and the resolution of the conflict that is set off in their respective communities when the two people come together as a couple. This question, however, takes on new interest: Bâ initially focuses on the white woman only to later introduce a black female character, whose increasing importance in the story is achieved at the expense of the white woman. The tension of the struggle between them creates a new dynamic.

I would like to consider the nature and function of the character of the white or foreign wife, and I will pay special attention to the relevance of the author's gender. I will first consider the very notion of the couple both as the choice and the union of two individuals and as the union of two families. "It takes two to build a home [la case se bâtit à deux]," says a Rwandan proverb. So in the case of an interracial marriage, the overlapping of two cultural systems adds a number of parameters that multiply the number of people with a stake in the relationship. The specificity of the two families that are geographically separated, one living in France and the other in Africa, becomes just as much the dual specificity of a black and a white community and gives special importance to the geographical location of the couple and, therefore, also to their displacement to the husband's native land. This particular repartition of groups and of the couple both literally and figuratively places the experience of the white wife in the interracial couple in the literary category of the journey.

The mixed marriage is more of an adventure than others; it is a journey in the sense that the husband returns to his native land, thereby displacing and transferring the white woman to Africa.[2] By its very nature, the journey is a form of change and is therefore a priori favorable to exploration and discovery. Travel is favorable to the discovery of both others and the unknown as well as to the discovery of the self. At the same time, the tropological function of the journey produces or provokes the most possible tension between one character and another or between character and place. It is precisely this system of tensions and the white woman's self-discovery that allow these authors to establish what Hamon defines as the semiological status of a character in the black-African novel.[3]

From the very beginning, *Scarlet Song* shows a consensus of negative reactions on the part of both the black and white communities. There is a strategy here that functions on several levels. People attempt to discourage the husband by pressuring him, either by accusing him of forgetting about his family, of renouncing his mother's love, or of renouncing his African soul and having "whitened" through contact with the West. At other points, people challenge his manly reputation, describing him as having submitted to his spouse and as renouncing the pleasures of other women. The husband is the first to be placed in the line of fire, implicitly threatened with marginalization. His friends especially react with hostility toward his wife. Thus both husband and wife are subjected to constant pressure.

In the white community, the reaction is even more visceral and entirely hostile at all levels of society. Her parents are quick to judge. The mother declares that she is sick and has to stay in bed all day. Mireille is quarantined and shut up in her room. The physical violence of her parents' reaction places everything within a tragic setting: "A resounding blow in her face! She choked on the words she was about to utter. She had just time to see her mother collapse on the floor as she fled out of the room, sobbing loud and desperately, and took refuge in her bedroom" (Bâ 1986, 27). The violence of the reaction allows a discourse with racist implications to appear.

The parents' attitude is one of open refusal. There is a parallel reaction in the black communities. On both sides, the union is resented as a misfortune, a source of shame, and a personal affront. The status of the parents is affected and imperiled in their respective communities. The union between a white woman and a black man is reduced to a physical, sexual exchange. All of the joking and verbal aggression illustrate a refusal on each community's side to see one of its own having sexual relations with a member of the other community. There is also an obvious jealousy in the community that cannot accept the idea of sexual relations between a black man and a white woman, a jealousy which Thérèse Kuoh-Moukouri elucidates in her sociological analysis of interracial relations "Les couples dominos":

> Their racial hostility increases with jealousy, envy, covetousness, and a will to ruin this union that shames their race. . . . The white wife of the Black Man is harassed by other Whites . . . but there is always a White Man who wants to devote himself to "whitening" a woman by having sexual relations with her. (Kuoh-Moukouri 1981, 179; my translation)

The white community thus persists in its ideology of whiteness wherein the marriage between one of its daughters and a black man is still interpreted as a loss of one of its own and as a threat to its integrity. The fruit of the mixed couple's union, a "café-au-lait" child, is thought of as a regression. Once again, the white community persists in reducing the woman to an anthropological value assigned by society: Woman, the source of life, is not a "being with rights [être de droits]" but an object of exchange or some kind of possession of her clan. This viewpoint is the source of the extremist measures taken.

The image of the white woman that emerges from *Scarlet Song* incorporates certain archetypes from colonial and postcolonial literature: The white woman is beautiful, attractive, fascinating. Through successive descriptions of distinctive physical features, the author portrays her as having long silky blond hair, a fair complexion, thin lips, and shapely legs. She appears as a loose and highly sexual woman, arrogant by nature, although also frail and ill equipped to adapt to the African lifestyle. This image is not far from that of the colonial woman described in *Un blanc vu d'Afrique:* "The colonial white woman in the black African novel in French is a more or less stereotyped character. She is often beautiful, blond, well-dressed, and extremely preoccupied with maintaining her youth and beauty. She likes to dress elegantly and does everything to attract the attention of men, if not to seduce them" (Schipper de Leeuw, 165; my translation).Through their focus on one specific point or another, the methods used and the sources of the descriptive gaze (a husband, the people from the community, the narrator) nevertheless allow more of the nuances of this feminine image to be revealed. The character has been classified and identified as a woman and as being of the white race. Her portrayal is the result of a progression in the appropriation of an identity (or, symbolically, in the conquest of a name, of a designation [*dénomination*] other than "her" or "woman"). A limited number of adjectives typifies the description of her physical appearance. Indeed, the adjectives are few, but they are adjectives that implicitly stress the contrast with the traditional beauty of black women.[4] Mireille's distinctive traits are those of the white race; her portrait is sketched out in strokes of contrast (her narrow lips appear alongside thick lips, her light shoulders next to dark ones). The recurrent descriptions of some of Mireille's body parts stress the sexual attraction that Ousmane feels for her. Mireille's image is first that of a dream, a product of the imagination, a memory played over by the mind as it becomes an erotic suggestion. At the onset, love is defined in its essence as anonymous and free of any questions of race or background: "A bare shoulder can bring it to life, . . . a half-turned head . . . a face seen in profile, . . . Here, a man, a woman. Elsewhere, a man, a woman!" (*Scarlet Song*, Bâ 1986, 17).

As in *O pays, mon beau peuple!*, at least in the beginning, Mireille, as a white woman, is regarded unfavorably; she is too strong-willed and too individualistic. This image is similar to the one Schipper de Leeuw depicts in her study of novels of the colonial and early postcolonial period.

> Before coming to Africa she dreamed of this continent of paradise, but once she arrived there, she conformed to the colonial custom of complaining about the African country, its climate and its inhabitants. . . . A petty bourgeoise in her native country, the colonial White Woman feels

superior to the Blacks and calls them derogatory names. She distances herself from them to the extent that she needs them only in order to be served. (1973, 165–166)

The character is not seen as an individual but only as a representative of a community upon which the archetypes of colonization have been projected. She is the "Toubab," distant, haughty, and incapable of adapting to the customs and responsibilities of the African woman. Her individualism threatens to separate the husband from the rest of his family. In *Le roman camerounais d'expression française* (1989), Claire Dehon remarks that contrary to the short descriptions for nonwhite characters, the purpose of which is to allow readers to grasp whatever composes the specificity of the character's soul through his or her body and mind, the white woman is generally the object of longer descriptions that insist on her authoritarianism, her lack of concern for others, and her absurd behavior (as, for example, in *Une vie de boy* [Oyono 1956]). Dehon further observes that when an African man falls in love with a white woman, she is idealized and described as an imaginary person, as, for instance, in *Rencontres essentielles* by Kuoh-Moukouri (1969) and *L'amour en noir et blanc* by Remy Mvodo (1973).

Whatever the novel, this game of antisymmetrical descriptions on the one hand and descriptions consisting in successive details on the other seem to be a distinctive characteristic in the depiction of the white woman. First, the play of successive descriptions is an attempt to bring out two points: (1) the community's reactions can be understood in light of the image of the white woman developed by the author; (2) the character's physical evolution becomes an inscription of her experience, which in the case of Mireille is one of rejection manifested in her physical degeneration and the simultaneous appearance of psychosomatic disturbances.[5] From this point, we can deduce the vital importance of the character's physical and psychological development as a sign of the evolution of her experience of interracial relations and of her being accepted in both the black and white communities. Therefore, as we will soon see, psychosomatic disturbances appear as a constant feature in each of the following cases involving wives who have been imposed on their husbands' families, whether they belong to a different nationality or a different ethnic group.

Juletane: Between Two Identities
(Myriam Warner-Vieyra's Juletane)

Like Mireille's, Juletane's experience can be placed in the category of a journey, as it involves her displacement from France to Africa when she follows her husband, Mamadou. Also as in Mireille's case (Mireille grew up in Senegal), this new land does not represent something entirely un-known; through her Antillean heritage Juletane hopes to reestablish contact with the land of her ancestors. Once in contact with African culture, however, Juletane's character falls apart. She loses her ability to maintain a fixed and stable identity. Although Antillean, she was raised by her god-mother in Paris after the death of her parents, and her godmother is now also dead. So Juletane has been cut off from her origins, removed both from her country and culture and from any source of familial or emotional support. The only culture that can provide her with a common point of reference is France. Like Mireille, she takes refuge in classical music, rejecting the tam-tam and anything cultural that reminds her of Africa.

Moreover, in her relations with others, she is not considered Antillean but a white woman, which is what N'deye derisively nicknames her. She is thus given a status like that of Mireille, the status of a foreigner and of a woman who knows neither how to understand nor how to adapt to the habits and customs of the social group that she has joined. As a white woman and as the spouse of an African man, Mireille is stigmatized from the beginning as a foreigner, an intruder, and someone who cannot manage to adapt. Paradoxically, Juletane is assimilated into the same position: "This homecoming to Africa, the land of my forefathers, I had imagined it in a hundred different ways, and it had become a nightmare. I no longer wondered how Mamadou's family would receive me: I knew I would be an intruder, out of place, lost. . . . And I, I was there, absurdly alone to face them, I was the stranger" (Warner Vieyra 1987, 15). In the eyes of the Africans, and because of the fact that she comes from France, Juletane is associated with the white community in spite of her Antillean ethnicity. This lack of recognition by others is also at the root of the collapse of her personality, as she loses the ability to identify even partially with either group.

As in Mireille's case, her status as a foreigner puts her in the position of an "immigrant," a role of subservience. In her analysis "Framing Marginality: Distinguishing the Textual Politics of the Marginal Voice," Sneja Gunew explores this question of marginality and voicelessness in great detail. She establishes a parallel between the status of marginalized people, women in particular, and that of children.

> Migrants are those whose initial socialization has taken place in a lan-guage and a culture other than the hegemonic one, so that when they enter a new culture, they are repositioned as children negotiating the lan-guage and the entry into the symbolic. (1985, 144)

If such a comparison is relevant, we should stress a key difference in the attitude toward the subject (child/woman) and the treatment it receives:

The child is in a natural learning situation, whereas the (foreign) woman has the learning situation imposed on her. Moreover, she lacks the advantage of the patience or the interest that one grants the child in view of his or her promising potential. Instead, the community rejects the idea of her possible integration and starts out with the notion that she is incapable of learning the cultural traditions of her husband's country.

As in *Scarlet Song,* the antisymmetrical descriptions of the character accentuate the difference between present and former times, either in the form of some physical deterioration or through some sign of psychosomatic disturbances. People compliment her on her long hair and her thin figure, but she looks like a ghost, a shadow of her former self. This deterioration occurs while she consciously attempts to self-destruct: "It seems as if I found nothing and that with time I have become accustomed to living a half life" (Warner-Vieyra 1987, 5).

Her self-portrait in her diary is more than harsh: "I was an *ingénue,* an ignorant yes and foolish girl" (Warner Vieyra 1987, 7). She attributes her relatively late discovery of the world to Mamadou alone. It is through him and with him that she gives herself a reason for being and for being defined as a human being. This self-portrait gives rise to the disappointment that she feels all the more when she believes that her most intimate self has been betrayed. She also identifies with the (religious) sign of bad fate. Her diary presents her through the anonymous forms of forgetting and negation. Her fate is characterized by an absence (of parents, of children, of friends). She is a nonperson insofar as she is lacking all the elements that compose a real personality. She no longer even has a name; "the Madwoman" becomes her only designation. Aside from the traces that are left in her journal, she is bound to be forgotten.

Character Development: Madness and Withdrawal

The experiences of Mireille and Juletane evolve negatively, as each of them sinks deeper and deeper into neurosis and madness. On the one hand, their respective failures derive from the African community's rejection of the foreign wife, whom it deems incapable of adapting to its lifestyle. On the other hand, each character is indeed unable to adapt to the demands placed on the African wife, and each rejects certain elements of the culture that she has entered. Basically, these obstacles fall into three categories: the material, the social, and the cultural.

Material obstacles: Housing and community life. The mixed couple's arrival in the community simultaneously requires living with the extended family for a time. In the case of the interracial couple, however, having to share the African lifestyle and experiencing its limited privacy are strongly resented by the spouse and by Mireille in particular. For her, sharing life as a couple with the family is synonymous with communal life and promiscuity: "She made an effort to get used for the time being to the community life, which upset her" (Bâ 1986, 81). Mireille also interprets the constant presence of her husband's friends as an intrusion. She believes that their attitude smacks of bad manners and parasitism. She cannot understand why they invite themselves over for meals, scorn whatever she prepares, and then, to top it all off, decide that the meal was too sparse and poorly seasoned. In each instance, she feels put to a test. Mireille suffers due to her misunderstanding (and refusal) of this lifestyle in which friends take precedence over the couple's privacy. This suffering leads her to keep to herself. She cuts herself off from the group and thus also from her husband.

As for Juletane, she cuts herself off from all collective life. She refuses to participate in the child Awa's baptism, refuses to join the group for meals, and goes out only to take showers after making sure that no one else is around. Her sickness finally secures her a certain freedom, the freedom of using her time as she sees fit. She does not have to participate in any community tasks and lives apart from everyone else. Her personal space is eventually reduced to the walls of her room and, finally, to the walls of the psychiatric hospital.

Social obstacles: The African mother and the friends. The considerable importance of the African mother's social status can be seen in Yaye Khadi's role in *Scarlet Song*. There is, first, an extremely close tie between mother and son: "Their frequent intimate conversations had woven an understanding between mother and son that made them both happy" (Bâ 1986, 8). The wife's arrival on the scene usually puts this relationship in doubt, although it may also offer the promise of succession, relief, and a certain reassurance regarding the golden years to come: "'There is no doubt,' she declared, 'one of the high points of a woman's life is the choice of her daughter-in-law'" (73). The choice of a white woman, however, destroys this given because it introduces the anomaly of her inability to assume both the role of the daughter-in-law and that primordial role of the African woman as a protector of the traditions of rural life.[6] Along with her role of protector and nurturer, the African woman has the additional responsibilities of being an educator. This explains the mother's fierce hostility toward the white woman who has taken her son away and deprived her of the prerogatives involving the love and complicity that bound her to her son.

Moreover, the white woman represents the real danger of the subversion of traditional values. The second type of portrait, of the African mother, appears relevant in this respect: It is one of the abandoned or frustrated mother, of the maternal taboo that forbids any contact. Moving far away from the mother becomes associated with a rift between cultures and a break with the past. The return to one's country, the period of rediscovery (especially of the mother) should therefore mean that contact has been reestablished and that the love of one's childhood is revived. However, the foreign woman's presence ruins this arrangement. Her presence pressures the husband to choose a different kind of life and forbids maternal love, at least in the form of its original bonding. With her authority, her image, and her love spurned, the African mother becomes a woman again: She will have no peace until the usurper has been chased away, and her son is well aware of it. The hostility displayed toward the white woman is that of rival against rival. Yaye Khadi exploits her rights as a paralyzing and castrating mother. Ousmane crumbles before her power. In fact, he has just come to her defense in a discussion with his wife ("You have to understand. You, you have me" [Il faut comprendre. Toi, tu m'as]) (Bâ 1981, 1986, 125). With these words, he actually signals that he is beginning to miss something, and this is a sign of Yaye Khadi's progress in breaking down her opponent.

In yet another situation, Yaye Khadi rejects the role that she might have played during Mireille's pregnancy. This rejection provokes discontent and a decline in relations with the community. Conducting the mixed child's baptism in secret constitutes a personal offense. Yaye Khadi opts to put her knowledge, her powers, and her prerogatives as a mother-in-law to malicious use against the mixed couple. Thus the mother exercises a major influence over the mixed couple's path in life and over the white woman's development in her African life.

Another influential element here is the role of the husband's friends. For the husband, returning to Africa means rediscovering his friends and resuming a traditional lifestyle. Going out at night with other men is an essential part of this lifestyle. For Mireille and Ousmane, the importance of friends and the nightly outings are instrumental in their inability to get along as a couple. Alongside these first obstacles, we can place a number of cultural factors that are completely opposed to the white woman's culture of origin—most notably the elements of language and religion.

Cultural obstacles: Language, traditions, Islamic religion. Scarlet Song and *Juletane* both focus on a common point: the difficulty that the foreign wife has when she first arrives in communicating with her in-laws because of the language barrier. If Mireille learns her in-laws' language, it is only because she has been pushed into it by her husband; the learning process is laborious and difficult. Juletane finds herself surrounded by numerous smiling faces speaking to her in a language she does not understand. Then, after the shocking revelation of a second wife's existence, she shuts herself up within her pain except for when she leaves her room to eat with Awa and N'deye, her two cowives, with whom she refuses to speak.

By their refusal to learn the new language, these two women fatally cut themselves off from the community. The impossibility of speaking the maternal language impedes or even completely prevents any communication with the in-laws, the eventual cowives, friends, and the people in the village, in the street, and in the market. This isolation positions the wife as a complete *foreigner*. The husband's explaining African ideas to her in French presents a number of difficulties as well, particularly because the translated concept is represented as existing within the original system of values and, therefore, is loaded with connotations that can impede its being understood.

The African husband's initial task is to help his wife understand the import of the words he is using and the matters they convey and thus help her decode the new reality that surrounds her. The husband's attitude is thus a predominant factor that will predispose his wife to a positive or negative experience of Africa. As a result of a failure to decode African realities for Mireille—especially the importance of the family, of friends, and of traditions—these same realities become daunting obstacles in her efforts to adapt. Because Mamadou fails to understand what his departure for the village means to Juletane, he cannot grasp the suffering he has caused. Overall, a lack of communication is the basis for the other sociocultural obstacles.

The concepts of family, language, and tradition are closely bound together. Traditions such as marriages, baptisms, and funerals occupy an important place in the African family structure. However, through the marital connection to what is foreign, the mixed couple is represented as depriving the family of a celebration; it therefore opposes tradition from the beginning. People expect the couple to make up for their slip by participating in other traditions, for instance, by attending a prayer ceremony, as Ousmane does; by properly celebrating every other festival to come; or by making small gestures displaying their attachment to the African community. Thus Ousmane and Ouleymatou's wedding ceremony and the baptism of their child make up for his marriage with Mireille and the baptism of the mixed-race child.

Faced with these many ceremonies, Mireille becomes stubborn and adopts a deliberately hostile position to the point of becoming irritated at the very sound of the tam-tam and interpreting these traditions in a racist way. She perceives the ceremonies as nothing more than noisy, vulgar, and primitive rejoicing. By adopting this position, she irrevocably closes herself off from from African life and society. In a similar fashion, Juletane shuts herself up in her room on the pretext of having headaches in order to avoid attending the baptism of Awa and Mamadou's first child. Juletane also refuses to participate in the funerals for Awa's children, this time because she has already cried too many tears over her own situation and the fact that she cannot be with Mamadou.

The religious element affects character development in a decisive fashion because it is not simply a choice for the spouse but an obligation.[7] Ousmane's Islamic family run their lives according to religious faith. The arrival of a white woman puts the principles of their daily lives in question even though she does not practice her religion. The family cannot renounce its religious practices any more than it can stand seeing one of its own turn her back on God. Satisfying the religious principle is therefore a sine qua non condition. In the case of Mireille and Ousmane, the husband signals his inflexibility on any religious matter: "Ousmane, uncompromising, relentlessly pursued Mireille to see that she carried out her religious duties correctly" (Bâ 1986, 84). The physical and moral image of the white woman assumes its full power here. Through her eroticized physical appearance and her willful and determined temperament that spurs her desire to change everything, she displays an individualism that is too strong for the good of the community. By projecting this image, she creates problems to the extent that she opposes the conception that the community has of woman's proper identity and social role. In *La femme dans l'inconscient musulman* (1986), Fatna Aït Sabbah offers precious testimony on this matter by discussing "the profile of the woman that a Muslim man should avoid at any price as a wife: the *chadaqa,* the woman who talks a lot." She specifically addresses the criteria involved in choosing a wife:

> Why would silence and immobility be the only criteria in choosing a wife and the primary qualities of the Muslim woman in general? (9; my translation)

The first point to be made here is that the white woman possesses none of the qualities of the ideal spouse. In fact, she seems to differ systematically from this definition in every sense and thus breaks the established balance between the sexes. A second factor of dissidence within the religious discourse—and thus with the well-being of the entire community—is the white woman's paid work outside the home. By having an existence outside the home, she establishes a new relation to time and space. Most of all, she challenges an economically specific relation that is at the base of relations between the sexes:

> Men have authority over women. Because of the expenses that they make in order to assure their upkeep.
>
> *[Les hommes ont autorité sur les femmes. A cause des dépenses qu'ils font pour assurer leur entretien.]* (*Le Coran,* trans. Masson, sourate 4, verse 34, Paris: Gallimard, 1967)

Mireille disturbs the traditional balance by virtue of her economic independence. The white woman represents an excess. The hierarchical relation within the couple seems to be destabilized, if not inverted. In the eyes of the community, it is she alone who would be the master of the house.

Another obstacle confronting the white woman is marriage within a polygamous arrangement. Ousmane takes a second wife, Ouleymatou. When Mireille learns this, it provokes a definitive break in their life as a couple and ultimately plunges her into madness. The African community has favored the polygamous arrangement precisely because it is aware that this construction will wear down the foreign woman's resistance; its very nature opposes her conception of marriage and life as a couple.

> In effect, polygamy creates an affective distance between a wife and her husband that does not favor the man's capacity for moral domination. In fact, what matters the most are the force relations that exist within the couple. (Sabbah 1986, 291)

It is clear that the relationship of the first couple has been pressured to the benefit of the second relationship initiated by the husband. Together with the white woman's character, these last two elements play a decisive role in the negative evolution of the interracial relationship.

In Juletane's case, the revelation of the polygamous arrangement surfaces when she is on the boat leaving for Africa, still full of her newfound joy. This news and the feeling of having been betrayed definitively destroy something inside her. She has been tricked about the most precious thing that she possessed, her exclusive love for Mamadou. Although Awa, the first cowife, receives her with kindness and later becomes the only person to take care of her, Juletane refuses any compromise. She is unable to accept the idea of sharing a husband. From the onset, she expresses tremendous hostility toward N'deye, the third wife, finally throwing a pot of boiling oil on her.

The other trials the young African wife has to face are only exacerbated when she is confronted with cultural, religious, and traditional obligations toward her in-laws, especially her mother-in-law and eventually her cospouses. Through the lens of the internal and external gaze concentrated on the foreign woman, the new wife's choices are problematized (especially her decision about whether to pursue studies and whether to pursue a professional career); the critique is taken to another level. In fact, in the novels that follow, one finds practically the same themes and the same difficulties (differences in language, cuisine, customs, traditions, religions, etc.). These novels center on a female character who is African but persona non grata because she is from another region or a different social or ethnic group and therefore subjected to her in-laws' hostility.

The Imposed Wife

In *Fureurs et cris de femmes,* Angèle Rawiri returns to the traditional theme of familial reaction to the announcement of a marriage that has been freely chosen between two individuals without consulting the maternal or paternal authority. Due to ethnic or social considerations (belonging to a different social group), the wife is considered to have been imposed on the family. The families of sons and daughters react in the same way. The marriage takes place against their will because it contradicts the voice of reason and tradition. Emilienne's determination parallels Mireille's in *Scarlet Song:* Emilienne pays no heed to her mother-in-law's reaction. Joseph's contrite silence and his need to reassure his mother about his filial love also parallel Ousmane's response to the situation. Once more, the background material presents nothing new; we have a story about the hostility and traditional opposition of two families to an interethnic marriage.

The mother's opposition in *Fureurs et cris de femmes* is particularly strong. As in *Scarlet Song,* she engages in a game of aggression and attrition against Emilienne. A claim about the daughter-in-law's sterility is the typical argument of choice. The mother favors the son's liaisons with other women and throws her support behind the mistress of the day by encouraging the son to take her as a second wife. Later on, it is she again who rushes her son to obtain a divorce.

The death of Emilienne and Joseph's daughter Rékia introduces a new element into the couple's relationship, since she was the only thing still keeping them together. In this couple in distress, each person suffers separately without supporting the other, even though the husband is aware of his wife's pain. Because of this awareness, he spares his wife the additional pain that he would cause by separating from her. Against his mother's will, Joseph displays a desire, albeit a weak one, to rebuild the couple, and he makes an effort to bring this about. He reminds Emilienne of the possibilities for his professional success and their future together. However, their dialogue is still stunted; Emilienne refuses to hear him out and will not believe that he is sincere. When she finally lends an attentive ear to his concerns, he turns away and becomes disinterested. Point by point, this scene refers us back to one that occurs between Ousmane and Mireille: Ousmane becomes dejected upon realizing that Mireille does not pay attention when he speaks of his childhood, his initiation, and what traditional music means to him.

Rawiri introduces a new aspect to this dynamic by adding differences in social status to the ethnic difference that provokes familial resistance. This time it is the woman who has a social status superior to her husband's. In this situation, he discovers his need for a woman who will be entirely submissive to him, in financial as well as other matters. We already found this element in a more basic form in *Scarlet Song*, when the in-laws took offense to Mireille's taking a professional position and, in doing so, let it be known that she would run her household as she saw fit. In this case, however, she did not hold a job that was better paid than her husband's. The important point here is precisely that Emilienne benefits from having professional status and regular pay that are clearly superior to Joseph's. Like Ousmane, who wanted to fall back on a simple traditional woman, Joseph takes a woman with little education as his mistress.[8] Thus the novel explores the lack of emotion and love that is experienced by the protagonist while recording whatever constitutes the couple's life and its happy and unhappy phases.

The truly original element in the novel is the introduction of a lesbian relationship between Emilienne and her secretary, Dominique. In the course of this relationship, they discover their own bodies as well as whatever was missing in their sexual and emotional lives. Although she has re-conquered an important part of life (she begins to take care of her body, looks younger, and pleases her husband again), Emilienne is ashamed of this lesbian relationship. As soon as she regains her husband's love and her own well-being, she is quick to dump her secretary. Lesbian love is presented as a dead-end, since the liaison is shown only in its relations to social taboos and mechanisms.[9] In effect, the relationship is depicted as nothing more than the result of manipulation. The secretary turns out to be Joseph's mistress, the one who was supposed to become his second wife. She had been pushed by Joseph's mother to approach Emilienne and befriend her in order to keep her under their surveillance and influence. In the hope of making Joseph revoke his decision to reconcile with his wife, Dominique records a conversation with Emilienne in which she announces her decision to end things with her husband. Dominique plays the conversation back to the husband, hoping to hurt him and to make him pay for her silence by marrying her; he categorically refuses, dismissing her on the spot.

If such a denouement seems somewhat artificial, the fact remains that the mother-in-law's approval of the two women's relationship is still the supporting frame of the plot. Her hostility toward her daughter-in-law reaches a high point when they exchange blows and threats that lead to the mother-in law's attempt to kill Emilienne's dog. Rawiri renews this theme of conflict by intensifying the hostilities between mother-in-law and daughter-in-law; moreover, she gives it a new twist because the denouement does not signal Emilienne's failure but that of her mother-in-law and husband instead. Both are ordered to leave her house, and this occurs when Emilienne is finally pregnant. According to tradition, her pregnancy means that she has returned to normal. By freeing herself from her shell of a husband, the protagonist reveals a new path for the Francophone African woman such as can be found in the works of Anglophone women writers (for example, Flora Nwapa's *One Is Enough* [1992] and *Women Are Different* [1986]). Rather than put up with an unhappy marriage and suffer her husband's infidelities and her mother-in-law's rebuffs, the young woman opts for a new beginning, alone and without marital constraints, a new life in which she can be committed to her own professional development.

Evelyne Mpoudi Ngolle, in *Sous la cendre, le feu* adopts a similar structure. Her story revolves around the hostility of the family of in-laws (here expressed in the person of the husband's sister) for reasons of ethnic and religious differences: The husband, Djibril, is from northern Cameroon, which for other ethnic groups is synonymous with conservatism, especially in the matter of conjugal relations; the wife, Mina, is a nonconformist who intends to continue her studies after the child is born and leave the child's care to the father.

Two new elements have been added to this basic structure: the protagonist's madness, which does not develop in the course of the work but which explodes at the very beginning, and the appearance of a first child, a daughter, Fanny. Fanny is not Djibril's child, a fact that he knows and accepts. This child is the joy of the family, especially for the father, and serves as a catalyst for the protagonist's madness. In her efforts to remember certain events, a contradiction develops between Djibril's public face and his inner character, displayed in contact with Mina. Since Mina is "sick," feels as if she is being persecuted, people think that she is making up things. On the surface, Djibril appears to be very caring toward his wife and seems to suffer because this illness afflicts her. Based on an alternation of therapeutic dialogues with the doctor and internal monologues that convey a sense of Mina's life and their first times together as a couple, the story moves forward to its climax when Mina's memory resurfaces and the truth breaks free: Fanny was sexually abused by Djibril.

Then it is the father's turn to make his confessions: He was acting under pressure from a fetishist who requested that he introduce him to a prepubescent girl in his family. He allowed this to happen because he was being blackmailed by Jo, Fanny's biological father, who threatened to take his wife and daughter back if he were not paid hush money for his silence. Djibril admits the causes of his gradual emotional distancing. He has suffered from constant teasing by his friends and his sister, who tried to wound his pride by pointing out that he had to change the children's diapers and feed them while his wife studied at the university. They made fun of him because he seemed to renounce the traditional virility expected of a man.

Once again, pressure from friends and family play a damaging role, even though Djibril had expressed his desire for a marital relation based on exchange and a sharing of work, including domestic and parental tasks.

This novel thus explores the difficulties facing young couples today in their quest to strike a difficult balance between their own convictions and familial pressures to respect traditions that generally imply a strict division of men's and women's roles. In a sharp reversal, the denouement signals a new beginning, as the entire family has recourse to tradition in the form of a collective ceremony with a cathartic purpose. Happiness is still possible, since love has been declared stronger than tradition and stronger than the male pride that has been challenged.

The Ideological Function of the Character

Through her use of the character of the white woman in *Scarlet Song*, Mariama Bâ returns to the basic message that can be found in *Rencontres essentielles* but gives it a more political twist. It is through Ousmane's voice that the entire political program of negritude reappears. Ousmane actually denounces African men who have denied their roots in order to adopt the lifestyles of their European wives.

> The man was out-and-out Europeanised. Mercilessly cut from his origins. "Wretched puppets!" Ousmane grumbled. There was nothing of the African left to them except their skin. . . . When the children of these marriages grew up they would become the harshest and most contemptuous racists. "This cross-breeding impoverishes Africa," thought Ousmane. (1986, 122)

Ousmane puts himself on trial as well and accuses himself of having denied his own identity; he was "smitten" for a time:

> Mireille? He admitted to himself that he had been drawn to her by the need to assert himself, to rise intellectually and socially. The European woman's qualities . . . her spellbinding beauty . . . the attraction of the unknown, a taste for originality . . . all these strengthened the links that bound us! (Bâ 1986, 123)

We must not mistake here the content of the actual message. Mariama Bâ has no intention of condemning mixed couples; on the contrary, in *Scarlet Song*, Lamine and his white wife form a happy couple and provide a counterexample of interracial marriage. However, considering the problems that she puts into play, Bâ stresses the danger of a negritude that would, for example, have Ousmane say no to the love of the other in order to preserve his own identity. It is precisely because he has not succeeded in finding balance within himself and has not been able to resolve his personal racial conflict that Ousmane remains "a prisoner of History" (Fanon 1952,

187). He is someone who "for fear of being considered a poor parent, an adopted son, a bastard reject, he attempts from now on, however weakly, to discover a black civilization" (186; my translation).

Thus Mariama Bâ emphasizes the danger of the black man's failure to find his own identity, a failure that leads to copying the white man. In a similar fashion, Mireille runs into failure when she refuses to acknowledge difference without having first questioned her own racial prejudices. The novel reveals the main source of misunderstandings within the interracial couple—the condition that arises when one member of the couple fails to come to terms with the racist prejudices that his or her own ethnic group projects on the other or, equally, when a man who has lived for a time according to European customs makes his white wife feel betrayed when he returns to the ways of his traditional milieu.

When we bear this initial message in mind, the question of the author's gender allows us to refine our interpretation. By creating black female characters who attempt to replace the foreign wife in the black man's heart (for example, Flo in *Rencontres essentielles* and Ouleymatou in *Scarlet Song*) and through the foreign wife's failure, female authors such as Mariama Bâ and Thérèse Kuoh-Moukouri articulate a problem that is unique to the black woman. The primary themes of the interracial couple and of the white woman's assimilation become reflections on the question of love in general and an account of couples' situation in the current African context.

Mariama Bâ goes even further in this dual task of making the African woman conscious of her own individual worth and of making clear to the reader the problems that face African women today. Bâ's efforts with *Scarlet Song* to represent woman's experiences center around two main characters, one of whom (Ouleymatou) becomes dominant at the expense of the other (Mireille); Ouleymatou's increased importance simultaneously signifies the other's failure. By opposing these two characters (Mireille, a well-educated white woman from an advantaged social class, and Ouleymatou, a black woman from a modest background with relatively little education), Mariama Bâ provides the means to make her reader sensitive to the array of problems that African women face. She shows that Mireille's failure is not caused so much by her color as by the fact that conditions for women are difficult in themselves. The narrator assumes the role of an alternative leader for the community, and this is a key role within the novel's structure. The narrator takes control of the discourse in order to force the reader to confront his or her part in perpetuating bigotry. If Mireille encounters so many difficulties, it is definitely because community members have banded together in order to ensure the failure of the interracial experience. However, this failure is primarily the result of the overall difficulties of women's lives in Africa, particularly in view of the political-cultural

goal of affirming a modern Africa while taking care to preserve its traditional heritage. Due to her symbolic role as mother and protector of
knowledge and tradition, the African woman finds herself at a critical
juncture in choosing her path. Her choice is one of either struggling for her
own emancipation at the risk of seeming like a traitor to the African cause
or of accepting the political goals at hand, goals that obviously have been
selected and determined by men. In pursuing this dilemma, Mariama Bâ
has managed to take the problems and conditions of African women into
account. Two of these are the generational conflict caused by the African
family's strong attachment to its children but also by the privileges of the
mother-in-law and the country's overall emancipation occurring through a
return to origins and traditions that the African woman is supposed to embody and protect.

In *Scarlet Song* (Bâ 1986), the empathy shown Mireille by the narrator and by Soukeyna, Ousmane's sister, is an empathy born of sex, not
race. In *Le deuxième sexe,* Simone de Beauvoir declared that until then
there had been no real solidarity among women. The bourgeois female
adopted the cause of the bourgeois male before taking the side of the
woman worker; the white woman adopted the cause of the white man before that of the black woman. Mariama Bâ depicts aspirations common to
all women, white or black. She takes into account problems that are specifically related to the condition of African women but also considers global
perspectives, creating a woman's point of view directed at other women, as
in the case of Madame de la Vallée, Mireille's mother. Mireille's mother
has been reduced to playing the role of a puppet. Ousmane's expectations
of Mireille are no different from Monsieur de la Vallée's attitude toward
his wife.

Although *Scarlet Song* begins as the story of an interracial relationship focused on two individuals, it becomes a reflection on African marriage and, by extension, marriage in general. For Mariama Bâ, the question
of the woman's choice is fundamental. In "Marriage, Tradition and
Woman's Pursuit of Happiness in the Novels of Mariama Bâ," Edris Makward (1986) explains Bâ's approach: She centers the novel on a couple
considered a single unit formed by a man and a woman who have chosen
one another freely. Since the idea of choice is prevalent, the author depicts
woman in a new way that is more faithful to reality.[10]

Following the example of Awa Thiam, who in *La parole aux Négresses* insisted that "Les Négresses" reestablish the truth, Mariama Bâ has
proven that women can mediate their own problems and, on their own,
correct the stereotypical image of the African wife-mother that has been
perpetrated too often in African novels. A final call arises from the novel.
It is neither a personal cry of lament nor a tragic chorus but a "cri de vie"
[cry of life]" (Groult 1975, 228). It is the cry of the African woman in

search of her own voice and path *(voix/voie)*.[11] It is in this way that *Scarlet Song* inaugurates a new phase in which a clear position is adopted by women writers as they open up to a rebellious form of writing.

With Juletane's character, Myriam Warner-Vieyra examines the Antillean woman's identity in the presence of two cultural universes, neither of which are truly her own. In that respect, *Juletane* can be grouped with other novels based on journey and exile as points of departure in search of the protagonists' roots (for example, Ken Bugul's *Le baobab fou [The Abandoned Baobab]*). Juletane indirectly illustrates the illusion of searching for a collective historical past through a return to Africa, an experience marked by failure.[12]

Echoing Mariama Bâ, Warner-Vieyra takes the many demands made on the African wife into account, particularly in regard to their restrictive effects on woman's individual emancipation. Through her refusal of the two cowives, Awa and N'deye, Juletane articulates her symbolic refusal of the two paths offered to the African woman. In Awa, she rejects the devoted wife for whom polygamous marriage is the only conceivable reality—the woman surrounded by children or kneeling and praying on her carpet. In N'deye, she rejects the coquettish woman in search of financial support, greedy for jewels, capricious, and proud of her privileges as the newest wife (on this theme, see Ngate 1986).

In Rawiri's *Fureurs et cris de femmes,* Emilienne and Mina offer variants on the character of the foreign woman, the stranger. Like others (Mireille, Juletane), they encounter the difficulties of integration into the African community. The only discernible difference arises in the definition of the group. The hostility that breaks out in the case of the imposed wife is limited to the family and close friends (the parents' or the husband's). Rejection of the wife arises because she has been imposed by the husband—the community has not been given the opportunity to make its own choice—and especially because the wife is different from her cosisters in her determination to lead a nontraditional marital life. In other words, the wife construes the couple as a pair rather than within the normative framework of the collectivity. She refuses to conceive of her identity as a woman as strictly circumscribed by the roles of mother and wife; she also wants professional development and, indirectly, the opportunity "to share in power [participer au pouvoir]" (Cornaton 1990, 40). The community perceives her choices as a threat to its traditional equilibrium and is increasingly hostile.[13] In fact, the imposed wife who is on the "wrong path" becomes excluded and estranged from her husband's community; as a result, she is also estranged from her own family because of the shame she brings on them.

The evolution of the imposed wife is similar to that of the foreign wife; that is, both are marked by negative physical and psychological changes. In both cases, the same kind of psychosomatic troubles develop: loss of appetite, severe weight loss, self-destructiveness, depression, fatigue, insomnia, nightmares, and the impossibility of communicating with the other. The character of the "foreign" woman (whether of a different race, ethnic group, or culture) by nature occupies the privileged position of an internal and external observer at the intersection of two philosophical and cultural systems. By using this character, women authors can undertake a detailed critique of society and its conceptions of woman's status as wife, daughter-in-law, and mother. The figure of the foreign woman (in both the specific and the general sense) therefore enables such a step, legitimizes speech that is critical of societal standards, and opens the way for the contestation of traditional roles.

Through a situational marginalization of race, culture, and sex, the character assumes a new corporeal status *(un nouveau corps statuel)*. The character associated with a nonnormative group is thus both individualized by being placed at the margins of a group identity and made generic in being perceived as attached to a collectivity (even if a marginal one).

On another level, this type of phenomenon reflects a general tendency in literature of the 1980s. I am thinking of the replacement of the traditional key concept of the African's alienation in contact with Western societies with the more ambiguous and more subtle concept of marginalization. It is through the marginalization of situation, race, culture, or sex that the character's body attains a new status.

It is important to equally emphasize men's attempts in discourse and in practice to stifle woman's ability to speak out and, consequently, to hold power. This repression is carried out with a combination of techniques and strategies, in particular, violence, humiliation, and marginalization. But marginalization is a double-edged sword. The women writers considered here have listened to male voices and have used the same strategies, but they have subverted them and endowed them with a new value. The choice of marginal characters such as the foreign woman, the prostitute, and the mad woman are the result of this revolutionary spirit.

Notes

1. In an interview with the American anthropologist Harrell-Bond, Mariama Bâ explains that she is interested in choosing only an interracial relationship in which the woman is white and the man is black, rather than the opposite, because it is equally shocking from both the mother's and society's point of view. The case I present here, which is generally more common, is the subject of more typical problems. In effect, making the relationship official is more frequent when the woman is white and the man black. The meeting has taken place in her native country, when he was a student. After completing his studies, he decides to return home with his new spouse. The marriage has already taken place (either for this

occasion or previously, after they had lived together for a certain period of time). In the opposite case of a white man and a black woman, the context is usually that the man has been called on to work in an African country for a period of months or years. The temporary nature of his stay makes any potential relation with a black woman rather temporary: there may be a relationship, but no lasting existence as a couple. Nevertheless, the officialization of the interracial relationship gives rise to conflict and tensions, playing a major role in the black or white community's attitude to the couple. The conflict takes on different aspects depending on whether it is the man or the woman who is white.

2. The couple either arrives together or the spouse's arrival is deferred; her husband precedes her in order to prepare their move and facilitate his wife's reception by his family.

3. In his article "Pour un statut sémiologique du personnage," Philippe Hamon shows that a postulate like this presupposes the preliminary choice of a "point of view" that constructs this object by integrating it into the message that is itself defined as a form of communication composed of linguistic signs (instead of accepting it as a given within a critical tradition and a culture centered on the notion of the human "person") (1977, 117).

4. One can find the same kind of image in *O pays, mon beau peuple!* The image appears again in the description of the rape scene when Isabelle's clothes are torn, letting her "sun-*coppered* and wind-polished skin appear along with her *rounded* breasts" (Sembène 1957, 114; my translation). The terms used here make the desirability of her body clear and likewise underline the jealous and aggressive reactions of the white community.

5. In the novels *O pays, mon beau peuple!* (Sembène 1957) and *Les deux mères de Guillaume Ismaël Dzewatama* (Beti 1983), the evolutions of Isabelle and Marie-Pierre accentuate their Africanization, which is made evident in their habits of dress, their tanned complexions, and their adoption of certain customs.

6. In *Emancipation féminine et roman africain*, Arlette Chemain-Degrange (1980) emphasizes the overdevelopment of the maternal image in black-African novels: "The cult of the mother or of a woman who replaces her is a constant feature of Francophone African literature. . . . In these novels, the growth of this image has been built around her supernatural powers. The mother ends up praising traditional beliefs. She is the one who consults the charlatans for the good of her children" (54; my translation); "The mother is made powerful by her connivance with the supernatural and her relations with the ancestors. She thus prefers that the son settle in her own milieu" (54–55); "The exploration of this image of the mother, bound up with the dreams of a patriarchal and rural society, allows us to identify certain key points regarding the attitudes that a mother can have when faced with the arrival of a white woman in the midst of her family. The image of the mother is inscribed in the great dream of a golden age preceding industrialization. The mother's character is inscribed in the quest for an impossible happiness, tied to a rural world where each thing was in its right place and where values were respected" (59; my translations). Because of her status, the mother-in-law feels authorized to rule over the new member of her household.

7. In *Mariages sans frontières* (1985), Augustin stresses the predominant importance of the religious element: "Religious distance is one of the most important factors, even if the newlyweds have chosen to turn away from their religion" (70; my translation). Isabelle and Faye decide to turn their backs on their religion, but here, as elsewhere, the family pressures the husband. In this case, the man is strong enough for both of them and imposes their choice of lifestyle, a choice that translates materially in their decision to build a house separate from the family.

8. One could explore the parallels with *So Long a Letter:* Modou has also taken a second wife who is entirely submissive and has no education; as such, she is the opposite of his first wife, Ramatoulaye, who was one of the first women to benefit from an education and to participate professionally in the education of the upcoming generation.

9. On this same point, d'Almeida (1994b) quite justifiably criticizes Rawiri's choice of ridiculing the lesbian relationship and giving it an artificial twist by turning it into a machination of the mother-in-law.

10. In "The Concept of Choice in Mariama Bâ's Fiction," (1986) Irène d'Almeida also raises the question of choice as a central point in the works of Mariama Bâ, with which she associates the concept of responsibility in *Une si longue lettre* (So long a letter) and *Scarlet Song*. She identifies the decisive stages as the rejection of parents (of Mireille and Ousmane), Ousmane's decision to marry Ouleymatou, Ouleymatou's decision to seduce Ousmane and to thereby steal Mireille's husband, Mireille's decision to adhere to her own culture and to reject the traditions of the other, and, finally, Ousmane's decision to deny his love for Mireille, which throws her into a vicious circle of depression and madness. As d'Almeida observes, each of these choices converges toward Mireille's destruction, and this destruction will touch each of the implicated individuals. Mariama Bâ thus raises the question of individual responsibility. D'Almeida draws the conclusion that both characters are responsible for their failed relationship; not only have they failed each other as individuals, they have failed in living up to their responsibilities as a couple. Because they both are weak and incapable of compromise, they destroy each other. Furthermore, they are both responsible to society as a couple and as members of a community (d'Almeida 1986, 170–171; see also d'Almeida 1994b, 98–122).

11. I should also add that Mariama Bâ considerably expands the scope of the theme of the foreign woman and the interracial couple. This is accomplished through the exploitation of narrative techniques as central to the dynamic of the text and by the inclusion of new elements, either the couple's stake in the child of their union as a key factor in its evolution or the white woman's character and the presentation of the black and white communities in their reactions to the couple. The issue of self-alienation takes a new turn here. In the place of the white woman, we find the new marginal character of the *métis*. Through a situational marginalization of race and culture, the character assumes a new bodily status *(un nouveau corps statuel)*.

12. For Antillean novels that present the displacement of their protagonists to Africa for the purpose of reconnecting with a lost past and discovering their true identity, see, for example, *Sapotille ou le serein d'argile* (1960) by Michèle Lacrosil, *Hérémakhonon* (1976) by Maryse Condé, and *Ti-Jean l'Horizon* (1978) by Simone Schwarz-Bart.

13. In her analysis of *Scarlet Song*, d'Almeida points out precisely this aspect of the conjugal relation's deterioration; that is, the couple fails not simply because of racial and cultural differences but also because of Ousmane's refusal to consider Mireille as an equal in any decisionmaking process. He prefers Ouleymatou, who has had practically no schooling and no professional ambition. D'Almeida notes: "It is interesting that Ousmane is attracted to Ouleymatou because of her adherence to traditional roles prescribed for women by men. He does not seek an African counterpart of Mireille, and it is clear that his disillusionment is rooted in something more than differences of race and cultures—he cannot accept her independence, her desire for equality" (1994b, 120–121).

2

Prostitutes and Prostitution

From an economic perspective, her situation is symmetrical to that of the married woman. For both of them, the sexual act is a service. The married woman is committed to a single man for life; the prostitute has several clients who pay as they go.
   —Simone de Beauvoir (*Le deuxième sexe*, 2:247; my translation)

There is no need to demonstrate the frequency of the literary theme of prostitution. The prostitute is one of the most commonly treated characters in modern literature, whether in Europe, the United States, or the countries of Asia, Africa, Latin America, or the Caribbean. In their introduction to *The Image of the Prostitute in Modern Literature* (1984), Horn and Pringle state that the character has traditionally been used by male authors either as a symbol or an object and that the representation of the prostitute is limited to a type rather than to a character endowed with individuality.[1] In Third World literature, geographical and historical parameters and the factor of colonization in particular play a fundamental role in this character's treatment and reason for being, which have taken on a political dimension. Of particular note, in her essay "The Prostitute in Arab and North-African Fiction," Evelyne Accad (1984) emphasizes the fact that Arab and North African authors utilize the figure of the prostitute in order to depict woman's dehumanization in their culture while at the same time making a satirical judgment about their society as a whole.

In the section on North African and sub-Saharan literatures in *The Prostitute in Progressive Literature,* Khristain (1982) adopts Accad's analysis. In Khristain's interpretation, the theme of the prostitute functions as an instrument of political critique aimed at the newly empowered African bourgeoisie and its haunts—"whitened" Africans and their nightclubs, balls, and other places of corruption. Khristain singles out two Anglophone authors for their treatment of this character: Cyprien Ekwensi of Nigeria and Ama Ata Aidoo of Ghana. In *Jagua Nana* (1961), Ekwensi describes the archetype of "the prostitute with a heart of gold, generous although weak and vain." Although the character functions as an archetype,

41

it nevertheless takes on a certain depth that allows us to understand the protagonist's perspective. Khristain stresses, however, that the novel "falls into the category of African works that portray the dregs of the industrial and commercial parts of the city as a trap for Africa's original innocence and virtue" (1982, 84). Ama Ata Aidoo is one of the first African women writers to have treated this theme. In her play *Something to Talk About on the Way to the Funeral,* she depicts the fate of the unlucky girl who drifts into prostitution as a result of having left her village to find work in the city.[2] Until the 1980s, Francophone authors depicted the prostitute only as part of the novelistic background.[3] Angèle Rawiri and Calixthe Beyala are two of the first African women novelists writing in French to have explored this theme and to have given it a comparable intensity and dimension. The character is no longer a traditional prostitute in the sense that she serves to represent only the vices of colonization. The traditional character dissolves, giving way to woman-as-object and body-as-merchandise. This portrayal is no longer limited to the single domain of prostitution but applies to the larger context of society in general.

In this chapter, I examine the nature and function of this character in the following texts: Bugul's *Le baobab fou* (1983; *The Abandoned Baobab,* 1991); Rawiri's *G'amàrakano, au carrefour* (1983); and Beyala's *C'est le soleil qui m'a brûlée* (1987; *The Sun Hath Looked Upon Me,* 1996), *Tu t'appelleras Tanga* (1987; *Your Name Shall Be Tanga,* 1996), *Seul le diable le savait* (1990), *Le petit prince de Belleville* (1992; *Loukoum, the Little Prince of Belleville,* 1995), and *Assèze l'Africaine* (1994).

Self-Prostitution, or the Loss of Identity, in *The Abandoned Baobab*

Although *The Abandoned Baobab* indeed belongs to the autobiographical genre and, as such, continues the long tradition of autobiographical tales of Africans who have departed for the Western world, in many regards, Ken Bugul's story breaks with this tradition. First, let us recall that Ken Bugul is a pseudonym for Mariétou M'Baye. At the time of the novel's original publication, the publishers pressured her because the novel was perceived to be daring, if not taboo, in its depiction of the life of a black female Muslim.[4] In fact, in Wolof the expression "ken bugul" means "No one wants. . . . " In *Journeys Through the French African Novel* (1990), Mildred Mortimer explains the reference as a name typically given to a newborn child in order to protect it (usually after a series of stillbirths) by warding off the attention of evil spirits. Mortimer identifies the protagonist—also named Ken—with the orphan girl who leaves in search of her own identity after being abandoned by her mother and the rest of her family.[5] In this case, she goes to Belgium, the illusory site of a possible identity, only to find that after experiencing drug addiction (to soft and hard drugs including alcohol), prostitution, and a flirtation with suicide, her identity can be found only within herself and she must return to Africa and the baobab tree she had abandoned. She returns to find after all those years that the tree is dead. Mortimer's analysis follows the journey of suffering that Ken must undergo before being able to single out the causes of her illness or malaise. Bugul stresses the importance of the protagonist's internal journey as opposed to her journey to Europe; a focus on the physical journey is more typical of autobiographical stories from male African literature.[6]

In her analysis of *The Abandoned Baobab,* Irène d'Almeida (1994b, 44–45) sees the choice of the pseudonym Ken Bugul for Mariétou M'Baye as symbolic of the author's refusal to be silenced. D'Almeida remarks that by making such a choice the author can play upon the very ambiguity of the term in Wolof, which, having no object, can be completed in any number of ways such as "no one wants me," or "no one wants this." "This," in this case, would designate the book itself, and so by choosing a name generally attributed to the newborn as a sign of protection, the author seeks to protect her work and to allow it to live.

In addition to the air of mystery surrounding the story's creation, the novel also breaks with tradition in its use of a narrative voice introduced through two different time frames, that of "Ken's prehistory," and that of "Ken's story." The narrative voice navigates between these two times, thus breaking with the traditional linear narration of previous autobiographical works. By contrast, the earlier novels describe the passage from childhood to adolescence, the discovery of the West through school, the departure from Africa and the stay in a Western country, usually France. Here, however, the author alternates between analepses (flashbacks) and prolepses (projections) that are filled with reflections on life and that always return to the protagonist's taking leave of her mother and the immense anguish that she feels as a consequence. However, particularly through the protagonist's search for her identity, she ends up with a clear analysis of the pathological aspects of Western culture and of the pathological behavior of Africans of her generation. Through the open and decisive tone of her formulations, Ken Bugul is a precursor of the lucid and visionary writing of young writers today. Through the amount of psychological suffering that the author expresses, through a new awareness of her body and the sensations that pass through it, through fear of going over the edge, she opens up a fierce and violent new style of writing that can be subsequently found in the works of Beyala, Rawiri, and Tadjo.

Through her experiences and encounters, Ken shows us the world of artists and intellectuals, including phony ones—as she herself emphasizes—and drug addicts, prostitutes, and other marginal types. She is able to slip between these two worlds with such ease because of her power—the effect of her beauty and skin color. She discovers her body and becomes aware that she has lost important points of reference and is fragmented:

> The front of a shop window mirrored glass reflected my face. I couldn't believe my eyes. This face couldn't belong to me, I quickly told myself. My eyes were bulging, my skin was shiny, the face terrifying. . . . How could this face belong to me? I understood why the saleswoman told me that she couldn't help me. Yes, I was a Black Woman, a foreigner. I touched my chin, my cheek, to better realize that this was my color.
> Yes, I was a foreigner, a stranger, and this was the first time I realized it. (Bugul 1991, 38)

Her second realization is about skin color and her own fascination with white skin, a fascination that has existed since her adolescence and her initial flirtation with Louis, her first companion in Belgium. The fascination endures even though she feels somewhat uncomfortable about it in the presence of her compatriots. Ken gets pregnant, has an abortion, temporarily feels a revulsion for white skin,[7] and then breaks up with Louis. From this point on, her lack of resources and growing self-alienation almost completely lock her into a trajectory of uncertainty and the underground milieu, which is always a white milieu. Her path seems to lead inevitably to prostitution.

Her growing awareness of her alienation and lack of identity develops through the idea of the importance of skin color and the phenomenon of fashion and exoticism that encourages Western men to seek out the company of African women and vice versa:

> I concluded that this student was part of a clique of all those foreign students who were out to date white women to make things easy and also to obey the myth of the Black man's hyper-sexuality. Furthermore, the white woman continued to be part of the repressed fantasy of the colonized attacked by her provocative attitudes. . . . Sexuality is culture and atmosphere. (Bugul 1991, 52)

In *The Abandoned Baobab,* Bugul offers a reading of race similar to that of Fanon's *in Peau noire, masques blancs* (1952); she suggests that color assumes this importance precisely because the scene is set in Europe, whereas in Africa it would attract hardly any notice. It is in Europe that Ken becomes aware of the attraction that she exercises on men because of the color of her skin. One after another, all of her friends point out the possible advantages of being exploited. Prostitution appears at first in a softer light, as a pretext for highlighting certain pathological aspects of the author's contemporary Western and African worlds.

> It was the period when the West was becoming enamored of the exotic. (Bugul 1991, 59)

The West was choking itself, and those trying to escape were people in their death throes. (74)

Ken's growing alienation comes from an awareness of the mask she wears, her game of playing the role of the Western woman, the woman who "takes charge" (as her friend Jean advises her to do), within a one-way identification: "I had played a character too long: a woman, a Black woman, who had for a long time believed in her ancestors the Gauls" (Bugul 1991, 111). Ken moves from one disillusion about the West to another. She also becomes disillusioned with the people who surround her as she uncovers new realities about sexuality, love, and friendship. The feeling of being estranged from herself and of prostituting her thought continues to grow, along with the fear of emptiness and solitude. Faced with a growing anguish, Ken enters the world of drugs, dealers, and marginalized people, sinking deeper and deeper into an abyss at the edge of madness.

> I was trying to shock society by wearing transparent dresses of infuriating colors, with a shaven skull, in huge hats, seeking to advertise an upside-down surrealism, intellectual frenzies, the game of the color black, in other words: to be a black woman who appeals to the white man. (Bugul 1991, 82)

Ken progressively slips from psychological self-prostitution into physical prostitution, a consequence of not being able to find an essential meaning to life. But her prostitution stems from a desire to please, to be loved even for a brief moment even if that means moving to a more advanced stage of alienation:

> I spent a great deal of time with white people; I found it easier to converse with them, I understood their language. For twenty years, all I had learned were their thoughts and their feelings. (Bugul 1991, 52)

Her desire to be with a white man is exploited, and she is tricked; she does not see that Gaëlle had arranged everything that first time in the sauna, that "brothel in disguise." Ken later becomes a prostitute through the intermediary of the "Suissesse" who gives her a series of rendezvous in spots ranging from a tiny restaurant to a chain of luxury hotels. In each of these instances or stages, the element of color is predominant; once again the people who surround her are the ones to point out the possibilities:

> Ah! you Black women, you're divine. (Bugul 1991, 72)

> You could do more. Men like you. You know what I mean, you bewitch them without even trying; you are Black and you are beautiful. You should exploit that. (101)

> You are a *Black woman,* you could make yourself a fortune. (104)

When Ken comes away from her experience with the client at the Hilton, she is faced with what she has become. She is conscious of having been reduced to her body and her color. From this point on, following another even more painful meeting with the man with the little dog who is old enough to be her father and after having been a hair's breadth from suicide, she brusquely confronts the truth. She needs to return to Africa even if she can no longer hope to retrieve her childhood. When she faces the dead baobab tree, she composes a silent funeral speech that will accompany the baobab in its death and reestablish her ties with tradition and ritual.

With this prostitution of her body and above all of her mind, Ken has become the allegorized figure of a tormented Africa, the image of a generation that learned no other model than that of identification with the other. Ken tells us this when she recalls her childhood and the stories based in Western culture that she read as a girl. Through a direct exploration of her conscience and sentiments, but also indirectly through the portrait of two of her compatriots and their Western lifestyle, Ken reveals the extent of the psychological trauma that educated Africans of her time undergo. If she has succumbed to an actual prostitution of her body, her parents and her brothers and sisters have succumbed to a prostitution of the mind with far more serious consequences. Whereas she is utterly aware of the mask she wears, they are not. For the first time, an African woman writer has dared to put Africa with all its neocolonialist ambitions on trial. With *The Abandoned Baobab,* Ken Bugul widened the scope of the traditional autobiographical narrative in order to reach an analytical reflection on her society and the behavior of her generation as well as on Western reactions to Africa and its men and women.

Angèle Rawiri, in turn, adopts this theme in order to explore it in all its fullness. Using the same temporal frame, she places it in the African context. Rawiri tends to place more emphasis on the bodily transformations of her characters, suggesting simply by her depiction of her society the transformations in mentality that lie at its roots.

Prostitution as a New Way of Life in *G'amàrakano*

G'amàrakano, au carrefour does not deal uniquely with prostitution but rather with one of its derivative forms that can be defined as a sort of semiprostitution.[8] The novel follows the paths of its protagonist Toula and some peripheral female characters who confront the primacy of appearance for women and their seduction of men as a means of obtaining financial and social success.

The novel opens with Toula's frustrations. She rejects her body and revolts against her poverty when faced with a situation where survival is an issue. Her problem is made all the more difficult when she discovers another lifestyle through contact with her colleagues at work, in particular Ekata. The mother, Moussiliki, a widow who has been abandoned twice by men, is in charge of the family. Her complaints against a girl who does not put her charms to work add to the gravity of the situation;, the neighbor's girl has used her wiles to catch a wealthy man: "Here is a girl who will pull her mother out. I am not counting on Toula to get me out of this" [En voilà une qui fera faire du chemin à sa mère. . . . Je ne compte pas sur Toula pour me sortir de là] (Rawiri 1983, 23). Gnaré is a friend of Moussiliki. Her advice insistently repeats the point: "Make yourself look beautiful and hang out in the places where you might meet rich men. It really doesn't matter if they are ugly as long as they have money" [Fais-toi belle et traîne dans les endroits où tu peux rencontrer des hommes riches. La laideur n'a pas d'importance pourvu qu'ils aient de l'argent] (23).

A new conception of society and man-woman relations appears through their voices. It is already understood that any success for a woman will come through a man. Attracting a man, any man, in order to obtain financial support becomes the norm: "If you wanted, you could have us all drinking champagne. To manage that, all you have to do is imitate the other girls" [Si tu veux, tu peux nous faire boire du champagne. Pour arriver à cela, tu n'as qu'à imiter les autres filles] (Rawiri 1983, 24). Refusing this type of financial compensation (what is it other than a form of prostitution organized by the mother?) is perceived as abnormal and pushes the girl to the edge of the family and the social group.

Toula actually has to resist two forms of pressure, that of her mother and that of her friend who is trying to get her out of Igewa, a social milieu that she deems suffocating and stagnant. After this, the novel describes the stages of Igewa's rejection, which results in the rejection of Igewa's men, Mebalé and Ipeké, who are deemed uninteresting and as having no hope of social ascension. It is in a symbolic manner that the first dies beneath the blows of the second. They both fight over Toula, and Ipeké has to flee into exile after Mebalé's death. A chapter in her life has closed and nothing could reattach her to this milieu. From this point on, Toula is described according to the changes in her body and mind, and her rise is related to her success with men. The various mechanisms of seduction and semiprostitution are examined in detail. These consist of dietary and aesthetic advice, an analysis of man and his contradictions, an analysis of the role and the status of the wife, a short guide to the behavior a woman needs to adopt in order to keep men's attention, what gifts to insist upon—everything appears as the characteristic sign of a mercantilization of relations.

The fact is in itself not new, but its organization and principle are completely different. Until now, a number of novels focused on the commodification of relations only in the very specific framework of marriage and the dowry. Both attribute an essential importance to the family's decision and the choice that it makes to raise the sum and the allotted gifts for the dowry. When the seduction of one or several men by a girl was described, the stress was placed on the commotion caused by such behavior and the community's unanimous disapproval. For example, this is the case in *Le fils d'Agatha Moudio* (Bebey 1967), in which Agatha is treated like dirt. Here, on the contrary, the narration stresses the reverse: A woman is pushed by her mother, in fact by the entire community, to enter into this mode of relations based on financial compensation.

Rawiri exposes a veritable ideology of appearance as a support system for the practice of semiprostitution: First, like the youths, the parents no longer believe in education as the path that leads to success. At the most, a diploma is an advantage (virtually necessary for men) to gain social recognition. Second, the traditional virtues embodied here by Okassa, the grandmother, and in a broader context by the elders, have been rejected because they lead nowhere. Third, what counts most is the appearance of success, which for the man can be recognized by his dress, his car, and the generosity he displays with women. For the woman, success is made manifest in her dress but also in her physical allure and the small accessories that denote her polish and chic. Fourth, it is important to be seen in places that are in fashion, preferably in the company of someone prominent. Fifth, anyone who fails to satisfy these preliminary conditions is considered a loser and relegated to the outer margins of the group.

Rawiri describes this philosophy of life in order to show the dangers of such a dominant trend, especially for women. Toula becomes symbolic of lost equilibrium in a society of temptations that creates not only new needs but obligations. The woman is the first to be thrown off balance, intoxicated by a false mastery of her body that actually leads to her loss. Okassa's thought summarizes this problem:

> Toula has become a victim of this world of mirrors that creates desires and jealously keeps what it possesses. She is crying because she is no longer happy with what she has. Because she has seen what a sensitive person of her condition is not supposed to see.
>
> *[Toula est victime de ce monde de miroirs qui crée des désirs et garde jalousement ce qu'il possède. Elle pleure parce qu'elle ne se contente plus de ce qu'elle a. Car elle a vu ce qu'une personne sensible de sa condition ne devait pas voir.]* (Rawiri 1983, 28)

The novel gives an account of the social expansion that took place in the 1980s, during which there was an insane competition to appear successful. Especially for women, the signs needed to attain this appearance, typically cosmetics and designer clothing, are clearly beyond their means. It seems obvious that somehow and somewhere the woman must devise a strategy to obtain the financial surplus needed to acquire these miraculous new elements of the success everyone dreams about. She will find this surplus "somewhere" in man, who becomes a source of income to be gleaned by performing several petty services: appearing at his side, being beautiful and vibrant (and thus letting her sexuality rub off on him), offering him sexual and emotional comfort in exchange for payment. Furthermore, girls utilize their charms to attract one or several men because their mothers encourage it. In Toula's case, her mother's influence is the determining factor in her decision. On the one hand, she wants to help her family; on the other, she paradoxically has the problem of finding a path that is radically different from her mother's.

Unlike Beyala's characters (see the next section), Rawiri's protagonist is not the least bit fascinated with her mother. As a matter of fact, the mother's misery, her almost tangible suffering and other physical traces of her failure, drive the daughter to try anything to counterbalance this threatening mirror image. Toula starts out under these conditions. The novel accurately describes a social trend in which occasional prostitution becomes a way of life for men as well as women.

In *Prostitution en Afrique,* Paulette Songue (1986) studies this phenomenon in the specific case of Yaoundé (Cameroon), although her remarks apply every bit as much to the situation described by the Gabonese author Rawiri, and perhaps even more to the texts of Beyala. Her sociological analysis notably singles out "the ideology of appearance" as the main grounds of support for semiprostitution. In order to show this, Songue examines the country's independence and the emergence of a new elite along with the creation of so-called white, or office, jobs. Both of these elements encouraged Western habits, especially the acquisition of more expensive imported products. Songue observes that confronted with a new elite engaged in ostentatious expenditures, the lower classes begin to show the same ambitions. In this context, "prostitution will favor the woman or the girl who discovers that she can live off of the 'fruits' of this profession" [la prostitution sera à la faveur de la femme ou de la jeune fille qui découvre qu'elle peut vivre des 'fruits' de ce métier] (139).

Elsewhere, Songue looks at the social strata affected by the problem. Predictably, the phenomenon of the lower classes taking on elite lifestyles affects a majority of rural girls who come to the city looking for a job in order to help their families. Failing to find any significant work, they gradually drift toward prostitution, concerned as they are to preserve their image as city women and not wanting to return to their villages empty-handed. Toula in *G'amàrakano* (Rawiri, 1983) represents a certain version of this first type of situation. Songue also points out the even more surprising fact that to a considerable extent, this phenomenon involves the daughters of civil servants, high-school and college students whose recourse to prostitution is sporadic and considered a source of extra income rather than their primary source of financial support. The second type of situation perfectly describes Ekata's case (in *G'amàrakano*), as she comes from a rather well-to-do background. A third element appears here now: the desire to assert oneself in relation to one's family or to freely explore one's sexuality.[9] For Ekata, seducing men and getting expensive gifts from them is not a necessity at first but becomes one as a sort of game that is symbolic of her freedom. When her father refuses to give her permission to go away with several friends for the weekend, she would rather run away from home than obey. Another characteristic of prostitution that Songue uncovers is that the phenomenon is not strictly limited to women; it is practiced by a significant segment of the male student body as well. Male prostitution appears on numerous occasions in Rawiri's *G'amàrakano*, for instance, in Rembeyo's character. He is Onanga's boyfriend and uses her and her connections with well-heeled men in order to procure the funds needed to continue his studies.

Songue's point of view on the role of prostitution in Camerounian society is worthy of note. According to her, prostitution has a triple regulating effect. Economically, it allows certain financially underprivileged individuals to dispel their frustrations by procuring the symbols of success that they are supposed to possess if they do not wish to appear marginalized. Sexually, it regulates the tensions experienced by women as well as men. Through the mechanism of prostitution, men can mimic the effects of polygamy by surrounding themselves with several women. Socially, prostitution enables the man to demonstrate his power, a potency that is financial as well as sexual. The cost and the frequency of the gifts he distributes to his various mistresses become signs of his prestige. This last element appears very clearly in *G'amàrakano* through the character Eléwagnè. Furthermore, Songue stresses that prostitution constitutes an important economic mechanism; it is a privileged domain that favors not only consumption but also investment by the former prostitute in hotels, bars, clubs, and boutiques. In *G'amàrakano,* Ekata and Onanga in their old age are symbolic of the possibilities available to prostitutes in general. Onanga finds a man that she marries, thus gaining a certain respectability, and Ekata becomes the owner of a fashionable restaurant, thereby realizing her ambition "to own an African restaurant where the foreign businessmen and all the celebrities of the town meet on a nightly basis" [tenir un restaurant africain qui réunit, tous les soirs, les hommes d'affaires étrangers et tous les grands noms de la ville] (Rawiri, 1983, 183). For each of these characters, however, a certain element is still sorely missing—love. Toula fails miserably for having wanted to privilege this element; as a result, she can no longer manage to maintain her personal stability.

Finally, Songue identifies two elements that have favored the development of the trend of prostitution. On the one hand, society has entered into "a period in which more importance is given to sexual gratification and to pleasure in the broad sense of the term" [une période où plus de place est accordée à la jouissance sexuelle et au plaisir (au sens large du terme)] (1986, 141). On the other hand (and related to this first effect), "the image of the chaste mother has lost more and more prestige, while that of the mistress has become more important. The household itself no longer has the almost sacred consideration that it used to receive and has been disturbed by forces of sexual freedom experienced both inside and out" [l'image de la mère chaste perd de plus en plus de prestige, et celle de la maîtresse se valorise. Le ménage lui-même n'a plus la considération quasi sacrée qu'on lui donnait et est bousculé par les élans de liberté sexuelle vécus en son sein et à l'extérieur de celui-ci] (141–142). The implications of this sociological analysis are clear:

> If these tendencies continue to be followed and are amplified, as marginal as prostitution now may be, it will eventually become just another lifestyle among others, particularly in this form of semiprostitution. (142)

> *[Si ces tendances suivent leurs cours et s'accentuent, la prostitution, de marginale qu'elle est encore, se transformera en véritable mode de vie proposé tout comme les autres, en particulier dans la semi-prostitution.]* (142)

Such a conclusion summarizes the entire viewpoint of *G'amàrakano*. There is an actual contamination of each young woman and girl. The novel achieves a documentary effect through its tone, ultimately seeming like a chronicle. Toula, Onanga, and Ekata are only several examples among so many others. They represent a serious social problem that male and female readers alike need to confront. It is everyone's responsibility to recognize the active part they play in this system. The novel calls on us to become aware of behavior that each one of us may reinforce, whether in drawing up our budgets, in concerning ourselves with external appearances, in purchasing magazines, in choosing the people we associate with, or in pursuing success with persons of the opposite sex. The novel offers indirect criticism through the grandmother's words. And Toula's dramatic and brutal evolution as a character speaks for itself, retrospectively revealing all the insidious phases of the phenomenon. Through the tone and the clarity of its vision, the novel resembles those by other women writers of this period. However, it makes a significant innovation in its exploration of certain subjects that were previously considered either trivial or of secondary importance (clothing, makeup, diet, and so on). Rawiri's novel also significantly breaks with its predecessors in its approach to areas such as sexuality and desire, subjects that are often considered taboo.

Because of her completely different approach and general tone, Calixthe Beyala depicts a more raw, immediate, and horrid reality in her works. She projects her reader into a completely different world. It is the world of real prostitution, approached at its lowest level.[10] The mechanisms exposed by the author displace the novel's center of interest from the superficial sociological explanations for the phenomenon and from the phenomenon as a lifestyle onto woman's intimate reactions in her relationship with man in this context.

The Female Prostitute in Beyala's Work

C'est le soleil qui m'a brûlée (1987; *The Sun Hath Looked upon Me,* 1996), *Tu t'appelleras Tanga* (1988; *Your Name Shall Be Tanga,* 1996), and *Seul le diable le savait* (1990) all involve the systematic recurrence of the same types of characters, and in what is almost always the same social environment of violence, horror, and abject poverty. There is no comfort zone where the reader can take solace in contemplating something beautiful, pure, or relaxing. Each of these novels is based on the life of a female character (Ateba, Tanga, and Megri, respectively). Each explores women's relationships as daughters, lovers, and mothers who are developing and trying to make their way in a world based on commodification and prostitution. In each of these texts, the prostitute's character plays a central role and appears as a determining factor in the protagonist's passage from adolescence to adulthood.

The family structure is consistently identical: a mother (or an aunt as surrogate mother), a daughter, the lover(s) of the mother, and the daughter's lover(s). I will accordingly study the configuration of the figure of the prostitute in the following representations: the mother, the daughter, the friends of the daughter. In light of these different "situations,"[11] I would like to analyze the implications of such a context for woman's identity and the protagonist's conception of love. Through these considerations, I wish to determine how the image of the female prostitute is specifically different for Calixthe Beyala.

Each of these three novels has its own particular orientation, centered on either a character or a concept of the body as a form of merchandise. *The Sun Hath Looked upon Me* thrusts us into a world composed almost entirely of women, all of whom are prostitutes (the mother, Betty; the aunt, Ada; the close friend, Irène) with the sole exception of the protagonist, Ateba. In *Your Name Shall Be Tanga*, the protagonist has the role of the prostitute. Finally, in *Seul le diable le savait,* the entire society in which

Megri, the main character, develops, exposes a global condition of loose manners (*moeurs relâchées*) in which everyone lives off of the mercantile principles of prostitution.

The Prostitute Mother

In *The Sun,* the prostitute in the narrow sense of its definition appears in the role of the mother, Betty.[12] In *Seul le diable,* she appears as a prostitute in a broader sense; she has two official husbands and offers her services to a third man, the village chief. In both cases, Beyala stresses the notion of freedom and economic independence, especially in *Seul le diable* when Dame maman controls the ménage-à-trois and makes it perfectly clear that she considers herself free to use her body as she sees fit: "I am free! Whoever doesn't like it can get lost. The door is open" [Je suis libre! Celui qui n'est pas content peut se tirer. La porte est ouverte] (Beyala 1990, 36).

This freedom of the body is the defining characteristic of maternal love, as illustrated in *The Sun* when Betty abandons her daughter in order to pursue one of her lovers, the "Titulaire" (the bureaucrat). The prostitute mother thus offers a problematic mirror image for her child to emulate. Obviously, we have the image of a woman who puts seducing men before communicating with her child, but we also see a beautiful woman who is well made up and who smells delicious, someone whom a young girl wants to resemble:

> As a child, Ateba wanted to resemble Betty. She'd wear her pagnes and her shoes much too big for her little feet. She'd put on her makeup. She'd study herself. She was a woman. She was Betty. She resembled her physically and she enjoyed imagining that her life would be nothing other than a continuation of Betty's. (1996, 52)

Betty's appearance has been idealized. She is a woman who charms in every sense of the word. Her attributes produce a complex combination of differing and sometimes contradictory reactions of attraction and repulsion in the mother-daughter relation. On one hand, the daughter is well aware of the fact that her mother sells her body, and she reacts with a possessive, exclusive, and jealous love. Ateba, and Megri (in *Seul le diable*), are happy only when they have their mothers to themselves. It is only with difficulty that they accept the presence of a man inside the house, whether it be the "official" lover (in *The Sun*) or the official father(s) (in *Tanga* and *Seul le diable*). On the one hand there is a claim to property—the body has become a form of merchandise—and the title to this property confirms the identity of the person who holds it.[13] On the other hand, there is a girl's judgmental gaze that falls upon a mother who is indifferent and physically or mentally absent, or upon a woman who appears weak in her relationships with men who treat her like an object. When the daughter is positioned as a judge, her hostile disapproval is particularly noteworthy in *The Sun.*

> Sure, I knew her, Mama Lady, the woman who would run away with a brain that could reject anything that bothered her. . . . With a brain that could never deal with any regrets or suffering.
>
> *[Certes, je la connaissais, Dame maman, la femme des fuites, un cerveau capable de rejeter tout ce qui la gênait. . . . Un cerveau incapable d'emmagasiner la souffrance, les regrets.]* (Beyala 1987, 46)

The mother is the pivotal figure, as she represents a primordial object of criticism. In *Tanga,* the eponymous protagonist cries out, "I destructure my mother! It is an act of birth. . . . I escape her and I evacuate her" (1996, 64). For all of the protagonists, passing from the stage of infancy to that of adulthood requires them to violently reject their mothers as women and as symbols of woman. It seems logical, then, that alongside the prostitute-mother, the status of the father figure appears problematic as well. In *The Sun,* his absence is his most remarkable trait. In *Tanga,* the father sexually abuses his daughter in plain view of the mother, who eventually forces her daughter into prostitution. In contrast, *Seul le diable* presents a number of fathers including "Papa bon Blanc" and "le Pygmée." With undependable family support and the complete lack of any organizing principle other than submission to men, the daughter is led to reject the mother's status and to consider the man as the oppressor. What each daughter is actually rejecting is not so much that the mother is (or acts like) a prostitute but the fact that the mother submits herself body and soul to a man's desires while remaining unable to conceive of relations in any different terms. From this point on, the main question in each text involves determining whether the girl will manage to reject this model that has been offered to her in order to discover her own way of life.[14] This decision conditions both her rejection of woman as she has been defined by the patriarchal social system and her search for a new kind of woman. This search becomes a veritable plan of action in *The Sun,* Beyala's first novel, in which writing, speaking, and communicating with one other allow women to see that there is some means of escape other than the streets and prostitution.

In Beyala's next two novels—*Le petit prince de Belleville* (1992); *Loukoum, the Little Prince of Belleville* (1994) and its sequel, *Maman a un amant* (1993)—the principal relationship is no longer between mother and daughter but between mother and son. The implications change and the approach differs a bit. There is a tenderness here that develops in the opposite direction. In other words, it is the mother who wants to reestablish ties with her son after having abandoned him to his father's (and M'am's) care. She expresses her joy and affection in so many effusive words and gestures. The first meeting between them is symbolic in this sense, because it is the child who identifies her with a prostitute through his description:

> There stood a very pretty and even attractive woman, except for her eyes which looked like the eyes of a dog that's just been kicked in the arse. . . . She's wearing a coat made of some kind of skin like fur, but it isn't real fur. She's really dolled up. A very short, black-leather skirt with a little jacket that leaves her belly bare, like a tart. That's what M'am calls it, a tart, a girl worth nothing at all. (Beyala 1995, 85)

It is ironic that the child borrows from the point of view of his mother (the one who raised him) and his father in order to describe his biological mother. When he learns the truth that this person and his mother are one and the same, it shocks him considerably.

> I almost fall over from the blow. I clench my fist very hard. I can't let the words I have in my heart out of my mouth. M'am looks at her without saying a word, as if someone had just cut off her tongue. . . . You'd think she was an old madwoman from Mali. (Beyala 1995, 87)

His initial reaction is one of disappointment. "Allah! That, that can't *possibly* be my mum. I don't feel like singing the mothers full of grace, holy shit. . . . No, this woman just cannot be my gentle mum, this slut who shows her tits like that." (Beyala 1995, 87). The language he uses to describe his mother is far more harsh than that used to describe Ateba, Tanga, and Megri. However, with time, his relation with his mother changes under the effect of what is nearly a taming process (hence the allusion to Saint-Exupéry's *Le petit prince*). Loukoum grows accustomed to this unusual image of his mother, the image of a prostitute. This idea seems all the more bizarre to him because the normal or normative referent is his two adoptive mothers, who appear as settled women and faithful wives, and these are, by definition, maternal images.

Once the period of "taming" has passed, Loukoum feels a certain fascination for his mother. Just as Ateba in *The Sun* admires her mother Betty's beauty, Loukoum admires his mother's looks.

> The shorts hardly cover any of her long legs. She makes you think a little of a very ripe mango when you see how well she fills out her little shorts and the thing she is wearing over her chest, and how all of it is smooth chestnut-coloured and plump. (Beyala 1995, 145)

When Aminata finally manages to bring Loukoum to stay in her apartment with her for several days, Loukoum feels more joy spending time with her than fascination with what she is. He admires her talents as a cook and plays with her: "In short, she is having fun like a kid, which she isn't any-more, and I am too" (Beyala 1995, 158). Their relation is characterized by their closeness in body and thought.

> Afterwards we watch the news because it's always the same. . . . But what I like above all is the happiness I enjoy with Aminata. It's true that I feel nothing anymore while I am happy. (159)

Aminata is completely different from Betty (Ateba's mother in *The Sun*) and Bertha (Megri's mother in *Seul le diable*) in that she gives her son maternal love. She prepares large dinners before leaving for work and cleans the apartment. The mother is fulfilling her role here, unlike Ateba's and Megri's. Also, the child here accepts his mother's position as a prosti-tute, describing with simplicity her activities when she gets ready to go to work: "Aminata works late and gets up late" (Beyala 1995, 157).

> She puts on short leather trousers, boots that come all the way to her thighs and a sweater with a rolled collar that fits around her breasts, since that is what a client notices first. She's gone all night and comes home in the morning, her eyes all red, with dreadful breath, and smelly, as if she'd spent the night with the homeless of Belleville. (159)

Loukoum's love is not possessive. Of course, Loukoum feels a certain jealousy toward his uncle Kouam when his mother sings for him, but his jealousy is easily calmed when Aminata sings a song that is for him alone and asks him what he thinks of her relationship with his uncle. The child is an important individual for whom Aminata shows great consideration. For example, she wants to be alone with him and to be left alone by her "protector" during the few days that Loukoum stays with her. The prosti-tute's position does not interfere with the child's development, although we must still consider that it makes all the difference that the child has been raised far away from this social context and that, unlike Ateba, Tanga, and Megri, he has benefited from a normative family structure.[15]

In her later novel, *Assèze l'Africaine* (1994), Beyala returns to the tra-ditional concept of the prostitute with the character of Assèze's mother, a village woman with almost no financial resources. Because her two chil-dren, Assèze and the newborn Okenk, have no acknowledged father—even though the reader is led to believe that Awono is probably the father—the mother seems deviant. As the story develops, Assèze is often reminded of her illegitimate origins by her stepsister. Sorraya reminds her of the dan-ger of following in her mother's footsteps. Thus the same question arises of whether Assèze will be able to follow her own path and succeed even though she was not born into the same privileged milieu as Sorraya.

Another primordial question is implicit here, the question of the meaning of *success*.

The Prostitute Daughter

In exploring the situation of the prostitute daughter, *Your Name Shall Be Tanga* represents a sort of continuation of *The Sun Hath Looked upon Me,* an answer by procuration. The novel opens in a prison cell, where the prostitute Tanga is suffering and finds comfort in speaking with Anna-Claude, a French Jew who has come to Africa in search of herself and love. Anna-Claude has been locked up for her subversive religious ideas. Like Tanga, she has been thoroughly disappointed in her search for love. Her past includes a father who abused her and a mother who forced her into prostitution and then had her incarcerated when she refused to continue turning tricks.

In telling her story, Tanga confronts her past and has a cathartic experience that finally enables her to discover her true identity through the mediation of Anna-Claude, who agrees to take Tanga's place. Some of the social implications of prostitution are brought to light, especially in the collective nature of the pressure hanging over Tanga. The first link in this chain is the emotional blackmail that her mother inflicts on her. The second link is the mother's act of making the disagreement public when her individual pressure fails. Tanga's mother calls on the entire village to judge the matter, and the village supports her position.

This conception of familial pressure and especially of the mother pressuring her daughter, reappears in the works of a number of African women novelists, most notably in Rawiri's *G' amàrakano, au carrefour.* These instances point to a disruption of the family unit's equilibrium. In his analysis of *G' amàrakano, au carrefour* (in *The African Quest for Freedom and Identity,* 1991) Richard Bjornson considers this disruption a key point in Beyala's argument in the sense that Tanga becomes a symbolic reflection of the living death that African children are exposed to from the start.[16] This position translates directly into the fact that, like Ateba and Megri, Tanga refuses to bear children, since giving birth is the equivalent of exposing the newborn to numerous dangers:

> I do not want to multiply myself. . . . I do not want to lend my womb to the unfurling of life. (*Tanga,* Beyala 1996, 120)
> After all, what does one kid's life matter in this country where everything is constantly in an embryonic state? The kids will always be skinny and never have the opportunity to grow sturdy. The adults will always be looking just over the edge of the abyss. (*The Sun,* Beyala 1996, 89)

This condition results in the search for another kind of love as a path to redemption. In this context, the love and comfort that Tanga discovers in Anna-Claude are symbolic of the potential solidarity between women as a way to achieve redemption. Bjornson comments on this possibility: "The merging of the two women's identities symbolizes the possibility of achieving the ideal love they had formerly associated with their illusory images of Jean and Ousmane" (1991, 419). Nevertheless, the example of Tanga and Anna-Claude clashes considerably with Beyala's usual depiction of the relations between female characters.

The Prostitute Friends

Considering the situational pressure in which the protagonist evolves, the prostitute friends are key characters because they are close to the protagonist and because they are representative of so many different paths. In these friends, we can find several of the archetypal variants of the prostitute character, for example, Ekassi *(The Sun),* the prostitute who has fallen, a victim of her own generosity. Ekassi prostitutes herself for a man she loves in order to obtain his release from prison. Because she doesn't acquire the necessary sum, she fails in his eyes. He abandons her, and because he leaves her completely exposed, she is forced to continue leading a life of prostitution.[17]

Paradoxically, Ekassi retains a sense of hope along with the notion that there is some other place outside their world of abject poverty: "On the cloudy horizons of the *QG* [*quartier général,* or shantytown] horizons, she stood for the future. . . . Men carried her in their blood, women within their unconfessed desires" (*The Sun,* Beyala 1996, 38). The second part of this sentence is ambiguous and can be interpreted in two different ways: as indicative of women's sexual attraction to the prostitute and also as representative of a woman's concealed desire to identify with a prostitute.[18] The second possibility means something completely opposed to the first: Woman's profound desire would be to be placed in the position of the object with no purpose other than pleasing and serving man. This possibility represents a return to nihilism and to a feminine identity that denies itself within a sadomasochistic desire.

Laetitia's character (in *Seul le diable*) allows us to probe into this question of the protagonist's fascination with the female prostitute and what she represents. Laetitia's initial meeting with Megri corresponds to Papa bon Blanc's departure. Their meeting is thus placed at a key transitional moment in Megri's life, just when she has been abandoned. Laetitia then offers the only moral support that Megri has ever known, playing the role of a substitute mother. There are many examples of this behavior, for instance, the song that Laetitia sings in order to calm Megri, and her concern that they not be surprised together so that Megri's reputation will never be damaged. For Megri, Laetitia represents the first and only example of solidarity between women. She has never experienced such solidarity any-where else, neither with her mother, the Foreigner's mother, nor the sister she has discovered late in life. The meeting with Laetitia also coincides with a phase in which Megri is confronting doubts about her own direction in life. As she admires Laetitia's beauty, Megri comes to wish that she could be her: "If only I were Laetitia and she could be me! Ah! if I were Laetitia!" [Si au moins j'étais Laetitia et si Laetitia était moi! . . . Ah! si j'étais Laetitia] (Beyala 1990, 77). In Megri's eyes, the female prostitute is the only person who brings light into her life, a light that is synonymous with salvation. Thus she has an unusual, idyllic view of prostitution:

> There would always be men with sweet smelling mouths. They would bring me flowers on leafless stems. They would bring me light to drink from their faces. If I were Laetitia, if Laetitia were me, the day would al-ways light up the night of my body.
>
> *[Il y aurait toujours des hommes, avec les bouches qui sentent bon, ils m'apporteraient des fleurs séparées de leurs feuilles. Ils m'apporteraient leur eau à boire sur leur figure. Si j'étais Laetitia, si Laetitia était moi, la lumière du jour entrerait toujours dans la nuit de mon corps.]* (77)

Old Missy Esther is described in similar terms; the protagonist Louk-oum also shows signs of a certain fascination with her. However, his ad-miration is somewhat different from his father's. He is touched by her kindness, her natural manners, and by the fact that she takes care of him, taking him out alone with her and allowing him to discover other things in life, such as beauty and peace during their walks in the park. His admi-ration is also that of a budding young man who is sensitive to her feminine qualities.

In *The Sun,* Betty's close friend Irène contrasts sharply with this model. She exemplifies the cynical prostitute. Betty and Ada, Ateba's aunt, also exemplify this character of the "hard and pure" woman who either willingly or unwittingly becomes indifferent to the world of misery and falsehood in which she lives. There is something almost infantile and des-perate about Betty and Ada. They need to trick nothingness and exhaust themselves in any way they can (playing the sex game) so as not to see themselves. Betty and Ada discover how to establish some (relative) per-sonal stability that is (paradoxically) detached from men. In her stubborn will to forget daily life, Irène "fucks" instead in order to somehow take re-venge on men, although she loses her life in the end. The prostitute's image has become emblematic of all the gestures used to conjure away the vertigo felt at the edge of the abyss.

The world discovered by Ateba, Tanga, and Megri is therefore a world in which men and women are limited to their sexual value and in which woman is reduced to being an object, a piece of merchandise. Nonetheless, in contrast to their mothers and their friends, all the protagonists manage to escape the vicious circle that would relegate them to an existence as female victims of man, because they manage to decipher man's double language. In order to do this, they have to deconstruct love in a systematic fashion so as to be able to expose it and examine it in all of its minute facets. They do this by reinterpreting love in such a way as to attain a complete awareness of the new woman's position in a relationship different from one where love is seen as a commercial object.

The countess's character in *Assèze l'Africaine* illustrates both a newly formed awareness of woman's power over man and the dangers women risk in searching for the easy success attained through a tacit or explicit financial contract with man. In such a position, the countess becomes a voice for all women, expressing both her frustrations and a lucid critique of her situation, confronted as she is with patriarchal domination. In fact, due to her influence over Awono, Assèze's probable father, she even manages to voice certain truths and to work for the benefit of either Sorraya or Assèze:

> "Assèze won't go to school anymore?" the Countess asked. . . . "Well? . . . She won't go to school anymore just like the married women and the young girls who are sacrificed for the boys. She won't go to school anymore like all the whores in this country that you fuck, and yet you say you want to send her there like the tiny minority of women you have no chance of fucking."
> "But . . . but what will she become?" Awono asked.
> "Just like everyone else," answered the Countess, who was tired of speaking by this time. "A woman, just another woman."
>
> [*"Assèze n'ira plus à l'école?" demanda la Comtesse. . . . "Et alors?" demanda-t-elle. . . . "Elle n'ira plus à l'école comme les femmes mariées, les jeunes filles qui sont sacrifiées au profit des garçons. Elle n'ira plus à l'école comme les putes de ce pays que tu baises, et tu voudrais l'y envoyer comme l'infime minorité de femmes que tu n'arrives pas à baiser."*
> *"Mais . . . Mais qu'est-ce qu'elle va devenir?" demanda Awono.*
> *"Comme tout le monde," dit la Comtesse qui en avait marre de parler. "Une femme, une femme, tout simplement."*] (Beyala 1994, 168–169).

The countess is also a duplicitous character who tries to have her cake and eat it too. She tries to reinforce her own power over Awono to the detriment of Sorraya and Awono's brothers. In this respect, she is stuck in the vicious circle that the other protagonists try to break out of. The countess represents the epitome of what they have to reject precisely because she "succeeds" in following the norms of a society in disarray, perpetuating exactly what has been undermining Africa, as Assèze points out in her final account. I will return to this point in Part 3, "Toward a New Political-Novel."

The Functions of the Prostitute in Beyala's Work

In this world of women where men appear only as intruders and are reduced to their financial or inseminating functions, Beyala strips relations between man and woman, woman and woman, and mother and daughter to their essential elements. By using the context of prostitution, Beyala achieves an intensity of vision that extends to the limits of what is tolerable. By immersing us in a world of horror and violence, but also of fantasies and dreams, Beyala forces us to rethink our ideas about the world in order to find some remedy for society's indifference. Like her fellow writers, she utilizes the character of the prostitute as an instrument of political criticism. However, this critique is no longer aimed at the colonizer or the elite but at all of African society in its "fundamentality," especially in its apathy: "Do they think that one day they can extricate themselves from their wretchedness? For now, nobody seems to want to take up the reins" (*The Sun,* Beyala 1996, 91).

The criticism is all the more biting in that it touches men and women alike. In order to accomplish this critique, Beyala uses a procedure that differs from that of most male writers, accentuating the similarities between prostitutes and other women rather than their differences. In an article on the image of prostitution in the works of two female Argentine writers, Louisa Valenzuela and Amalia Jamilis, Amy Katz Kaminsky detects this same principle.[19] Like her Latin American sisters, Beyala constructs individuals rather than archetypal figures, giving each character its own life and development, creating it from the inside according to a feminine point of view. The male writer endows this character with a feminine quality that illustrates a political or moral lesson. The female writer approaches the character with empathetic examination; the prostitute is a woman with traits common to all women. Beyala engages in this perspective, although she diverges radically from other writers on the following point: Far from avoiding any identification with her reader (by creating a suturing effect, for instance, by minimizing the protagonist's intelligence and clairvoyance), as the two Latin American authors have done, she pushes the reader to identify with Ateba, Tanga, or Megri. Each character embodies a model of clairvoyance that is symbolic of the new woman and of the potential new society. In fact, Beyala takes apart and contradicts the traditional literary definition of the character at every moment. The prostitute is no longer an "other" character who exists only for man, who barely exists for other women, and who does not exist at all for herself.[20] Instead, she is an incarnation of all women. The character exists through and by other women and, furthermore, it is in discovering her sisters that she finally discovers herself.

In addition to raising the question of how women define themselves, Beyala denounces prostitution as dangerous for contemporary African society. In particular, she singles out the daughter's exploitation by the mother who encourages attracting and pleasing a man in order to live off of him as if such an arrangement were part of the financial system. Through this denunciation, Beyala explores society at its lowest level in order to define a new ethic for society and the sexes. Finally, the daughter's revolt unearths a key question about women and all of society: Can woman break free of the vicious circle to which she has been confined in her relationship with man on the one hand and with the family on the other? In other words, what kind of future exists for the daughter whose eyes are fixed upon her mother? Is there any other viable solution that would not put her at the margins of the group? In addition to these questions, we must ask whether African societies can rid themselves of the habits and dreams that dominate them and whether the contamination of relations is itself capable of being reversed. The questions have been asked, and the reader is invited to participate in the exploration of areas heretofore unexplored. I undertake this exploration in Part 2.

Notes

1. They identify nine basic archetypal figures. To mention only a few, there is "the bitch witch," who embodies meanness and cruelty as she leads men to their ruin. This type is represented by Zola's Nana. There is also "the weak but wonderful prostitute," the one with a golden heart who is loving and innocent, like Marion Delorme in Victor Hugo's novel of the same name and, more recently, Adriana in Alberto Moravia's *La femme de Rome*. Another example is "the saved prostitute," an essentially virtuous woman who is reconverted and saved from her profession. We also find "the seduced-and-abandoned prostitute," who is victimized for her lost virginity and led into a life walking the streets. To consult the entire table, see Horn and Pringle 1984, 1–7.

2. Another Aidoo play, *For Whom Things Do Not Change,* follows the same basic program, blaming the city and the new elite for exploiting traditional communities, particularly by seducing their daughters with the lure of easy gain.

3. For example, the prostitute appears as a secondary character in *Le fils d'Agatha Moudio* (Bebey 1967), *Mon mari est capable* (Boucoulon 1988), and *Un bouquet d'épines pour elle* (Ndao 1988). These are not all prostitutes in the strict sense of the word but women whose manners have been judged as lax or shameful by their communities. In *Le fils d'Agatha Moudio* in particular, the village and especially the mother blame Agatha for "hanging about" and "advertising" her presence with whites and thereby rejecting her own kind.

4. For details concerning the choice of this pseudonym, see Bernard Magnier, "Ken Bugul ou l'écriture thérapeutique," *Notre Librairie* 11 (1985): 151–155.

5. Irène d'Almeida (1994b) stresses this point in her analysis as well, calling our attention to the fact that the protagonist's feeling of being abandoned by her mother as a child is the source of her lack of direction and the search for her identity.

6. In particular, we might recall Cheik Hamidou Kane's *L'aventure ambiguë* (1961), in which Samba's encounter with the West involves a difficult search for

balance between both worlds and their respective systems of value. Samba's journey ends in death upon returning to his native village.

7. She writes: "I began to detest everything about him, including his skin, the very skin that used to fascinate me, down there in the village. . . . I no longer found his skin to be but yellow, sometimes pink, especially when he came in from the cold as pale as a ghost in the desert" (Bugul 1991, 49).

8. I am referring here to the definition provided by Paulette Songue in her analysis *Prostitution en Afrique: L'exemple de Yaoundé* (1986). She makes a distinction between prostitution and semiprostitution, which appears as an original condition in certain developing African countries. "It is the lot of those people who, in daily life, engage in an activity other than prostitution while often pursuing both activities at the same time or subjecting one to the other. They are usually students, housewives, office workers, or other workers at establishments with direct ties to prostitution such as bars, dance halls, and hotels. In certain cases, prostitution is only a rare or secondary activity. In other cases, the acquisition of a diploma is just another advantage in prostituting oneself" (15; my translation). Songue adds that semiprostitution is also practiced by young men. This can be observed in *G'amàrakano* in Rembeyo, Onanga's boyfriend.

9. In this respect, Songue notes that prostitution "regulates woman's sexual instincts that have been traditionally repressed by custom and confined to the home. The practice of monogamy and the choice of a spouse, much like celibacy, can open new horizons of pleasure for women to enjoy. She can take the initiative and use her body as she sees fit. With prostitution, certain social barriers that kept feminine sexuality in check begin to fall away" (1986, 140).

10. *Loukoum, the Little Prince of Belleville,* however, shows prostitution in a less serious and more humorous light, presented through the gaze and observations of its hero, Loukoum, a seven-year-old boy.

11. I refer my readers to the term *situations* as used by Simone de Beauvoir in *Le deuxième sexe* in order to describe different contexts in which woman can find herself. She dedicates part of one chapter to prostitutes and hétaïres (2:246–276).

12. To this point, I have been using the definition of *prostitute* given by Paulette Songue: someone who regularly exchanges sexual services for payment and whose clientele is diverse. Songue remarks that the engagement between two partners, one to pay and one to give, is explicit or implicit depending on the social status of the prostitute. At the lowest level, it is explicit; at the highest level it is a tacit contract. When the primary objective is payment, "she will make no fuss over physical appearances, nor over temperament, nor the marital situation of the person nor of any consideration other than profit" (1986, 12). To this comment, Songue adds, however, that in Cameroon prostitutes work independently and therefore possess a certain theoretical freedom in choosing their clients. Finally, the sanctioned aspect of the transaction is tied to cultural values and can be modified with time and so does not have the same character in the African situation.

13. Naturally, the daughter feels hostility and jealousy regarding the men who take her mother away and pollute her body as they pour their bad blood into her.

14. Irène d'Almeida (1994b, 74–87) draws similar conclusions in her analysis of *Tanga*. She particularly identifies different strategies that the mother uses in order to force Tanga to submit to her duty as a daughter, which in this case means prostituting herself. Likewise, she stresses the successive stages in which Tanga becomes aware of her need to free herself from her mother's control if she wants to go on living. Elsewhere, d'Almeida declares woman's allegiance to a new dream, a dream that is not far from typical Western bourgeois materialism: a house

and a husband whom she loves. The same dream can already be found in *The Sun*, then reappears again in Beyala's *Assèze l'Africaine* (1994), this time in the form of a desire to get married and to thereby establish some kind of stability or social promotion.

15. The situations of Megri and Loukoum are comparable in that they both remain ignorant of their origins. Megri knows nothing about her father, and Loukoum knows nothing about his mother. Both question their remaining parents in their search for the truth. A difference exists in the fact that Loukoum learns the truth only much later.

16. Bjornson states: "The meaning of Tanga's life is crucial to Beyala because it reflects the living death to which African children are born. It also helps explain the breakdown of the African family as a sanctuary for the love that people need in order to lead decent, emotionally fulfilling lives" (1991, 419).

17. Tanga offers a variant on the same character type; because she was abused by her father, her commodification appears almost inevitable.

18. The attraction of a female "client" for a female prostitute has not really been explored. Mutual attraction between women has been treated by Simone de Beauvoir in *Le deuxième sexe* in the chapter entitled "Situations." In the section entitled "The Prostitute," she emphasizes the fact that in a world where man is valued only in a contractual context, a woman represents the only comfort and support that another woman can experience. The situation therefore arises in which prostitutes are brought closer together, often within homosexual relationships.

In her preface to *The Prostitute in Literature* (1960), Aron Krich insists on the distinction between the feelings of men and women toward the prostitute. For men, he emphasizes, the prostitute represents the possibility of abandoning responsibilities; for women, the prostitute becomes a sort of unconscious rival who is inaccessible and invulnerable, simultaneously hated and envied and sometimes imitated (see, for example, p. 3).

19. Amy Katz Kaminsky (1984, 121) writes: "When a woman writer confronts the figure of the prostitute, she can see her creation as 'other' only on the most superficial level. She comes to understand the 'other' as somehow being connected to herself."

20. The original phrase here can be attributed to Katz Kaminsky. I have translated it and slightly modified it for the convenience of the text.

3

Madness and "Mad" Women

All deviations from the dominant stream of thought, that is to say, the be-
lief of a permanent essence of a wo/man and in an invariant but fragile
identity, whose "loss" is considered to be a "specifically human danger"
can easily fit the category of the "mentally ill" or the "mentally unde-
veloped." . . . What if the popularized story of the identity crisis proves
to be a story and nothing else? . . . How am I to lose, maintain, or gain
a (female) identity when it is impossible for me to take up a position out-
side this identity from which I presumably reach in and feel for it?
—Trinh T. Minh-ha (*Woman, Native, Other*, 96)

An overview of black African literature of the 1980s reveals a number of novels that have a depressive female character as the main protagonist. These characters often live in marginalized situations on the fringe of madness. In the works of some women authors, these characters seem to recur in a virtually systematic fashion. I shall set out here to define this character's function and the rationale for its selection by the author.[1]

Using the following corpus—*Scarlet Song* (Bâ 1981), *L'appel des arènes* (Sow Fall 1982), *Juletane* (Warner-Vieyra 1987), and *Etrange héritage* (Ami 1985)—I shall examine the archetypal physical, psychological, and sociological traits common to these feminine characters who live in the midst of depression and fall prey to madness.[2]

In addition to these common traits, a more detailed analysis will reveal the layering of certain narrative leitmotifs chosen to fully render the protagonist's violence and suffering. I shall study the writing of madness and violence through the insertion of a diary within the text, the (re)reading of epistolary fragments, and, especially, the implicit or explicit presence of multiple narratees in the position of the reader or interlocutor.

The Archetypal Traits of Characters

To begin, I would like to establish a preliminary classification of characters in order to make the comparisons more meaningful. The different protagonists can be divided into two categories: those considered from the start as existing at the margins of some group and those whose marginalization results from the character's evolution. Mireille (*Scarlet Song*) and Juletane (*Juletane*) fall into the first category; Diattou (*L'appel des arènes*) and Déla (*Etrange héritage*) fall into the second. Because they have been imposed on their husbands' families and because they have come from France, Mireille (a white woman) and Juletane (an Antillean woman) appear as foreigners in a situation of immediate exclusion. Diattou and Déla form a second category of characters. In light of their initially promising situations, their slip into madness defies our expectations. Another possible subcategory is the cause-and-effect relation that is responsible for the character's madness, whether brought on by emotional disappointment in love (Mireille, Juletane, Déla) or professional and familial disappointments (Diattou).

If the circumstances that cause each character's marginalization are different, the evolutionary process remains the same. Mireille (*Scarlet Song*), Diattou (*L'appel des arènes*), Juletane (*Juletane*), and Déla (*Etrange héritage*) evolve along a single line that runs from the positive pole (of socioeconomic success, beauty, decisiveness, confidence in the other) to the opposite pole (involving a serious decline in social conditions, the character's marginalization, the indifference of a husband or loved one, physical deterioration, and madness.) A number of external signs denote this passage from the positive to the negative extreme. On the one hand, the character gradually loses her powers of seduction, a loss signaled by a physical degeneration consistent with the appearance of psychosomatic disturbances such as anorexia (Mireille, Diattou, Déla) or obsessive fixations and paranoid reactions (Mireille, Juletane).

> I was no longer alive and was indifferent to everything around me. Everyone was tired of having comforted me so much and so they left me to my own sad fate. I made an effort to swallow a few mouthfuls of food for my parents' sake. A relapse was imminent. . . . I even ignored my own son.
>
> *[Je ne vivais plus et étais indifférente à tout ce qui m'entourait. Tout le monde, fatigué de m'avoir assez réconfortée me laissa à mon triste sort. Pour mes parents, je fis l'effort d'avaler quelques bouchées de nourriture. . . . Une rechute me guettait. . . . J'ignorais même mon fils.]* (*Etrange héritage*, Ami 1985, 150).

> Mireille no longer laughed. Mireille no longer spoke. Mireille no longer ate. Mireille no longer slept. . . . Suffering had become an integral part of the rhythm of her existence. (*Scarlet Song*, Bâ 1986, 163)

> I was losing weight, my skirts which were now too big, made me look like a scarecrow. . . . I remained locked in my room without eating or drinking. (*Juletane*, Warner-Vieyra 1987, 24)

Juletane in particular details the protagonist's pathological behavior in its slightest phases and developments, from mental anguish and collapse to full-blown rage: "I turn around: it is Diary. . . . I know that Awa has sent her. Am I not mad in their eyes? It is natural. I am being watched. . . . I want to scream. Why this sudden anger? . . . So, I carefully tear the sheet into tiny pieces. That keeps me busy, entertains me and calms my anger" (Warner-Vieyra 1987, 16–17).

The character's social status changes as she loses her initial position of strength. Diattou, for example, initially projects an image of the socially successful and emancipated African woman. She is the midwife in charge of the maternity ward; professionally trained in France, she symbolizes professional success for women. Her absence from the hospital and a spate of negative rumors about her (incited by the jealousy that her exceptional status has provoked) gradually knock her from her pedestal. For Mireille, Déla, and Juletane, the decline is signaled by their being increasingly neglected by the man they love. This decline is translated externally by a lack of interest and appreciation for their daily environment in addition to a loss of sleep and appetite. Juletane seems almost like an extension of Mireille's character insofar as she goes deeper into her experience of madness. The insertion of a diary into the narration provides access to the character's inner feelings and allows us to separate the different stages in the transition from the character's marginalization to her extreme alienation.

In fact, looking at Mireille and Juletane respectively, we find nearly identical descriptions of physical and mental characteristics as well as a number of other common features, in particular their inassimilable status. They are both foreigners—Mireille because she is a white woman and Juletane, paradoxically, because she has been assimilated into French culture. Their status as foreigners pushes them to the edge of the society in which they exist. In contrast to this category of marginal female characters, Diattou represents another type of marginalization. As a result of her foreign education and her rejection of African traditions for European customs, Diattou is gradually excluded from African society. In contrast to Mireille and Juletane, from the very beginning Diattou voluntarily excludes herself from her community by rejecting African traditions as "outdated" and "atavistic." Among the traditions she refuses are the celebration of baptism, the importance of the family and the village, the polygamous social structure, and traditional festivals and practices such as the wrestling in the arenas, the dances, and the tam-tam.

This rejection of traditions and ritual dances and entertainment must be emphasized as something that all the characters considered here share (with the exception of Déla, who displays a general passivity, absorbing everything that is imposed on her). This characteristic is especially evident in Mireille and Juletane. In their cases, however, this rejection is given as a primary factor in their failure to adapt to the society in which they live. Mireille, Diattou, and Juletane exhibit the same irritation with the tam-tam and prefer classical music to drumming. (Mireille and Diattou prefer Mozart; Juletane likes Beethoven.) Once again, this preference is a sign of their subscription to European standards of taste and judgment.

An Archetypal Context

In the novels under consideration here, the theme of madness also involves another type of behavior, that of the hero-victim or, in this case, of the heroine who refuses to play an active role or even participate in basic social functions. Each of the protagonists shuts herself up within a form of solitude that constitutes a response and a system of defense in reaction to a specific event that has deeply disturbed her sense of identity and definitively pushed her to the edge. On the one hand, their alienation is caused by a combination of factors—their status as outsiders, such as the hostility of the community (the mother-in-law's in Mireille's case and the third cowife's in Juletane's); the continuous and invasive presence of the husband's friends (for Mireille and Juletane); and the barrier of the foreign language, which inhibits any ongoing communication with the family of in-laws and the other members of the community (Mireille, Juletane). On the other hand, a specific event—the discovery of a lie within the couple's relationship—acts as a catalyst: The spouse learns about another wife (or woman) whose existence is revealed a posteriori, indirectly, by a third party (by the lover's sister in the cases of Mireille and Déla). The evidence of the lie destroys the world that the character has constructed for herself. There is a sharp break with the past that leads to an irremediable process of physical and psychological deterioration.

A number of the points made here complement those mentioned by Evelyn O'Callaghan (1990) in her analysis of the character of the "mad" woman in Caribbean literature. Based on a study of novels by Jean Rhys (*Wide Sargasso Sea,* 1966), Myriam Warner-Vieyra (*Le quimboiseur l'avait dit,* 1980), and Zee Edgell (*Beka Lamb,* 1980), O'Callaghan observes that in spite of their different racial, sociological, and historical contexts, these protagonists share the same history of rejection by one or both of their parents and the same experience of solitude, insecurity, and despair while growing up.

This kind of background fatally leads to the character's withdrawal, a gradual marginalization, and a fragmentation of the self that when carried to its extreme, leads to the character's madness:

> The characters are portrayed as reacting with feelings of anger, guilt, frustration and hopelessness. They exhibit behavioral abnormalities such

as extreme violence, paranoia, and, in the case of those whose mental world we are permitted to enter, hallucinations. (O'Callaghan 1990, 90)

This description is appropriate to our characters, and we can probe deeper into the causes of this madness within an African context.

The Character's Evolution: From Marginalization to Madness

Disillusionment in love (Mireille, Juletane, Déla) and professional life (Diattou) provokes the character's withdrawal into madness. This condition often involves megalomania, paranoia, hysterical crisis, and violent outbursts as well as a withdrawal into the self and an incommensurable sadness (in Déla's case). This transformation is signaled by the voluntary solitude of the characters. The final separation with the outer world is accomplished symbolically through the gesture of acting violently against their children (Déla in *Etrange héritage,* Mireille in *Scarlet Song,* Diattou in *L'appel des arènes*) even if this was the one thing that initially kept them alive and served as their sole reason for fighting. Through the act of infanticide, Mireille and Diattou attack their positions as mother and wife. In Diattou's case, the infanticide is indirect in the sense that her behavior is responsible for the anorexia of her son, Nalla. Juletane reacts in a similar way. Once she is deprived of the possibility of becoming a mother (her husband's attitude toward her changes after her miscarriage), she takes revenge on her husband Mamadou's indifference by poisoning the children of Awa, her first cowife, an act that leads to Awa's suicide. In these three cases, the woman attempts to erase any ties to the past—by denying the flesh and genes of her husband (Mireille); by attacking her husband's most precious thing, that is, his child(ren) (Mireille, Juletane); or by simply forgetting the past (Diattou). In contrast, Déla becomes preoccupied with her newborn son; the entire narrative is, in effect, a long explanatory letter to her son, his only inheritance.

Confronted with rejection and their resulting marginalization, Mireille, Diattou, Juletane, and Déla share a common reaction: the absence of desire. Julia Kristeva explains this absence of desire as an element of neurotic and psychotic behavior.[3] Each of the characters displays evidence of this absence of desire in one form or another, whether it be detachment from the external world, continual daydreaming,[4] neglect of her body, a refusal of conversational or sexual contact with the opposite sex, or closing herself off from others through verbal and physical aggression, anger, and silence.

In the context of this atrophy of the self, writing assumes increased importance as a sheltering, therapeutic activity. In relation to this subject, Sneja Gunew (1985) investigates the authority speaking and writing grants to marginal characters and notes the importance of the personal voice occurring in the form of homodiagetic narration.[5] According to her analysis, this form in particular requires a minimal amount of justification and is therefore more easily accessible to the marginalized character. Indeed, the narrative use of the first person is of primordial importance in *Scarlet Song, Etrange héritage*, and *Juletane*.

As Linda Kauffman shows in her critical analysis *Discourses of Desire* (1986), writing becomes not only a substitute for desire but the very source of desire. Kauffman refers to the example of the *trois Maria* in which the question of passion takes precedence over the object of passion within an exchange of letters:[6]

> Granted, then, that all literature is a long letter to an invisible other, a present, a possible, or a future passion that we rid ourselves of, feed, or seek. (1986, 1)

Writing is an erotic practice and initiates a series of exchanges between addresser *(destinateur)* and addressee *(destinataire),* between the writing subject *(l'écrivant)* and the receiver *(le récepteur).* In *Sade, Fourier, Loyola,* Barthes points out the fluidity of the reader's and writer's roles in creating a space to be explored, "nature and culture, the past and the present, desire and the law, the body and language." Barthes therefore analyzes writing as a process of research into the laws that preside over the desires of the writer and reader.

In *Scarlet Song, Juletane,* and *Etrange héritage,* we find elaborate work on the text as a place for interaction, notably in the epistolary form (or one of its variants such as the diary or the confession story).

Written as a letter addressed to a particular reader—the heroine's newborn son, Désiré—*Etrange héritage* recalls the narrative technique of Mariama Bâ's *So Long a Letter.* The letter, however, does not support any dialogue between mother and son. It is only in the second paragraph that the narration assumes a truly epistolary form: "Désiré, the joy of my life was having met your father. If I had only known what this very joy had in store for me" [Désiré, mon bonheur était d'avoir rencontré ton père. Si j'avais su ce que ce même bonheur me réservait.] (Ami 1985, 7). The next line already introduces the evocation of the past, the narrator's inner gaze cast on her past. From now on, the name Désiré will appear only in the third person in order to refer to his birth, his growth, and finally in these last lines, as the addressee of this long letter—which is, however, not directly addressed to him:

> I won't see Désiré grow up anymore, but he will know that he was the most beautiful thing that I had in my short life. . . . These pages will constitute his inheritance. He will understand and won't be too upset with us

for having brought him into this world and for having left him alone. From heaven we will try to help him with love.

[Je ne verrai plus Désiré grandir mais il saura qu'il était ce que j'ai eu de plus beau dans ma courte vie. . . . Ces pages constituent son héritage. Il comprendra et ne nous en voudra pas trop de l'avoir fait venir dans ce monde et de l'avoir laissé seul. De là-haut, nous essaierons de l'aider avec amour.] (152)

Only the supposedly posthumous signature is directly addressed to the son and follows, in its textual position, the format of a letter:

Adieu my son,
　　　　Your Mother Déla, who died for having loved too much,
　　　　　　　　　　　　　　　　　　　　　Adieu.

[Adieu mon fils,
　　　　Ta maman Déla, morte pour avoir trop aimé.
　　　　　　　　　　　　　　　　　Adieu.] (153)

The letter ends with the announcement of Déla's death, but the reader learns from the epilogue that the attempted suicide has been averted, and the character fades away into a lifelong madness that leads her to the psychiatric hospital. The greatest difference between *Etrange héritage* and *So Long a Letter* is that in the latter, the narration itself plays a curative role in two specific ways: The letter is systematically dated to observe the passage of time required for a respectful observance of mourning and widowhood; thematically, the letter is a dialogue between two friends, Aïssatou and Ramatoulaye, who have gone through similar trials. In *Etrange héritage,* Déla's letter simply stands as a confession to proclaim her guilt and suffering; she believes that she caused her husband's death by resorting to the services of a marabout. The text leaves us, unofficial narratees, somewhat dissatisfied; the melodramatic tone and the narrator's obstinacy in shutting herself up within her own sadness for a love that has been scorned and betrayed— when obvious signs of difficulty and instability existed in their love from the start—make it harder to empathize with the character.

Scarlet Song is composed not of a single letter but of a series of letters whose addressers and addressees vary. These letters function on two levels and within two different time frames. The alternation of letters sent to the respective parents of Mireille and Ousmane and their reading by the concerned parties attest to the similarity of reactions by parental authority in both the black and white communities. The regular correspondence between Mireille and Ousmane reveals their parallel feelings and ideas in pursuing a common political ideal (Mireille as a demonstrator in 1968 and Ousmane as an activist during the strike at the University of Dakar). At the same time, this correspondence foreshadows their different attitudes toward their engagement. Mireille's letters confirm her extremism *(jusqu'au-boutisme)* in her love for Ousmane and in her resolve to wait for him and follow him back to his country. Circulating in the opposite direction, Ousmane's letters include a proleptic warning about the hardships involved with this course of action, as well as a clear declaration of his integrationism. Marrying Ousmane would be marrying into his religion and the customs of his country.

Later in the story, the rereading of fragments of Ousmane's letters acts as a catalyst and sets off Mireille's hysteria. Because the letters reveal the rupture between a before and an after, exposing the lie of their current relationship, they push Mireille into the irrational. Mireille's violence is revealingly concentrated on these letters as obvious proof of the lie; hence her shredding them with a pair of scissors. Feeding on a constant desire for vengeance, she moves into a stage of verbal violence directed at Ousmane and the mixed-race child before turning to extreme violence and ultimate revenge: the infanticide of Gnouloule Khessoule and the attempted murder of Ousmane.[7]

In *Juletane,* the protagonist's diary also plays a dual role, acting as both therapy and confession. Here, too, writing functions as a mechanism of *jouissance* and as a substitute for the object of desire. Writing in her diary is Juletane's only source of peace and well-being. In "The Discourse of the Imaginary," Gregory L. Ulmer comments on the role of writing as an agent that first affects the writing subject *(l'écrivant)* from within—one writes for oneself as a sort of ethical exercise. It is also Juletane's only pastime and, through the dating system of the diary, her only tie with reality. For Juletane, who exists outside of society, the process of time has nearly ceased altogether; ironically, she is caught short of time when Mamadou dies before she can complete the diary she was writing for him. Her purpose in writing the diary to Mamadou is both to confess and to exact revenge. A reading of the diary is supposed to make Mamadou aware of his responsibility in Juletane's sufferings and, moreover, of the true cause of the death of Awa's children—the fact that Juletane poisoned them (even though the writing seems to cast doubt on who might have poisoned the children). For the time being, Mamadou's premature death deprives Juletane of her vengeful pleasure.

A second mechanism of exchange between addresser and unintended addressee is superimposed on the former through Hélène, the Antillean medical assistant who comes across Juletane's diary. The narration is thus interspersed with Hélène's reaction to what she reads in the diary. As a professionally successful Antillean woman who is well integrated in Senegalese society, she functions as Juletane's counterimage. Hélène's reading of the diary acts as a catalyst for her to examine her own life and confront her own image, and thus Juletane is also a countermirroring image for

Hélène. The "given literary text" (Juletane's diary) is transplanted into Hélène's life, and the "text of the other" manages to transcribe a fragment of Hélène's life. By imagining Juletane's experiences, Hélène succeeds in representing her own life. The diary has therapeutic value, since it finally forces Hélène to recognize an emotion. Thus the alternation of Juletane's diary and Hélène's reflections, her shifting impressions, dissolve the borders between analyzed and analyst.[8] By inscribing their history between the two, they articulate a fundamental revolt. The personal has become political.

Linda Kauffman's analysis of *Three Marias* is quite relevant to Juletane and Hélène, who through their interaction expose "the codes responsible for the reduction of woman to a 'legal fiction'; these codes grant her an individuality and a legal identity, reinscribing her in the books of Law and the books of life" (1986, 290). By constructing a narrator/narratee system, Juletane and Hélène demolish the fixed traditional literary code of hierarchies (active writer/passive reader). On the topic of the epistolary love discourse (of which Juletane's diary is one form), Linda Kauffman notes that it becomes acrobatic and thus reproduces the different positions of passion. Writing accordingly becomes a mimesis of "the double, of duplicity and dissimulation" (294).

The claim to madness also offers the character the power of unlimited creation, by which the woman acquires the means to denounce the patriarchal colonizing discourse. Until recently, madness had been viewed as a dead-end, an abdication of the subject confronted with the difficulties of the surrounding world. In *La folie et la chose littéraire*, Shoshana Felman analyzes the psychological, social, and material condition of the woman facing madness:

> Madness is the complete opposite of protest; it is a dead end for those whose cultural conditioning has denied them even the means to revolt. "Mental illness" is the expression of a cultural impotence and a political castration, the social and psychological manifestation of a request for help, of a cry for help, which are all still a part of woman's conditioning, of the ideological stereotype of her role and of "feminine" behavior. (Felman 1978, 139; my translation)

In fact, psychotic characters in literature have always denied their madness, as O'Callaghan (1990) shows regarding Caribbean literature. Such characters have always accused their entourage of using this label against them in order to shut them up within a behavior and a world associated with madness, understood in both the literal and figurative sense. With *Scarlet Song* and *Juletane,* the theme of madness becomes political protest and demand *(revendication)*. In *Archetypal Patterns in Woman's Fiction*, Annis Pratt writes about this matter: "Escape through imagination is not escapist but strategic, a withdrawal into the unconscious for the purpose of personal transformation" (1981, 177).

In an initial phase, Juletane refuses to be referred to as the madwoman, which is what N'deye, the third wife, calls her. Juletane doubts the existence of her madness while projecting the responsibility onto others: "And my madness, whose will was that? That is, if I could be considered mad. . . . My madness is the private property of Mamadou Moustapha's house and in particular of N'deye" (Warner-Vieyra 1987, 62). She draws a distinction between different types of psychoses and in her diary records her observations on the patients around her, whom she classifies as "mad," thereby dissociating herself from such behavior. In her second phase, however, she lays claim to this madness. She not only accepts its reality but actually manages to benefit from it, enjoying the privilege of not having to participate in common chores and thereby escaping the duties of the other wives. From her situation as a victim, she moves straight into a position of power. She becomes the person with a right to special consideration and one who therefore also has the leisure to write.[9]

Both Hélène's presence as a reader of Juletane's diary and her indignation make the writing not only political but unifying *(solidaire):* "Reading her compatriot's diary made Hélène more determined than ever. She was ready to avenge her. She wanted to make every man on earth suffer, to humiliate all men and emasculate them" (Warner-Vieyra 1987, 46).

When considered together, the novels disclose a common political engagement and a discourse of denunciation. In "Geographies of Pain, Captive Bodies and Violent Acts in the Fictions of Myriam Warner-Vieyra, Gayle Jones and Bessie Head," Françoise Lionnet comments on the subversive character of such a text as follows:

> For whereas murder is generally considered to be a crime of the individual against society, in these texts, it is present as a symptom of society's crime against the female individual. . . . The narratives thus construct each of them as a heroine who takes justice into her own hands, revealing a profound conflict of values between the dominant culture and its "weaker" members. (*Callaloo* 16, no. 1 [1987]: 135)

This discourse is, first, one of lack and frustration. Considered separately, the discourses of Mireille, Diattou, and Juletane each expose the same fundamental elements: nostalgia, desire for revenge, anger, and the need for expiation and exorcism. At the heart of this system lies the principle of alterity, in other words, the fact that one can feel total empathy for the other and even become the other, as Cixous describes in *Le rire de la Méduse:*

> Women for women: the wonders of being several others, she does not defend herself against these unknown other women that she catches

herself perceiving herself to be, enjoying her gift of alterity. (1975, 50; my translation)

This possibility of alterity also holds out hope against the pathological. If, however, each of the characters is examined in terms of her distinct experience, we notice a difference in tone. Diattou and Mireille can be grouped together on one hand, Juletane and Déla on the other. Because they were not able or because they did not know how to create the possibility of an interlocutor for themselves, Diattou and Mireille remain complete prisoners of their neurosis. Through the creation of an other—through the creation of a substitute for what is missing in love by writing or telling her story—Juletane initially escapes her madness. Mireille simply remains in the stage of nostalgia and desire for revenge, so her discourse only reproduces what is lacking or revolting: Questions are still unanswered, and the marginal language includes slang, interjections, sexual/erotic terminology, and insults. Juletane's discourse goes further, breaking apart language's normalizing frame through dialogism. In her analyses of the discourse of love, Kauffman demonstrates that the use of dialogism results in a political decentralization of language. Moreover, recourse to homodiagetic narration creates a more direct empathy and requires the reader to compare the story with his or her own experience of life. The "I" becomes a political *autogynography*.[10]

Lionnet states the importance of *Juletane*'s dual narrative in this regard:

> *Juletane* relies heavily on the principle of doubling, on both the levels of theme and structure. The text constructs a dialogue between Juletane's diary and Hélène's reading: it is thanks to the personal narrative of a fellow Guadeloupean that Hélène reorganizes her own "face" and her own predicament in the mirror of the story. Doubling also occurs among the three cowives, Juletane, N'deye and Awa in a way that is suggestive of the echoing patterns of disfiguration, death and castration that are at the center of Warner-Vieyra's works. (Lionnet 1989, 139)

Lionnet explores this aspect of mutual and substitutional reflection/reflexivity between Juletane and Hélène. She equally stresses the interest of the play of contrasts between the three cowives. As she explains,

> It is among the three co-wives that textual specularity is established in a non-binary fashion: for if N'deye and Awa are each other's opposites—the modern, superficially educated, vulgar, spendthrift, urbanized wife, and the illiterate, but refined traditional African wife—they are also the figures whose fate incorporates elements of Juletane's own predicament: Awa commits suicide by jumping into a well, while Juletane keeps feeling trapped in a well of loneliness and despair . . . ; and Juletane appears

to enact her own anxieties about her loss of self by disfiguring N'deye. Juletane's diary thus constructs each of her co-wives as a "substitutive exchange that constitutes [her] as subject" (De Man, 921), since the specular structure of their relationships points to Juletane's implicit recognition of their shared predicament as faceless/nameless women occupying the position "wife" and hence easily substitutable or permutable within the familial economy. (1989, 140)

The creation of a fluid system (between the reader in the text and the readers of the text) allows an active exchange between the writing/narrating figure and its receiver. It is through the intermediary of language and writing that desire reappears. In contrast to the traditional discourse of love, however, the discourse of these characters is above all negation and denial *(dénégation)*. The possibility of an alternative, the possibility that things could have happened differently, is certainly evoked (Diattou, who dreamed of a certain kind of future for her son, Nalla; Déla, who imagines that she will finally be accepted by Koffi's father and become his wife; Mireille and Juletane, who imagine that they will return to France). This appeal, however, is more an attempt to explain the negative charge that drives the character who is faced with the impossibility of alternatives. There is the multiplication of rage (for Mireille, who rips up all her letters) and the reinforced desire for revenge (for Juletane, who imagines Mamadou's body and different tortures to inflict on N'deye). The character enjoys combining the imaginary (resting on an irrational foundation of violence and castration) and the reality of her marginalization in relation to the group. Furthermore, the weaving of the two discourses, that of narrator and narratee, create a web that spawns desire. The discourse becomes a "dramatization of the exercise of passion as spectacle" (Kauffman 1986).

This combination of two discourses constitutes a fundamental difference from previous texts on women's madness. A new space has arisen in the place of woman's textual silence, the sign of her exclusion from society, a space in which the discourse of madness finds its own expression. It is given to woman to elaborate her own discourse on the exclusion and the silence of women. These texts thus offer an indirect response to certain questions asked by Felman: "The alterity of woman as a subject of the enunciation" [l'altérité de la femme comme sujet de l'énoncé] is "fully assumed" [pleinement assumée] and questioned in "the place of its enunciation" [le lieu de son énonciation].[11]

In this sense, Warner-Vieyra's text goes further in its claims for madness. In "Les naufragés" (*Femmes échouées,* 1988), she probes even deeper not only into the question of the threshold of consciousness for psychotic individuals but also into the question of the margin of power granted to whoever has been labeled mad. The protagonist, To de Blocoto, plays this card fully aware that she is allowed to do anything in words or in actions on account of her illness. This last element of being able to say or do anything may define exactly what sustains the author's interest in a psychotic character. Placed at a certain spatial and temporal distance, freed from any normative constraints, this character presents an unlimited capacity for denunciation. Because the marginal, alienated character refers to the center as a complement, he or she ends up shattering the aberrations of the central normative structure. The dramatization of the lack and of passion but also of madness, the recurring reliance on certain textual leitmotifs and common archetypal character traits, and the use of specific narrative strategies all beg the question of whether there is a system and of what rationale guides women writers in their choice of the neurotic or hysterical female character.

Choosing a Neurotic/Psychotic Character

Reading Déla's character raises the problem of her passivity, her sense of resignation and submission. In contrast to Mireille and Juletane, Déla displays no signs of resentment or any desire for revenge but only a sadness that infiltrates the permeable narrative. The text does not go beyond the level of woman's traditional social and sexual victimization and falls within the limits of writings cited by Phyllis Chesler in *Women and Madness* (1972). As Felman shows in her analysis of Chesler's study, "the book identifies and questions 'a psychology of woman' created by an oppressive and patriarchal male culture" (Felman 1978, 78). She quotes the following passage on this subject:

> It is obvious that if a woman wants to be sane, she has to "adapt" to the behavioral norms of her sex and accept them as such, even if the kinds of behavior in question are generally thought to have a lesser social appeal. . . . In our civilization, the ethic of mental health is masculine. (Felman 1978, 78, quoting Chesler 1972)

By behavioral norms of the feminine sex, we are supposed to understand that "the social role assigned to woman" is either one of serving the primary authoritarian figure of man, in other words being a daughter, mother, or wife (Felman 1978, 139). Déla accepts this triple role at every point in the story. She is an exemplary case of the perfect daughter, attentive to her mother's advice and happy with her parents' love. She is an ideal example of the woman in love, feeding on the classic dreams of the future happiness that she is supposed to discover in becoming the wife of the man she loves, in tending to his needs, in making him happy and bearing his child. Finally, she is a loving mother who wants to be cured of her illness (love!) and to find the strength needed to be at her son's side. If she consults the marabout (not on her own initiative but at her friends' request), it is in the hope of regaining her place in Koffi's heart. But she does so only under a condition defined from the start—that the marabout's interference will cause Koffi no harm. When Déla learns of her lover's death, she believes that she is responsible for this sad result. Her parents reveal what really happened: Déla's friend Affi never returned to the marabout, and thus Déla is not responsible in any way for Koffi's death.

Déla neverthelesss feels guilty and sinks into the role of a victim, preferring to be alone with her sadness. Her only opportunity to revolt escapes her own control, and she becomes anorexic. Her physical weakness and her depression all lead to an attempted suicide from which she is saved, but only to sink once and for all into madness and live out the rest of her days in a psychiatric ward. These are all so many signs of revolt against victimization, a victimization that she has, however, consented to. With its first-person narrative, the novel recalls an earlier literature of testimony, yet its portrayal of the African woman's submission to misguided dreams does not engender much sympathy in the reader.

Mariama Bâ's writing, on the contrary, takes a political turn. Through Mireille's failure, the author accounts for the problem of cultural differences in the concepts of the family, marriage, and the couple. Bâ makes us aware of certain obstacles facing African women in the postcolonial situation. In this sense, the novel is a continuation of *So Long a Letter,* transposing Aïssatou's problems into a third-person world. These problems include a conjugal relation that deteriorates because of pressures from the husband's mother and friends. These pressures give rise to the husband's indifference and convince him to take a second wife, to whom he grants all possible favors including financial preference.

Aminata Sow Fall uses Diattou's character in *L'appel des arènes* in order to single out one of the specific aspects of postcolonialism—the danger of systematically copying the European model at the risk of losing one's own identity. She equally demonstrates, however, that any step backward to a precolonial Africa is a utopian dream and that only a balance between modern Western technology and African traditions—which is yet to be found for each individual and for each woman in particular—can ensure the viability of African women and men. This choice seems all the more delicate for woman insofar as she is expected to act as the upholder of traditions. And so her emancipation is often branded as subversive by the community at large.

Through Juletane's character, Warner-Vieyra explores the topics of alterity and marginalization. Inassimilable as a foreigner, Juletane contributes to her own marginalization and willingly shuts herself up within the solitude of writing. Through the character's reflections on polygamy, rivalries with cowives, and the strength of the traditions that have recaptured her husband's way of thinking, the author describes the multiple obstacles in African women's daily life. In an interview with Mildred Mortimer, Warner-Vieyra answered a question on the autobiographical elements of this character:

> Of course, my writing is not concerned directly with my own personal life but presents parallels. Like Juletane, I was born in the Antilles, left the islands to go to France and then to Senegal. Although Juletane does just that, people who know me know that my life and hers are not the same. My husband was neither Muslim nor from the same country as hers. Yet I tried to put myself in my character's place and see what would happen. . . . I make Juletane react the way I believe I would in identical circumstances. . . . My character acts somewhat the way I do. If my husband were polygamous and I were confronted with Juletane's dilemma, I wonder if I would have chosen to leave. . . . Since psychological problems, particularly women's struggles with depression have always fascinated me, I placed her in a situation where I believe the only possibility of getting out that she has is through inner escape. (*Callaloo* 16, no. 1 [1993]: 111)

Juletane's criticisms regarding N'deye and Awa elsewhere take on an important metaphoric value. In "Reading Warner-Vieyra's Juletane," Jonathan Ngate stresses that Juletane's rejection of these two women is a meaningful instance of the rejection of feminine types deemed inadequate. In Awa, Juletane rejects the submissive woman for whom the husband remains the master. In N'deye, she condemns the African vamp, the Europeanized coquette full of vain demands. Yet Juletane's example is a warning and a reminder for the woman who may be lulled by the illusion of the sentimental and who may privilege the discourse of love as it occurs in the Western context. Françoise Lionnet emphasizes Juletane's obstinacy in clinging to her exclusive love for Mamadou to the detriment of any other potential interests. By this refusal, she sanctions her failure to overcome the fixed symbolic order of patriarchal relations.

> For Warner-Vieyra, . . . madness and death seem to underscore the triumphant reinscription of the symbolic order since the heroine's rebellion fails to dismantle or transpose the patriarchal narrative: Juletane never actually loses the desire to please her husband Mamadou. (Lionnet 1989, 134)

If the novel deals with the problems of African women, it also evokes the difficulties of the foreign woman and beyond these, more specifically, the hardships for the Antillean woman of being in France or Africa. Warner-Vieyra develops this point in greater detail and further pursues the theme of madness in "Les naufragés," although this time as a meta-discourse on madness in Caribbean society. Here, we can refer to Evelyn

O'Callaghan's analysis, which interprets the recurrence of the psychotic character in Caribbean literature as a metaphoric inscription of the "ontological insecurity" that is prevalent in Caribbean society: "The interior schisms dramatized in fiction may be interpreted as the symptoms of the dangerous lack of ontological security still prevalent in our region—manifested in continuing 'outward directness': continuing regard for foreign culture, denigration of local traditions, the need to seek an elusive 'reality' in the metropolis, or to play out roles adapted from imported models/ ideals—all revealing a lack of secure pride in our society and its image" (1990, 104).

The interpretation of the "mad" female character who is at odds with herself—usually read as a metaphor for the subsequent ills of colonialism and a passive, fatalistic mentality of victimization in Caribbean society— can be extended to African society, as Bâ and Sow Fall illustrate in their novels. In the final account, the systematic occurrence of the neurotic or psychotic female character in the works of these women authors, and the recurrence of certain images and narrative techniques such as the diary as the preferred choice to communicate the character's psychological disturbances, raise the question of whether there is an artistic method common to women writers of the diaspora. These elements also raise the question of the use of archetypal linguistic effects as a response to the alienating effect of the patriarchal system in these societies. Why has the subject of madness been taken up uniquely by women authors? Why does it necessarily deal with a female character?

I shall limit myself to a single response, arguing that this type of subject and character, madness and the mad woman, represents a strategy *(biais)* for dealing with political questions. Such a strategy enables women to enter a domain that used to be mainly the prerogative of male writers. Finally, we have come to a signified for this character, as opposed to what the signifier revealed (psychosomatic disturbances, the breakdown of the personality, withdrawal into the self). Certainly, the character of the mad woman possesses all the attributes of a heroine-victim (in the sense developed by Vladimir Propp[12]). She is characterized by her inaction, her refusal to participate in the life around her, preferring to close herself into her own world. By her presence *(son être-là)*, she nonetheless functions as a catalyst. She becomes the inscription of woman's refusal of the limited normative framework to which her social status confines her. Her discourse carries the important sign of her rebellion against this system. What is more, she operates as a cathartic character whose intermediary enables the reader to purge her own frustrations. From her marginal position, the character becomes central and vital in women's texts. Lionnet's analysis shows that the value of this protagonist, characterized by violence, death, and/or murder, involves a transgression of the symbolic decapitation to which the patriarchal order has subjected her. Using Hélène Cixous's *Castration or Decapitation*, Lionnet remarks that it is through her hysterical laughter that the mad woman succeeds in freeing herself from the masculine economy and thereby threatens the normative environment. Nevertheless, she concludes that *Juletane*'s denouement (and the same can be said of *Scarlet Song* and *Etrange héritage*), death and/or murder, is indicative of the character's failure to triumph over patriarchal order. According to Lionnet, there is a sense in which this ending returns to a traditional patriarchal form in conforming to social order: *exit* she who attempted to disturb it. If I partly adhere to this conclusion, it also seems that we can read this outcome against the grain and see it as a textual victory of madness and of the mad woman's character, especially in the sense that the author has succeeded in reaching her audience and in communicating what was incommunicable: the pain that woman feels in confronting a society that oppresses her, what Lionnet has referred to elsewhere as "geographies of pain."

Likewise, the characters of the foreign woman, the imposed wife, and the prostitute have similarities and differences that allow us to understand woman in her multiple expressions and conditions. They depict (self-)representation in its multiplicity:

> Not one, not two either. *"I"* is therefore, not a unified subject, a fixed identity. . . . *"I"* is itself *infinite layers*. Its complexity can hardly be conveyed through such typographic conventions as I, i, or I/i. . . . Whether I accept it or not, the natures of *I, i, you, s/he, We, we, they,* and *wo/man* constantly overlap. They all display necessary ambivalence, for the line dividing *I* and *Not-I, us* and *them,* or *he* and *her* is not (cannot) always (be) as clear as we would like it to be. Despite our desperate, eternal attempt to separate, contain, and mend, categories always leak. (Minh-ha 1989, 94)

I am not saying that women writers attempt to understand woman simply by portraying her different facets but that beyond such attempts these writers demonstrate that woman is not a singular identity, cataloged and labeled once and for all according to a normative description. Understanding woman means recognizing woman's changes, that she is not *one* but *many*. In the African context, this approach confirms not only the impossibility of defining woman in her essence but also, and especially, the danger of enclosing woman within a notion of difference.[13]

Through the use of outside-the-norms female protagonists, these authors rebel against the dominant language and ideology; through their preference *(biais)* for an antiheroine, they create a necessarily oppositional speech, a breath of freedom. I shall return to the heart of these questions in Part 3, where I will link them to the global effects of a form of writing that uses margins and taboo as a privileged mode of representation.

Notes

1. One part of my analysis of *Scarlet Song* and *Juletane* has previously appeared in an article entitled "Inscription de la folie et de l'irrationnel dans les textes de femmes," *Revue des Etudes Francophones* 7, no. 2 (1993): 107–129.

2. Warner-Vieyra's entire work is built around female characters who have fallen prey to madness or phantasms. *Le quimboiseur l'avait dit* (1980) and the collection of short stories *Femmes échouées* (1988), especially "Les naufragés" and "Sidonie," examine different degrees of alienation and madness. In *Le quimboiseur l'avait dit,* Suzette is traumatized by being tricked by her mother into being her maid when Suzette believed she had come to Paris to catch up on her schooling. Then she is seduced by a stepfather who is trying to convince her to marry one of his business partners. Suzette has no alternative but violence and the memory of the past to escape from the reality of her present situation. Sidonie ("Sidonie"), married to the man responsible for the car accident she was injured in, then cheated on by this man, finds herself in the position of the woman who is in the way and has to accept the finality of what has been done. To de Blocoto and her friends ("Les naufragés") are recognized and labeled as mentally ill. The story deals with conditions in a psychiatric institution that is revolutionary in its rules and structure. I should also mention other novels that are representative of a female character who falls prey to madness, among them Evelyne Mpoudi Ngolle's *Sous la cendre, le feu* (1990) and Komlavi Jean-Marie Pinto's *Les mémoires d'Emilienne* (1991). The first novel shows the ravages of the madness into which the character sinks and her efforts, at the behest of a therapist, to reestablish ties with the present by exercising her memory. The second combines a treatment of love and hate, madness and violence, also through recourse to memory.

3. On this subject, Kristeva writes: "This is to say that some existences are not sustained by any *desire,* in that desire is always a desire for objects. Such existences are founded on *exclusions.* These are clearly distinguished from those understood in terms of neurosis or psychosis which are articulated by negation and its modalities, transgression, *dénégation,* and foreclosure" ("Approaching Abjection," *Powers of Horror* [1982] 129).

4. As in Warner-Vieyra's two previous novels, *Femmes échouées* (1988) brings out certain key elements associated with madness, particularly the room or psychiatric hospital as the story's primary space and the presence of a doctor (such as Doctor Edouard in *Le quimboiseur l'avait dit*) or a paramedical authority (such as Hélène, the medical assistant in *Juletane*). These elements create an oral or written dialogue with medical authority, a dialogue of therapeutic value. However, the playful tone of the extradiagetic (third person) narration and the choice of focusing on the doctor from the very beginning give this text a different tone. For a detailed study of the different types of pathology represented by Warner-Vieyra, see the article "Représentations de la folie dans les textes de Warner-Vieyra," *Actes du Colloque APELA: Littérature et Maladie* (1994).

5. Whereas in autodiagetic narration, the first-person narrative coincides with the protagonist's voice, as in autobiographical testimonial literature, in homodiagetic narration, the first-person narrative can be that of a character who is not necessarily the protagonist.

6. See the chapter "Poetics, Passion, and Politics in the Three Marias: New Portuguese Letters," in *Discourses of Desire* (Kauffman 1986, 280–311). Here, Kauffman analyzes the diagetic universe in detail (especially the role of epistolary exchanges) in Maria Isabel Barreno, Maria Theresa Horta, and Maria Zelho da Costa, *The Three Marias: New Portuguese Letters* (New York: Bantam, 1976).

7. In *Etrange héritage,* the child plays the same role as catalyst, plunging Déla into madness. When she is still showing signs of physical improvement, she loses her head when her son is brought to her, as the very sight of him irremediably reminds her of Koffi, her husband, and of her pain and her failure: "We thought that she was going to be cured and someone brought her son to her. It was fatal for her. She descended into madness once and for all and her only words were: 'Koko, take me away, wait for me.'" [On crut qu'elle allait guérir et on lui ramena son fils. Ce lui fut fatal. Elle sombra pour de bon dans la folie et ses seules paroles étaient: "Koko, emmène-moi, attends-moi"] (Ami 1985, 155).

8. The same flow of exchange between analyzed and analyst exists in *Tanga,* except this time it is transposed in the form of direct narration with an interlocutor who is present (Anna-Claude). Here also, the reception of Tanga's story operates on two levels. On the one hand Tanga has a didactic intention; through her faithful reception of Tanga's narrative, Anna-Claude will become Tanga. A complete transference takes place between one character and the other. On the other hand, Anna-Claude's stay in an African prison and her contact with a black woman function as self-revelation. Anna-Claude finally discovers a purpose and a reason for being. Paradoxically, however, this role will prove destructive of Anna-Claude's own self because it implies an annihilation of the white woman's prior personality. She discovers an identity, but one that is not her own in terms of race and culture. *Le regard du roi* (Laye 1954) already offered an example of a white man lost and in search of himself, a story in which the white man is in the position of initiate and receiver. His experience, however, occurred through a multiplicity of contacts and initiations with men and women. In *Tanga* we are instead confronted with a closed universe and harsh conditions including incarceration and the violence of the male guards; within this closed world, their encounter acts and develops like an experiment in chemistry, where some elements play the role of *révélateurs* and precipatate change. The only other characters that intervene in the story's development are the prison guards and Tanga's mother. Her appearance in the course of Tanga's narration bears witness to Tanga's transformation into Anna-Claude. Through the narration, both women triumph over the violence that surrounds them: the violence of the guards who strike them and defecate in front of them, the social violence of the pressures of the village and Tanga's mother, who insists that Tanga return to her profession. If the men are the masters of the bodies and spaces of these two women, the narration's transmission from Tanga to Anna-Claude enables the women to triumph over the patriarchal masculine discourse.

9. Myriam Warner-Vieyra explores this question of the limits of consciousness for those suffering from mental illness in greater detail in "Les naufragés" (*Femmes échouées,* 1988). She develops a veritable metadiscourse with a medical tenor on the subject. The credibility of this discourse is based on Célestin's status as a protagonist. A psychiatrist, he returns to the Antilles in order to implement the new techniques he has learned for treating the mentally ill. These techniques focus on the reconstitution of the patient's surrounding natural milieu. The discourse is a virtual transcription of a typical medical discourse. The principles of his therapy are a compromise between modern medical techniques and traditional practices. Gradually the irrational and the marvelous infiltrate the narration. The author invites us to reflect on madness as well as on the world of false appearances and simulacra. To de Blocoto's diary and the curiosity of the "dames patronnesses" about her story serve as illustrations of Caribbean society's interest in the sensational and the magic. The journalist, motivated by profit, is a nonempathetic reader of To's diary and opens up the question of the addressee and the motives of any potential reader of a private story.

10. This term *autogynography* has been taken from Domna Stanton, ed.,

"Autogynography: Is the Subject Different?" in *The Female Autograph* (New York: J. Parisier Plottel, 1984, 5–22). The author asks whether there is any gender-specific difference in autobiographical writing. In other words, does a woman writing autobiography use any different tone or method when she rewrites the story in the first person? Without stating that there is any definitive difference, Stanton observes a group of characteristics, notably the fragmentation and narrative discontinuity of the feminine text as a basis for spontaneity and truth. Of equal note are the dichotomies of inner/outer and private/public; the woman writer tends to privilege the first. Finally, there is the importance of seeking the unsaid, the desire to show what remains hidden and to evoke it. This last observation is especially valid for Juletane's diary and in what she implies there in the play between what is conscious and unconscious: Did she or didn't she poison Awa's children? And if so, was it done consciously or because she was overcome by an impulse that she could not control?

11. See the questions Felman asks on the subject of theoretical problems encountered by feminism and the general questioning of our cultural codes. In particular, while stressing the merits of Irigaray's analysis in *Speculum de l'autre femme,* which recalls that "the oppression of women can be detected not simply in the functioning of social, political and medical structures, but also in the presuppositions of discursive reasoning itself, in the subtle mechanisms of the very process that produces meaning" (Irigaray 1974, 141), Felman investigates the site of discursive enunciation: "However, if the alterity of woman is fully assumed here as being *the subject of the enunciated,* it is not certain that she has assumed it and that she can lay claim to herself in the unquestioned place of her *enunciation*" (Felman 1978, 141; my translation).

12. In *Morphologie du conte,* Propp identifies a set of types of heroes and characteristic features for these types that are universal in all narrative structure. This is one of the types.

13. Trinh Minh-ha recalls the dangers of reducing woman to and confusing woman with sexual difference. See "Woman and the Subtle Power of Linguistic Exclusion," (1989, 100–101).

PART TWO

The Exploration of Taboos

4

Parent-Child Relations

In general, the feelings remained buried in our hearts. We didn't dare reveal them for fear of being perceived as Westernized and poorly educated. Deep down I cursed our education, its strictness and compunctions, its taboos.

[En général, l'affection restait enfouie dans nos coeurs; on n'osait la dévoiler sous peine de passer pour mal élevé, occidentalisé. Je maudissais dans mon for intérieur notre éducation, sa sévérité, ses componctions, ses tabous.]

—Nafissatou Diallo
(*De Tilène au plateau: Une enfance dakaroise*, 62)

Taboo is a strong word charged with numerous ideological connotations that have a cultural or religious basis and that assume a number of possible meanings. Every society has its taboos, and what is accepted or acceptable in one culture may be an object of prohibitions within another. The taboo can consist in the exclusion of a given thing; its use, proximity, or even its mention may be forbidden. The word, in effect, can apply to any "protected" object, word, or action. The prohibition results from collective religious and/or social conformity, thus from the need to forbid anything that opposes the norm. Its primary objective is to preserve the cohesion of the group through an observance of implicit or explicit rules.

In Africa there are a significant number of taboos placed on the position and role of women in relation to certain words and objects, diets, designated spaces, tasks to be carried out, and customs (collective celebrations, initiation rites). These taboos may also apply to anything that defines the important moments in life and that regulates (hierarchical) relations between men and women, parents and children, mothers-in-law and daughters-in-law, as defined by the patriarchal system.

I use the term *taboo* in its specific sense of any type of prohibition about words or actions that applies to African women in their collective group identity. As I demonstrated in the introduction, women writers of an earlier period concentrated on the very act of speaking up *(prendre la parole)* and *articulating woman (dire la femme).* In itself, this act already constituted an infraction against the social law. They escaped censure by maintaining a sort of intermediate position where they refrained from any direct and incisive critique of their society. In 1975, Régine Lambrech characterized female African writing as follows:

> If we were to draw a profile of the modern, Black African female writer of French expression, we would see a working woman who is well steeped in family traditions and customs and who is beginning to re-evaluate her position in society. She does not reject what she cannot reconcile, and above all, does not incite others to this action. She seeks to be accepted for what she is, and more importantly she wants to be free to be herself. (143)

This portrayal does not match the woman writer today. She wants to abolish the interdictions that have been imposed on her and to explore her self *(son être-soi)* and her being *(son être-là)* in society without any restrictions. She thus wants to break down the unspoken barriers *(les non-dits)* that circumscribe woman's condition in African society. This ambition leads to the exploration of areas considered off limits, such as questions concerning representations of the body, sexuality, desire, and passion, but also to the minute observation of the other in intimate relations. This exploration leads to a reconfiguration of the boundaries that define familial relations, including mother-son and especially mother-daughter relationships, the notion of maternity, and, therefore, of paternity as well. Until recently, such domains have been considered only within a narrow patriarchal framework.

To apply the term *taboo* or even *marginal* to parent-child relations may seem like an oxymoron. In fact, this theme played an important role on the African literary scene from the years of independence through the 1970s and early 1980s. Then, however, the context was different; it was that of an African's alienation in contact with the white world through the French educational system. The child was the first person to experience this new form of knowledge and the first to be immersed in the white man's world. In the 1950s and 1960s, the theme took on this typical form: A child or adolescent protagonist (almost always a boy) acquires a white education and gains access to the white man's world, first in Africa, then in France, where he is sent to continue his studies. On the one hand, his departure represented a break with his environment as a source of potential conflicts between himself and his parents or between his parents and the rest of the village. On the other hand, his departure signaled a break in parental ties and especially of the ties between mother and son.[1] As a "roman de formation,"[2] the novel focused on conflicts between generations about their ambivalent attitudes toward Western education.[3]

This theme persisted through the 1980s, although it was configured differently around three main points: (1) The center of interest was displaced onto the child's parents, who themselves belonged to that generation of young Africans who had left to study in France and who, after returning to Africa, faced the choice of how to educate their own children. (2) Depictions of parent-child relations no longer dealt exclusively with sons but with daughters as well. (3) It was the mother who occupied the key position in the relationship, whereas the father generally stood out by virtue of his absence.

I shall analyze this theme of parent-child relations along three lines: the mother-son relation, using the example of Aminata Sow Fall's *L'appel des arènes* (1982); the mother-daughter relation in the works of Beyala and Rawiri, Warner-Vieyra's *Juletane,* and Ken Bugul's *The Abandoned Baobab* (1991); and finally, the father's physical or figurative absence as a characteristic feature of this corpus of novels.

The Mother-Son Relation: Toward Independence

Even though *L'appel des arènes* presents the identity and education of the child Nalla as a central thread of the story, it is clear that the focus has shifted from the child to the parents.[4] Of course, the quest for an identity lies at the heart of the novel, but the search has become the parents' instead of the child's. In fact, the struggle (the real competition does not take place in the arena) in the novel dictates that either the parents or the child will attain this goal. The roles appear to be reversed from the start: The parents are the ones who insist on a Western education for Nalla, with a private tutor. Nalla would prefer a more traditional education, such as the one he enjoys with his grandmother and, especially, with André the wrestler. The novel opens with Nalla's mental and physical "health problems." According to his parents, he is apathetic, unable to concentrate, and virtually anorexic.

In addition, the parents, the mother in particular, reveal their ineptitude in raising the child. The theme of this inability to educate the child is not new in itself. The emphasis, however, is usually on the ignorance of parents who feel disconnected and unable to help when faced with this new world of Western values that their child is entering. The parents feel inferior to their child because of his newly acquired knowledge. They have no access to this knowledge, so naturally, the child becomes their guide.

In *L'appel des arènes,* the parents' shortcoming arises from their lack of time. Each of them works outside the home and is caught up in his or her own career (the father is a veterinarian; the mother is a midwife). The child is therefore deprived of intimate contact with his parents, especially his mother. This situation is exactly the opposite of the traditional image of close bonding between mother and son as analyzed by Arlette Chemain-Degrange in *Roman africain et emancipation féminine* (1980).

The stake in the struggle between mother and son is their own identity. Nalla's initial madness corresponds to his mother's madness at the end of the story. The structuralist analysis of *L'appel des arènes* conducted by Madeleine Borgomano (1989) provides valuable insight here. She sheds light on a focalizing system in which she identifies the dominant, privileged points of view as those of Nalla, the main character; André and Mallow, his original guides; and his grandmother, who symbolizes the traditional past. An over-Westernized mother, Diattou, represents the negative point of view. The novel's final message results from the specific combination of two authorities, the positive and the negative, and the positive and negative characters have been constructed in order to render a specific meaning. A positive time (the past) and space (the arena) exist, as well as a reciprocal negative time (the present) and negative space (the modern house). Borgomano thus interprets the novel as belonging to the category of traditional quest stories, "a moving quest to reassimilate the lost paradise" (55). In that sense, the novel could be identified as one of the first works by African women to glorify the past. On this issue, Borgomano points out a contradiction. According to her, the fact that the main character is described as a dreamer who seeks refuge in the past rather than tackling his present responsibilities undermines the meaning of the traditional past. Hers is obviously one possible interpretation. However, it seems more likely to me that the novel specifically depicts the child as a dreamer in order to criticize the more dramatic reverie of the parents, wherein the mother believes she must either renounce everything traditional or risk appearing ignorant. Fables, legends, and village traditions appear to her unworthy of her family, which she narrowly defines as a single cell limited to her husband, herself, and an only child.

By behaving as she does, Diattou commits a quasi-infanticide against Nalla in the sense that she deprives him of essential spiritual nourishment. She cuts him off from his instructor, whose teaching she considers harmful to a child's development in a modern world. Here too, her behavior is paradoxical; she renounces her role as the child's privileged educator by hiring a third party for the job while remaining highly critical of his methodology.

By distancing the grandmother and reducing the number of family visits to the village, she deprives Nalla of access to the things that make him what he is. She distances him from his African identity and aborts everything that could reconnect him to his ancestral past. Her rejection of the traditional family structure in favor of a nuclear family with a single child (to follow a Western model), her rejection of the traditional educational roles of his grandmother and the villagers, her scorn for the extended family whose influence she feels is a burden, contribute to her alienation from her own African identity. The extradiagetic narrative authority stresses Diattou's absurdity when she tries to dress European and prefers short, tight skirts to traditional African dress.[5] Her rejection of African songs and cooking is emphasized as well. Diattou unconsciously causes the development of her child's mental anorexia. Nalla seems to lose his ability to speak. He loses his appetite and cannot sleep; he can no longer lose himself in dreams. Dreaming in this case connects him to real life, the life of traditions. His fascination for the tam-tam and wrestling is in fact a sign of his awakening and plays a revelatory role. That the child takes back his life, resuming contact with the real life to which he belongs, enables him to regain his vital strength, appetite, and dynamic energy. This change is particularly evident in his sudden excitement when telling his parents about the arenas. In contrast, his mother gradually loses energy at the same time.

The tam-tam has a similar salutary effect on the father. The father and son's geographical displacement to the arenas allows the father to reposition himself in relation to his origins, leading him to a growing awareness. The father thus manages to strike a balance in his perception of traditional and modern life: The tam-tam and the collective traditional elements that he associates with the past do not exist solely for the people in the street, the plebs, but for every African. The tam-tam has therapeutic virtue. To refuse its attraction would lead to a loss of self. Like Mireille in *Scarlet Song,* Diattou is definitively alienated from the African world for refusing it. Not surprisingly, almost identical descriptions of Mireille and Diattou can be found. The two characters react to their roles as mothers in an almost identical fashion: Their rejection of motherhood translates into an act of infanticide, physical in Mireille's case and psychological in Diattou's, as she is the cause of Nalla's aphasia. I will return to this point later.

Sow Fall introduces a new element in the mother-child relation. The traditional bond between mother and son is absent because of the mother. Ironically, Diattou as a midwife exercises a traditional form of knowledge at the same time that she rejects it. This rejection of African values dates from her time as a student in France, when she did all she could to imitate and resemble the French girls of the same age.

> Diattou went to great lengths to transform herself. She submitted to the torture of taming her vocal chords and polishing them. She learned how to adapt her gestures and her gait to the speed of the West.
>
> *[Diattou mit le plus grand soin à se métamorphoser. Elle se soumit à la torture d'apprivoiser ses cordes vocales et de les polir. Elle apprit à régler sa démarche et ses gestes sur la vitesse de l'Occident.]* (1982, 88)

The choice of verbs—*torture, tame, adapt*—stress the weight of the changes she has undergone for the purpose of becoming something different.

In her systematic search for Western values and criteria of judgment, Diattou has lost her entire identity. Thus it is she and not her son who serves as an example of failure.[6]

Animata Sow Fall describes the deterioration of love between mother and son; Nalla judges his mother and takes a position against her. He pursues his own reeducation by resuming contact with traditional African folklore, ritual, storytelling, dance, music, and the fights in the arenas. Once he is initiated into African ways, he becomes a guide for his parents, trying to bring them back to their roots. His effort is successful for the father but ends in failure for the mother. Psychologically, this maturation begins when he leaves his familial environment for the arenas and chooses his own system of education, adopting a position opposed to his mother:

> You are mean to me just like you were with Mame Fari [the grandmother]. I don't want to live with you anymore! I want to go live with Mame Fari!
>
> *[Tu es méchante avec moi comme tu l'as été avec Mame Fari [la grandmère]. Je ne veux plus vivre avec toi! Je veux aller rejoindre Mame Fari!]* (1982, 86)

The interaction of several narrative voices confirms Nalla's revolt and the profound change in his relationship with his mother, as the journal of Mr. Niang, Nalla's instructor, reveals:

> The umbilical cord to the mother has been cut, but retied to the grandmother. A sign of our times. A somewhat encouraging sign, better than nothing. Maybe even salvation. . . . The grandmother is still the earth. . . . The tie to the earth.
>
> *[Le cordon ombilical coupé avec la mère, mais renoué avec la grandmère. Un des signes de notre temps. Signe encourageant, d'ailleurs meilleur que le vide. Peut-être même le salut. . . . La grand-mère, c'est encore la terre. . . . Le lien avec la terre.]* (1982, 86)

His revolt cannot be confused with the usual adolescent crisis and questioning of parental authority; Nalla rejects his mother's authority only to turn to the authority of others, an authority considered superior and adequate. His new instructors are his grandmother, Mr. Niang, André, and Mallaw. On this subject, Madeleine Borgomano points out the passage in Sow Fall's book on the grandmother's multiple role: "She was Nalla's mother, father, brother and playmate." [Elle était pour Nalla mère, père, frère et compagnon de jeux] (Sow Fall 1982, 13). She also notes the importance of the wrestlers' role as paternal substitutes. They double in this role as maternal substitutes because of the physical contact they offer to the child. In addition to this familial role, Borgomano identifies another, "which could have been familial, the role of the ideal model, of the hero" [qui aurait pu être familial: celui de modèle idéal, de héros], which she explains as follows:

> When Diattou chased away the Griot, she chased off the heroes and models with him, and created a lack that Nalla fills by creating new hero-models.

> *[Quand Diattou a chassé le griot, elle a chassé avec lui les héros et les modèles, et créé un manque, que Nalla comble par la création de nouveaux héros-modèles]* (Borgomano 1989, 53)

L'appel des arènes develops a dual theme. On the one hand, Sow Fall gives voice to the problem of the African woman who seeks her identity in the evolution of her own society and who has not been able to save her own identity. On the other hand, she raises the question of choice and of the parent's role in the child's education. She asks the difficult question of what path the African woman should follow, split between a desire for "emancipation" and confined in her role of guardian of ancestral values. Under the banner of modernization, Sow Fall points out, women have fallen prisoner to a world of appearances. By adopting new behavior, they adhere to a new style of colonization—more subtle but still present in many ways.[7] I will return to this point in "Inscriptions of the Female Body" in Chapter 5.

Rawiri's *Fureurs et cris de femmes* (1989) explores another facet of this burgeoning revolt of the son against his mother. The husband-son overtly rebels against her:

> "You are seriously annoying," her son replied sharply. "You are no mother. My word, you are more like a mothercop! When will you start treating me like an adult? Because I don't consider myself a child when I play with my nephews."

> *["Tu deviens sérieusement agaçante," rétorque vivement son fils. "Tu n'es pas une mère mais plutôt une gendarmette, ma parole!.... Quand vas-tu me traiter comme un adulte? Car je ne me considère pas comme un gamin en jouant avec mes neveux."]* (105)

In opposition to the traditional reaction of obedience to his mother to the detriment of his wife's well-being (which occurs, for instance, in *Scarlet Song* and *Juletane*), mother and son clash over the daughter-in-law's position and role within the conjugal home:

> Eyang raised her head high to better confront her son. In a movement of anger, the mother rips her scarf from her head.

"Are you using those words to remind me that I am not at home? Whatever I do or say inside this house annoys you, isn't that right?"

[Eyang relève la tête pour mieux affronter son fils. Dans un mouvement de colère, la mère arrache son foulard de la tête.
"Veux-tu par ces propos me rappeler que je ne suis pas chez moi? Tout ce que je peux faire ou dire dans cette maison vous irrite, n'est-ce pas?" (Sow Fall 1982, 105)

In Rawiri's *Fureurs et cris de femmes* (1989) the mother, Eyang, associates her son with his wife and instills a sense of guilt in him, convincing him that he is a bad son. Like Yaye Khadi in *Scarlet Song*, Eyang resorts to emotional blackmail, reminding her son of everything she did for him.

He lowers his head, disturbed and at the same time smarting with a feeling of guilt. He examines himself again. . . . These vivid memories tear a confused smile from him. He walks towards his mother with an uneasy step and holds her in his arms.

[Troublé, et en même temps animé d'un sentiment de culpabilité, il baisse la tête. Il se revoit . . . Ces souvenirs vivaces lui arrachent un sourire confus. Il marche d'un pas hésitant vers sa mère qu'il serre dans ses bras.] (Sow Fall 1982, 105)

Here too, the son experiences a feeling of guilt for his deficient filial love. There is, however, one small difference between Joseph in *Fureurs et cris de femmes* and Ousmane in *Scarlet Song*. It is through his wife Emilienne's eyes that Joseph discovers his own emotional dependance on his mother and the extent of her power on him. He responds by refusing to leave Emilienne, thus displaying a completely new desire on the man's part to save his marriage.

Joseph's example recalls the image of the castrating mother whose behavior is responsible for man's masculine identity and his "ulterior relations with women." In her study of masculine identity (*XY*: De *l'identité masculine, 1992*) Elisabeth Badinter stresses the necessity of a "safe distance" [bonne distance] between mother and son as a primordial condition for the "construction of the male" [construction du mâle]. The opposite condition implies the usual attitude of male domination of women, which is expressed in sexist tendencies, a need for multiple relations, and violence: "The more mothers burden their sons, the more their sons fear, flee or oppress women" [Plus les mères pèsent sur leurs fils, plus ceux-ci redoutent les femmes, les fuient ou les oppriment] (106). Badinter proposes an alternative to this condition, which involves including man in the tasks of mothering and thereby releasing woman from her exclusive role in these relations:

But, instead of accusing "castrating" mothers of engendering sexist sons (read: women are somehow responsible for the oppression of women), it is time to put an end to the mother's exclusive role in mothering in order to break this vicious circle. We know that men are just as capable of mothering as women when circumstances require it.

[Mais plutôt que d'accuser les mères "castratrices" d'engendrer des fils sexistes (sous-entendu ce sont les femmes qui sont responsables du malheur des femmes), il est temps de mettre un terme au maternage exclusif de la mère pour briser le cercle vicieux. Nous savons que les hommes maternent aussi bien que les femmes quand les circonstances le commandent.] (106)

I will deal with this subject in greater detail in "The Absent Father" later in this chapter.

In *Loukoum, The Little Prince of Belleville* (1995), Beyala plunges us into a different world in terms of geographic location, familial structure, and tone of writing. The seven-year-old protagonist, Loukoum, lives in Paris in the Belleville neighborhood. His family, which is from Mali, includes his father, Abdou, and his two mothers, La Soumana and M'am. It so happens that neither of these two women is his real mother. His real mother just shows up one morning. Her profession: prostitute. A fourth woman is added to the basic family structure, M'amzelle Esther, who lives off her charms and graces and who also becomes pregnant by Abdou.

The primary narrative voice belongs to Loukoum. His voice alternates with the narrative voice of the father in the form of letters. The unopinionated discovery of his true origins brings Loukoum to reflect on the question of parents and his biological mother.[8] Through the child's reflections and discussions with his legal mother, Aminata, Beyala examines the questions of maternity for the African mother and the familial structure of African immigrant families when in contact with a new set of rules. This theme will be developed later in the chapter in "The Rejection of Motherhood"

If we compare the novels produced before 1985 with those produced since, significant changes appear in the milieu that is represented, and therefore also in the depicted familial structure. Instead of a bourgeois family (of the lower-middle and middle class) and a woman preoccupied with the disillusionments of her marital relation (*Scarlet Song, Juletane, L'appel des arènes*), Beyala's novels produced after 1985 depict the underprivileged milieu of a lumpen proletariat in which the family unit has been reduced to a mother and her children. The woman has to confront her concrete material difficulties alone. If we return to the privileged milieu in such novels as Bassek's *La tache de sang* (1990), Rawiri's *Fureurs et cris de femmes* (1989), and Mpoudi Ngolle's *Sous la cendre, le feu* (1990), we find that the problems of female protagonists have assumed another dimension. For instance, marital and familial pressures are weighed against the possibility of pursuing a college degree, there is resistance or refusal to see the wife or mother leave the house in order to attend feminist meetings, the family exerts pressure about the responsibilities of motherhood. New difficulties appear, for instance, the husband's jealousy and feelings of inferiority brought on by his wife's better professional status.

The Mother-Daughter Relation: Love and Rejections

In this section, I use Rawiri's *G'amàrakano, au carrefour* (1983); Beyala's *The Sun Hath Looked upon Me* (1996), *Your Name Shall Be Tanga* (1996), *Seul le diable le savait* (1990), and *Assèze l'Africaine* (1994); as well as Philomène Bassek's *La tache de sang* (1990) as a counterexample.

The question of maternal love appears in a much sharper light when looking at the mother-daughter relationship. In fact, African literature from the 1960s and 1970s typically represents the mother in relation to her son, never in relation to her daughter. For women writers to consider this relationship is innovative in itself. The literary and sociological silence that hangs over this relation can be attributed to woman's status in African society, which dictated, on the one hand, that people were interested first and foremost in boys' development and, on the other, that when the story was about a child's departure to a distant city or a foreign land, the journey almost always involved a boy rather than a girl, in conformity with the colonial politics of education. Once again, one had to wait until the 1980s to see the daughter's departure constitute the main focus of the story.[9] The case of the daughter's leaving for abroad appears in the 1970s, but always in conjunction with the encounter of a male African student; the plot then focuses strictly on the couple and their conjugal difficulties when returning to their native country.[10]

Ken Bugul is the first to have dealt in depth with the question of the mother-daughter relationship. In *The Abandoned Baobab* the relationship is presented as something that is missing and is colored by the daughter's feelings of abandonment. Having been torn apart, Ken will wander between places and people in search of some meaning to her existence and a reason for her mother's abandonment.

Rawiri and Beyala explore mother-daughter relations even further, trying not only to identify a daughter's intimate feelings for her mother but also the ambiguity between them. This relationship is generally depicted as one of malaise; the daughter is sometimes in open revolt against the mother. One main common point emerges from a study of the texts just mentioned: the daughter's exploitation by the mother and the daughter's perception of that exploitation. The causes of this troubled relationship may differ slightly from text to text, but the result is the same. Exploitation arises in the form of the mother's pressure on the daughter to commodify her body. In other words, the daughter is pushed into a form of prostitution or semiprostitution that involves marketing her charms in one way or another.

Choosing One's Destiny: G'amàrakano

Like Beyala's works, Rawari's *G'amàrakano* (1983) unfolds primarily within a world of women. There is the mother (Moussiliki), the grandmother (Okassa), the daughter-protagonist (Toula), and their different friends, notably Toula's friend Ekata. The book opens in Igewa, where the family lives. There are also three boys in the family, one who is old enough to marry and two adolescents who are still dependent on the family. The mother is a widow who has since been abandoned in succession by two different men. (The first one left because he deemed Moussiliki's social status too inferior to his own; the second left after stealing all her money and emptying all the liquor bottles in the house.) Moussiliki has sunk into despair . . . and alcoholism, running a local bar. This milieu is modest at best, in contrast to Toula's work environment, where her elegantly dressed colleagues shun her for her obvious poverty.

Confronted with this environment and the prospect of being stuck in a dead-end life, the mother and the grandmother represent two diametrically opposed forces. Each of them tries to pull Toula in the direction of her own choice. The grandmother represents the typical voice of tradition and a past in which people were judged according to their inner qualities and individual merits, not on appearances. The comparison she draws between life today and life in the past is symbolic of feeling disposessed of a rich past full of true pleasures.[11] The mother, in contrast, pushes Toula toward social change, encouraging her to rise above her milieu and to lift them out of poverty. In order to accomplish this, Moussiliki suggests that Toula imitate other girls her age, such as the neighbor's daughter who uses her appeal to seduce men and procure financial support. The grandmother blames her daughter for wanting to sell Toula like some produce at the market and for forcing her into prostitution. The traditional conflict between generations takes a new turn, as the confrontation also occurs in the very heart of the younger generation. Toula must decide between the values that her grandmother has instilled in her (although this would mean staying in Igewa with people who no longer interest her) and the values of her coworkers, who seem to "live their life to the fullest" (although this would mean evolving in a world that is not her own).

The mother-daughter relation assumes a dual perspective, of two worlds and two generations. On one side, the mother constantly pressures her daughter to change her appearance so that she can escape their milieu. The mother confronts her daughter and accuses her of being ungrateful because she does not help her family escape their impoverished life. On the other, relations change between generations—between Moussiliki and

Okassa (mother and grandmother), who confront each other over Toula's fate; and between Moussiliki and Toula (mother and daughter), who are brought closer once Toula decides to change. The mother's pressure on her daughter to reject the traditional image of internal virtues in favor of external appearances in order to seduce a man constitutes a new phenomenon. Until now, the mother had been the guardian of traditions, especially for her daughter. She played an important role in watching over her virginity and in reproaching her if she lost any of her African personality by adopting ideas that were too European.[12] Here, it is the grandmother who takes over and adopts this position of control.

The new understanding between Moussiliki and Toula can be characterized in the beginning as a conversation from woman to woman. The elder confides in the younger and tells her of the burdens that she has endured as a woman, and not only as a mother:

> Toula is happy that her mother spontaneously came to sit next to her and worried about what could happen to her. What does a woman really know about her? Does she realize that she is engaged in an internal struggle that may require her help? Have they ever understood one another and have they ever tried to understand each other and to be closer?
>
> *[Toula est heureuse que sa mère soit venue spontanément s'asseoir auprès d'elle et s'inquiéter de ce qui peut lui arriver. Qu'est-ce qu'une femme sait réellement d'elle? Peut-elle imaginer qu'elle mène un combat intérieur qui nécessiterait peut-être son aide? Se sont-elles jamais comprises et ont-elles jamais cherché à se comprendre et à se rapprocher l'une de l'autre?]* (Rawiri 1983, 73)

The mother opens up about her remorse for not providing for her children and for sinking into despair: "After my lover left, the one who was almost rich, I drowned myself in alcohol. I lost interest in all of you" [Après le départ de mon amant qui était presque riche, je me suis noyée dans l'alcool. Vous ne m'intéressiez plus] (Rawiri 1983, 72). This confession is also a woman's reflection on her age and the beauty she has lost. Toula displays an empathy full of love when faced with her mother's pain and failures: "How you have suffered, Mama Moussiliki" [Comme tu as souffert, Mama Moussiliki] (80). Daughter and mother are also brought closer together in sharing Toula's secret transformations. When the neighborhood women attribute the lightening of Toula's skin and her loss of appetite to a pregnancy, her mother denies it while leaving the real reason shrouded in ambiguity. She defends Toula against her grandmother and expresses her maternal pride in her duaghter's change:[13]

> Between bottles, she was overjoyed with the privileges of being the mother of such an attractive young woman with light skin and an admirable figure, even if this miracle had not occurred within her body.

[Elle se réjouissait entre ses bouteilles des privilèges d'être la mère d'une telle jeune femme au teint clair et au corps admirablement taillé même si ce miracle ne s'est pas produit dans son corps.] (91)

This pride contains no jealousy, unlike the example of Dame maman's feelings in *Seul le diable le savait*. The only points of friction are those that could oppose her plan for her daughter's success, for instance, Toula's infatuation for a penniless boy over an influential man.

In contrast, Toula's feelings for her mother are contradictory. The narrative voice in *G'amàrakano* focuses in particular on Toula's mixed feelings about her mother's physical appearance. She gazes at her mother's body ravaged by alcohol and hard labor. She examines her mother's body with a fear of resembling her. Here, the author introduces a point that has not been brought up before: the potential repulsion of the child, of the girl in particular, for the mother's body. The rounded contour and loose flesh of the mother (as well as of the grandmother) are warning signs of what she might look like if she fails to take care of her own body. In *Voix et visages de femmes,* Madeleine Borgomano emphasizes this anxiety in portraying the grandmother, Okassa. Unlike Nalla's grandmother, Mame Fari, Okassa has not been idealized. Even if she represents the values of the past, which are considered better than those of the present, these values seem outdated and "the [present] situation of the old woman is depressing" (Borgomano 1989, 119; my translation). Borgomano points out that "the moral and physical decrepitude . . . and old age are seen from the inside, but perceived as much in the modern way as a terrible misery, as an extension of wisdom in the ancient" (119). Okassa internally ponders her physical appearance, her body's wrinkles: "She looks at the carcass that is no more than skin on bones. . . . She asks herself, what is this shape?" [Elle regarde la carcasse qui n'est plus qu'une peau recouvrant des os . . . Quelle est donc cette masse, se demande-t-elle?] (quoted in Borgomano 1989, 182). Once more, the old woman's body is an object of scrutiny.

In the context of this new importance of the body and its appearance, a girl's judgment not only of her mother's behavior but her physical appearance as well constitutes a new phenomenon. In her analysis *Motherself,* on the concept of motherhood and the mother-child relation, Kathryn Allen Rabuzzi (1994) explains that it is not infrequent for children, especially daughters, to find their mother's body repugnant at a very young age; a daughter's disgust may later be associated with the fear of resembling her mother. Rabuzzi writes: "Children of either sex may, for whatever reasons, find their mother's body loathsome. Some daughters, even at very young ages, will unconsciously judge their mother's slightly round and sagging flesh against the Western cultural ideal of firm smoothness. Her daughters may even shrink from the sight of her body . . . making them want to dissociate themselves completely from the maternal body" (182).

One point appears to be of particular interest in this context of African women and mothers: The child's judgment is formulated according to Western criteria. Toula in *G'amàrakano* is an example. She tries to detach herself from everything that reminds her of traditional Africa, including the status of motherhood. This observation is equally true for Diattou (in *L'appel des arènes*) in relation to her mother, whom she distances from Nalla, attempting to reduce her mother's influence over him because she rejects what her mother represents. The act of scrutinizing the mother's body marks the next stage in the alienation process of the African self. This attitude becomes an extreme example of the emphasis on social success and appearances to the extent that people deny their background and their origins. In this context, losing weight and taking care of the female body can be read as attempts not to resemble one's mother. Rabuzzi explains the daughter's rejection of her body as directly related to her view of her mother's body: "A daughter may deny her natural body, coercing it into a form she finds more acceptable than that of her mother" (1994, 183). It is up to the girl to challenge her environment and her social and genetic origins in order to transform herself and, in doing so, to climb the social ladder.

This desire to detach oneself from one's original milieu and everything represented by one's mother also plays a key role in Beyala's texts. Beyala, however, does not consider the question in terms of social ascension but in terms of identity. The matter is whether the girl can escape her mother's position and mirror image and whether she can escape the traditional male domination to which the mother has been subjected. This critique moves toward a radical rejection of society, especially the values associated with the Western model of success.

Revolts Against the Mother; Revolts Against Society: The Sun Hath Looked upon Me, Your Name Shall Be Tanga, *and* Seul le Diable

Each of Beyala's novels begins with a common basic scheme in which (1) we find a world composed primarily of women and in which men intervene only as passing characters—official or transitory lovers and/or oppressors; (2) the main relationship is between mother and daughter, mother and lover(s), or daughter and mother's lover(s); (3) either the mother or the daughter functions as a prostitute. Common to each of these texts is a mixture of fascination with and repulsion toward the mother on the daughter's part. The relation is played out in terms of power and domination. The mother is portrayed as distant and indifferent *(The Sun);* cold, authoritarian, and calculating *(Tanga);* weak and treated by men as a piece of merchandise *(The Sun, Seul le diable)*.

As seen in the study of the prostitute's character and in the mother's role as a prostitute, each novel represents the mother as a failure. The choice of this dual context of prostitution and failure underlies Beyala's assault on the traditional assumption about the mother as a designated totem figure for what Luce Irigaray in "L'argent, les femmes et le sacré" (in *Sexe et parenté,* 1987) defines as follows: "Our societies presuppose that the mother nurse the child for free, before and after giving birth, and that she remain the nurse of men and of society" [Nos sociétés supposent que la mère nourrisse gratuitement l'enfant, avant et après l'accouchement, et qu'elle reste la nourrice de l'homme et de la société] (97). In each of her positions, the mother betrays the institutionalized notion of maternal love. In *L'appel des arènes* and *Scarlet Song*, the mother does not seem to possess or even seem capable of possessing this so-called sacred love. Ken Bugul's *The Abandoned Baobab* is exemplary in this respect; the protagonist feels betrayed because she was abandoned as a child by her mother. Through writing and through her journey in space and time (her return to the past, her departure from Africa, and her displacement [exile] in Belgium), Ken evokes the pain and the loneliness she felt when her mother left her:

> All my life I shall curse the day that carried my mother off, that shattered my childhood, that reduced me to that little girl of five, all alone on the platform of some station long after the train was gone. (Bugul 1991, 66)

It is difficult for Ken to understand her mother's reasons for leaving her, difficult to understand the fact that her mother did not abandon her for any lack of maternal love but because she did not want to interrupt her daughter's education. By the time she sees her mother again, Ken has distanced herself, a distance marked, as Mildred Mortimer stresses,[14] by the abandonment of the possessive pronoun "my" in favor of the generic determinant "the": "That is why, when I arrived, *my* mother was no longer. All that was left was the mother. All was silence" (Bugul 1991, 112).

Approaching the mother-child relation uniquely through the mother-daughter relation amounts to attacking the traditional foundations of society in its myths and beliefs. The mother-child relation refers us in particular to the ancient myth of Oedipus and incest. As Irigaray observes in her analysis of maternal love, "Love between mother and daughter, rendered impossible by the patriarcal regime . . . has been transformed into an obligatory cult for the children of the legal husband, and for her own husband as a masculine child. It is all about the mother *of the son,* to the detriment of the mother of the daughter" [L'amour entre mère et fille, rendu impossible par le régime patriarcal, . . . est transformé en culte obligatoire pour les enfants du mari légal, et pour son mari en tant qu'enfant masculin. Il s'agit de la mère *du fils* au détriment de la mère de la fille] (Irigaray 1987, 14–15). Consequently, the Oedipus complex has always been limited to the mother-son (or father-daughter). Therefore, to speak of the mother-daughter relation is to attack the patriarchal structures of society and to demonstrate the writer's participation in an act of radical revolt. Viewed along these lines, the love-hate relationship between mother and protagonist assumes another dimension, confronting us with the daughter's physical attraction to her mother, for example, the scene in *The Sun* in which Ateba massages her mother's body:

> And Ateba enjoyed working on them, . . . massaging the woman's body that had passed through so many hands. . . . She used to want to say to her: "Betty, I love you." . . . She would have liked to enter into her so as to purify each vein, each artery from that bad blood, that blood of theirs they poured into her to cleanse themselves. (Beyala 1996, 68–69)

Another example is the description of Megri (in *Seul le diable*) as she sizes up her mother. The terms that are utilized denote the presence of two semantic networks, one signaling aggressiveness (they threw themselves, crossed themselves . . . two swords), another marked by sexual connotations (petting).[15]

An ambivalence in the girl's behavior is clearly formed from these ambivalent feelings toward her mother, as she simultaneously adopts the role of judge and mother. If she has a clear understanding of her mother's weaknesses, she is also the one who forgives: "As a child, Ateba admired Betty. Her body was beautiful. Her soul impure. But she loved her for all her impurities" (*The Sun,* Beyala 1996, 77). Ateba is also the person who takes care of the other.[16] In "Le Retour des mères dévorantes," Héloïse Brière (1994) associates this reversal of the roles of mother and child with "the image of an Africa that is unable to provide any tomorrows. . . . The survival of the family depends on child labor" [l'image d'une Afrique incapable de se donner des lendemains" in which "la survie de la famille dépend du travail des enfants] (68). She concludes on this note: "If the children have been devoured by their mothers, so to speak, their mothers themselves are victims of post-colonial African rapaciousness" (68; my translation).

Beyala's first three novels have a recurring feature, the daughter's fascination with the mother; this fascination is dominated by feelings of possessiveness and exclusivity claimed against the men who provide for her mother (either the lover or the official father). Two scenes are especially characteristic in this respect. The first, in *The Sun*, shows Ateba's immeasurable joy when she finally has her mother (or her aunt) to herself. The second is in *Seul le diable;* Megri expresses her jealousy toward her two fathers and cannot stand seeing her mother engaged in an activity from which she is excluded:

> Seeing her fingers running up and down his skin was such a marvelous sight that I was struck with the same anger that I would always get when Dame maman did or thought anything from which I was excluded.

[Le spectacle de ses doigts allant et venant sur sa peau était tellement merveilleux que me saisit une colère identique à celle que je ressentais toujours quand Dame maman faisait ou pensait quoi que ce soit dont je sois exclue.] (Beyala 1990, 51)

The daughter's attraction and admiration for her mother, and for her body in particular, offers a striking contrast with Rawiri's texts (analyzed earlier). In spite of their differences, however, the outcome is the same. The daughter is pressed into considering her own body for its value as merchandise. In Rawiri's *G'amàrakano,* beyond the familial pressure, Toula's fear of resembling her mother and remaining stuck in the same environment pushes her into the beauty contest, leading her to use her newly acquired attractiveness in order to seduce men. In *The Sun, Tanga,* and *Seul le diable,* the daughter experiences a fascination for the mother's body. She admires it and, therefore, can only dream of resembling it. In these novels it is actually the mother who offers the model of prostitution and the marketed body as a basic approach to life. The status of the prostitute-mother plays a key role for the daughter, who is presented with the image of woman's inevitable submission. Refusing the mother's path implies a new awareness on the daughter's part, an awareness that leads to a movement of revolt not only against the mother but also against man and therefore against the entire community.

We can find similar elements in Beyala's *Assèze l'Africaine* (1994). Although Assèze's mother is not a prostitute, she belongs to the most destitute rural environment and is considered as such by Sorraya, Assèze's stepsister. She thus treats Assèze like a prostitute's daughter, as if her future can only reproduce her mother's. Moreover, Awono's mistress, ironically nicknamed the countess, is a former prostitute, a fact that provokes Sorraya's disdain. The novel raises the question of a daughter's development in relation to her mother's life. Assèze's being deprived of both moral support and her mother's presence highlights the question of feminine influence and original milieu. Assèze's relationship with her mother is close to Ken's relation with hers in *The Abandoned Baobab.* For Assèze, just as for Ken, the feeling of being alone, abandoned, ignored after the arrival of another child, and separated by a great distance from her mother predominates. Whereas the birth of a niece replaces Ken in her mother's heart, the birth of a boy, Okeng, a first and only son, takes Assèze out of the running for her own mother's affections. Both characters attribute their lack of self-confidence, their trouble in finding their way in life, their feelings of unfathomable emptiness, to their lack of maternal love in childhood (for Ken mainly) or in adolescence (in Assèze's case).

Each novel repeatedly raises the question of whether one can avoid one's mother's mirror image and free oneself from the saying "Like mother, like daughter." The real question is clearly one of determining the nature and extent of this freedom.

In this regard, Philomène Bassek's *La tache de sang* (1990) presents a gripping counterexample in which the daughter takes responsibility for her mother and for breaking the vicious circle in which she has been trapped. What holds her mother captive?—an endless series of obligatory pregnancies conceived as a last resort to rewin a husband who fools around. Through the example of their two lives that differ in every respect, mother and daughter illustrate the distance that separates their two generations. The daughter, Patricia, has the ability to work, to lead an independent life, and to freely express her opinions, and she benefits from a cooperative and understanding relationship with her husband, who supports her in her struggle for women's social and political rights. In contrast, the mother, Ida, is exposed to constant mockery and sacrifice, is forced to put up with her husband's blows, to obey as if she were a child, and to live life only through her children, who became her only reason for being.

Their differences revolve around the question of maternity and the wife's role in the family. For Mama Ida, the fact that her daughter and son-in-law still have no child after three years of marriage constitutes an anomaly, and she warns Patricia about the danger of losing her husband. At the same time, in spite of age and poor health brought on by her many pregnancies, she becomes pregnant for the eleventh time. For her, the pregnancy represents receiving a moment of care and concern from her husband, Same. Patricia's reaction is exactly the opposite of her mother's. She receives the news with anger and fear. Because she cannot dissuade her mother from keeping the child, she persuades a doctor friend to perform an abortion (without her mother's knowledge). Complications develop and Mama Ida immediately is hospitalized. The diagnosis: stillbirth. Mandika figures out his wife's role in the affair and blames her not for breaking the law but because he feels his wife has been mistaken in her struggle for better women's living conditions and has failed to understand the importance of motherhood for a woman of Mother Ida's generation:[17]

> "Mama Ida is not a victim. You know you mutilated her. . . . She was happy to bear that child."
>
> "Did she have a choice? Has she ever had a choice?" Patricia asked pathetically.
>
> "There you go again, always as stubborn as a mule with your head full of illusions. You want to know something? Your mother will never forgive you for what you did. . . . That child was more than her life. I read it on her face a few hours ago."
>
> *["Maman Ida n'est pas une victime. Tu sais que vous l'avez mutilée. . . . Elle était heureuse de porter cet enfant."*
>
> *"Avait-elle le choix? A-t-elle jamais eu à choisir?" demanda Patricia pathétique.*
>
> *"Toujours aussi têtue qu'une mule, la tête pleine de chimères. Veux-tu que je te dise une chose? Ta mère ne te pardonnera jamais ce que tu as*

fait. . . . Cet enfant était plus que sa vie. Je l'ai lu sur son visage il y a
quelques heures."] (Bassek 1990, 152)

The discussion contains all the essential questions about the possibility of judging and understanding another woman's conduct, in particular, the mother's right to decide for herself. The novel introduces a fundamental difference between the two women on a number of basic issues. These issues are the role of motherhood for the African woman and the direction to be taken by a truly African feminism, one independent of the Western model.

As her sense of judgment breaks down, Patricia approaches her mother and admits her responsibility in Ida's losing the baby:

> Mama Ida felt someone's presence in the room. The two women were facing one another. There was a silence.
> "I came to talk to you, to explain."
> "That's useless. Your lady doctor friend Modi told me everything. . . . That you saved my life! I am really grateful to you."
> "I'm the person who should thank you for your understanding, Mama. I was so scared." . . . Patricia held fast to her mother's hands, overcome with some vague hope.
>
> *[Maman Ida sentit une présence. Les deux femmes se retrouvèrent en tête-à-tête. Il y eut un silence.*
> *"Je suis revenue pour te parler, pour t'expliquer."*
> *"C'est inutile. La doctoresse Modi ton amie, m'a tout raconté. . . . Que vous m'avez sauvé la vie! Je vous en suis reconnaissante."*
> *"C'est moi qui te remercie pour ta compréhension, maman, j'avais si peur." . . . Patricia serra fortement les mains de sa mère. Un espoir indéterminé l'envahissait.] (Bassek 1990, 154)*

A new understanding has been forged between the two women. Paradoxically, this trial brought mother and daughter closer together, and the daughter has reached the point where she can finally reveal her own pregnancy, engendering a new position for thc mother: her future grandchildren will now become her reason to live. This expression is hardly any different from her first inspiration, as the daughter tries to explain to her mother:

> "Mama! Children and the home aren't everything. That's not enough." . . .
> "No one ever taught me anything else."
>
> *["Maman! Le foyer et les enfants, ce n'est pas tout, ce n'est pas suffisant." . . .*
> *"On m'a rien appris d'autre."] (155)*

The message is both harsh and moving: Not everyone has a chance to start over. For the older generation, strongly rooted in its ideas, there can be no changing in life for the reason that any emancipatory messages oppose the ideological system that has guided it, for better or for worse, up to this point.

The feelings expressed here are comparable to those voiced by Ramatoulaye, the protagonist in *So Long a Letter*. She can make no decision based on what her friend Aïssatou has chosen to do, and so she has two different choices: either remain married and accept polygamy or refuse to remarry and remain in her own world, which is a courageous choice, for staying can be just as difficult as leaving. In a similar fashion, Ida in *La tache de sang* attempts to explain her position to her daughter:

"I was happy in my own way," continued Mama Ida. "I knew moments of happiness. But sometimes I began to think that my life could have been drawn up differently. I don't know how, but the idea was there, as a secret, formless and unspeakable. It was eventually lost down through the years and by learning to keep quiet myself. I never wanted to tell you about my sufferings, or even less about my friends', because I wanted to protect you from any pain and worry. I imagined that you would inescapably follow our harsh, cruel path. So, as our own mothers had done, I prepared you to courageously submit to the same torments. And Patricia, contrary to what you always thought, I struggled too, but in the shadows, alone and unarmed, far from any secret women's societies of bygone days, strong and powerful as they were, or relatively powerful, although they no longer exist these days. Sometimes I forget that you went to school, that you learned to speak and to write and, more important, to think and reflect on things. I am wrong. The secret admiration that I have for you and your comrades is great, but even greater is the fear that holds me back. Is there any mother who has voluntarily directed her children towards a path she fears, or whose condition and outcome she ignores?"

[*"J'ai été heureuse à ma manière," poursuivit Mama Ida. "J'ai connu des instants de bonheur. Pourtant, il m'est arrivé de penser que ma vie aurait pu se dessiner autrement. Je ne sais comment, mais l'idée était là, dans le secret, sans forme, inexprimable. Elle s'est perdue au fil des années à force de me taire et je n'ai jamais voulu te conter mes souffrances, celles de mes semblables encore moins, pour t'épargner peine et ennuis. Je pensais que tu suivrais inéluctablement notre chemin si rude et si dur. Aussi te préparais-je, comme le firent nos mères à notre endroit, à subir courageusement le même calvaire. . . . J'ai lutté, moi aussi, Patricia, contrairement à ce que tu as toujours cru, mais dans l'ombre, seule et sans armes, loin des sociétés secrètes féminines de jadis, fortes, puissantes, relativement puissantes, mais aujourd'hui inexistantes. . . . Il m'arrive parfois d'oublier que tu as fait des études, que tu as appris à parler et à écrire, mais surtout à penser et à réfléchir. J'ai tort. L'admiration que je te témoigne pour tes camarades et toi, en secret, est grande, mais plus grande encore est la peur qui m'étreint. Y a-t-il une mère qui ait volontairement orienté ses enfants vers un chemin dont elle redoute ou ignore l'état ou l'issue?"*] (Bassek 1990, 155)

Her words are like a revelation for Patricia. They expose the lucidity hidden behind "her mother's sometimes oppressive silence." She is invited to enter a new phase in her relationship with Mama Ida, of getting to know her and start anew: "She had not only regained a mother, but she was moreover discovering a new confidante and friend" [Non seulement elle retrouvait une mère, mais elle découvrait en outre une amie, une confidente] (156).

This example brings us back to the fundamental question of choice. On the one hand, the mother has to explain her behavior toward her daughter in terms of her desire to protect her, to spare her any unnecessary suffering related to the feminine condition. On the other hand, she has to explain it in terms of her conviction that every woman's fate is predestined in some inevitable way; that her duty as a mother is to prepare her daughter for everything, even the likelihood of suffering.

More than any exaggeration of maternal love, we find expressed here the younger generation's eagerness to shake off the old system, which is depicted as synonymous with the exploitation of woman and provokes her refusal to see her identity confined to motherhood. Ida's speech also demonstrates older women's inability to find any satisfaction in younger women's aspirations. Such ideas are too strongly opposed to the ones that were instilled in them during the first three-quarters of their lives. *La tache de sang* is much like Beyala's work in identifying the limitations that arise when motherhood is to be attained at any price.

The Rejection of Motherhood

Engaged in their search for a new identity, African women have come to question maternity as a panacea and in certain cases to reject it as a form of subjection. A number of novels from the 1980s focus on the question of maternal love.[18] In "Le retour des mères dévorantes," Héloise Brière (1994) declares:

> These writers have shaken the very foundations of the concept of maternity, dispersing the halo that has crowned the literary figure of the African mother in male writing since the beginnings of African literature. Ceasing to procreate becomes a means of renouncing not only this particular vision of the mother and the primacy of blood relations, but also the masculine post-colonial order in Africa. Questioning woman's life-bearing role is a change of major importance origininating in woman's exclusion from post-colonial power. (66; my translation)

Brière affectively shows that the literary treatment of motherhood has undergone a significant change that assumes the aspect of a "transformation in the relation between woman and her own fertility, and particularly between woman and society." According to Brière, this transformation is indicative of woman's mastery of her own body and therefore also "a modernization and a liberation from domination by the group" (67).

In *L'appel des arènes,* Sow Fall shows that there has been an inversion of maternal feelings and a related reversal within the mother-son relationship.[19] The child Pieds-Gâtés in *Tanga* presents another example of this phenomenon. When left to himself, he develops his own philosophy of life. Each of these novels calls for a reassessment of the child's status and of the image of the traditional bonding between mother and child.[20]

Lauretta Ngcobo's article on this topic, "Motherhood—Myth and Reality" (1988), provides precious testimony on the symbolic value of the child and therefore also on woman's status as a mother. She explains that a woman cannot be recognized as a complete being until she has become a mother. In this context, marriage is not seen as an end in itself anymore than it is considered for love or the notion of sharing that it may entail. Children and the official recognition that it gives women are what justify marriage. Naturally, this perspective results in an institutionalization of motherhood.[21] Ngcobo's analysis also presents mother-son relations in their true light. Yes, the traditional collusion between the two exists, but only within the limited framework of polygamy. Ngcobo emphasizes that generally, mother-son relations are actually emphasized when the family structure is monogamous because the mother in the polygamous structure finds herself in a noncompetitive relationship with other wives who are also mothers. Furthermore, the mother's severity is justified by her desire to see her child succeed. *L'appel des arènes* conforms completely to this pattern on all but one point. The demands that Diattou places on her son are actually unreasonable and lead to his loss. It is by rejecting his mother's authority that Nalla is able to rediscover his true calling. Diattou's failure in professional and personal life make us wonder whether she possesses any maternal love and, in a broader sense, lead us to question the educational model for the African child today. Until now, in both Western and African society, we were always assured that maternal love was inherent to every woman. In *L'amour en plus,* Elisabeth Badinter demonstrates that this notion has developed historically along with the concept of childhood since the formation of the bourgeoisie.[22] Maternal love, therefore, should not be thought of as existing naturally. Nonetheless, in the case of African women, no one ever dared consider such a possibility. *L'appel des arènes* and *Scarlet Song* (with the killing of the mixed-race child) draw the reader in this direction through the question of the African woman's alienation and the difficult search for her identity.

As indicated in Beyala's texts, the mother's inability to fulfill her maternal role in providing sufficient love and a decent upbringing surfaces within the mother-daughter relation.[23] Rawiri's *Fureurs et cris de femmes* (1989) is particularly symbolic of the question of the status of motherhood for women today insofar as the novel deals with both Emilienne's sterility and her lack of maternal love for her daughter, Rékia, who disappears and dies after being raped by a band of thieves.

Emilienne rejects motherhood as an end in itself. When her husband leaves in search of their daughter, she looks back on her years as a mother and her relationship with her daughter and is forced to recognize some important points. Among these, she realizes that her love for her daughter was in fact dependent on her love for her husband.

> Already, after the first years of joy and pride that had followed her birth, Emilienne, while still adoring her baby, had been drawn closer to her husband whose expressions of tenderness and love filled her heart every bit as much, if not more. Although she may not have realized it right away, the intensity of the love that she felt for her child depended on the love she received from her husband.

> *[Déjà, après les premières années de joie et d'orgueil qui avaient suivi sa naissance, Emilienne, tout en adorant son bébé, s'était rapprochée de son mari, dont les élans de tendresse et d'amour comblaient autant sinon davantage son coeur. Pour elle, et bien qu'elle ne le réalisât pas tout de suite, l'intensité de l'amour qu'elle éprouvait pour son enfant dépendait de celle qu'elle recevait du père.]* (Rawiri 1989, 32)

As a result of her husband's growing indifference, she displayed the same feelings toward her daughter:

> With some distance, she fully realized that her affection for her daughter had been tainted with a certain reticence that began the day she figured out that her husband had a mistress, although, at the same time, she represented her only security. Because of this, she would sometimes respond aggressively when her daughter begged for attention. With terror, she realized that her daughter had never really had enough of a place in her heart.

> *[Avec le recul, elle réalise pleinement que son affection pour sa fille avait été teintée par une certaine retenue depuis le jour où elle s'était aperçue que son mari avait une maîtresse, bien qu'en même temps elle était son seul refuge. D'où parfois quelque agressivité quand sa fille quémandait quelque attention. Elle se rendait compte avec effarement que cette dernière n'occupait pas vraiment dans son coeur la place qui aurait dû être la sienne.]* (Rawiri 1989, 32)

The feelings of guilt and remorse will make her ask two questions from now on: Was she a bad mother? Did she have a normal reaction?

> While many women find happiness with their children, instead I look for it with a man. Am I abnormal?

[Alors que beaucoup de femmes tirent leur bonheur de leurs enfants, moi je le cherche plutôt auprès d'un homme. Suis-je anormale?] (Rawiri 1989, 32)

Am I abnormal? This is the key question asked by women writers of the new generation. Rawiri describes motherhood in a new light. Certainly, wanting to have a child is central to the novel. However, the question takes a new turn when this desire is recognized as a product of social pressure and not of any innate physiological need. It is to win back her husband, to obey the traditions that demand that any home have several children, and to escape from her mother-in-law's complaints that Emilienne resorts to any possible solution. She has no intrinsic desire for a child but only responds to social obligations. Emilienne's sterility does not allow her to be a complete woman. The elders, her mother-in-law, from society at large to the members of her immediate family, are all authorized to encourage Joseph to look for another wife. Furthermore, the women are the first to reproduce this discourse through Joseph's sister and Dominique. According to Dominique, Emilienne's secretary, a woman must want to have children, and in order to get them, she is willing to do anything, even to make a deal with the devil.

> You know that men don't put up with women who put their virility in question. And as for the family, it won't ever forgive you for that. And then, madame, you know, a woman without a child is like a one-handed person. How can I explain that to you? For her whole life, she will be missing that other life that comes from her and without which she falls ill. She will be singled out all her life, ridiculed and blamed.
>
> *[Vous savez, les hommes ne supportent pas les femmes qui remettent leur virilité en cause. Quant à la famille, elle ne vous le pardonne pas. Et puis, vous savez, madame, une femme sans enfant est comme un manchot. Comment vous expliquer ça? Toute son existence, il lui manquera cette autre vie venant d'elle et sans laquelle elle devient infirme. Toute sa vie, elle sera montrée du doigt, ridiculisée et plainte.]* (Rawiri 1989, 100)

Dominique's opinion on women who refuse to have children is perfectly clear: "'You must be sick in the head to make a decision like that,' the secretary indignantly exclaimed." ["Il faut être malade dans la tête pour prendre une telle décision," s'indigne la secrétaire] (Rawiri 1989, 100).

Emilienne's thoughts bring us to reflect on woman's status, on the conditions that prevent her from succeeding in her professional, emotional, and family lives. To manage any two of these domains is a challenge. Her discourse takes raw reality into account. Even in a society that has experienced woman's emancipation, professional success is not enough to justify a childless marriage, because a woman owes it to herself to have children:

"Even today it still seems like a woman only wins consideration and respect from her entourage by being a mother" [Il semble qu'une femme, encore aujourdh'hui, ne suscite la considération et le respect de son entourage que par sa maternité] (Rawiri 1989, 91).

More disturbing, as her family warns her, the death of her child will quickly be forgotten, and she will be considered a barren woman even though she once gave birth to a daughter. Emilienne rejects this notion, portraying young mothers who can no longer smile for having sacrificed everything for their children.

> The smiles have not only disappeared from the faces of sterile women. Many mothers do not know how to laugh anymore either. Do you know one of the reasons for this sadness that can already be found in children and later on in adults who have become parents? This widespread sadness can be explained by the problems and traumas experienced by pregnant women. Children born in these conditions present significant character problems that sometimes affect them for their entire lives. Add to that the conditions in which they are raised, because it is obvious that noone takes care of them. And as soon as anyone mentions it, someone answers that the African man does not have any psychological problems because he lives in an a very large extended family unit.

> [*Les sourires n'ont pas seulement disparu des visages des femmes stériles: de nombreuses mères non plus ne savent plus rire. Connaissez-vous l'une des raisons de cette tristesse que l'on retrouve déjà chez les enfants, et plus tard chez les adultes devenus parents? Cette tristesse généralisée peut se justifier par les problèmes et les traumatismes que connaissent les femmes en grossesse. Les enfants qui naissent à la suite de ces conditions présentent des problèmes caractériels considérables qui les affectent parfois toute leur vie. Ajoutez à cela les conditions dans lesquelles ils sont élevés, car bien évidemment, personne ne s'en occupe. Et dès qu'on en parle, on vous répond que l'Africain n'a pas de problèmes psychologiques parce qu'il vit dans une cellule familiale très élargie.*] (Rawiri 1989, 92)

As in Beyala's works, the narrative voice in *Fureurs et cris* draws attention to the world these children live in: "In destitute families, these accidental or so-called wanted children are not adequately fed or maintained, and the rates of infant mortality and wasted youth are simply mindboggling." [Dans les familles indigentes, ces enfants accidentels ou soi-disant désirés ne sont pas convenablement nourris et entretenus, et l'on s'étonne du taux de mortalité infantile ou de la déperdition des jeunes] (Rawiri 1989, 91). Both Beyala's novels and Rawiri's *Fureurs et cris* focus on the instability and collapse of a family structure in which woman, abandoned by man, has to confront on her own the financial burden of a family. Both transcribe the problem of women's honor and dignity being related to pregnancies that result in many successful births. Women writers are putting their cards on the table for the first time. What can be done with so many mouths to feed? Who will bear the burden of raising these children? In all cases, the same answer rings out: Woman, of course. Beyala and Rawiri say no to this response. No, one must learn to refuse motherhood in this inhospitable world that holds no future for the children of tomorrow. In her last novel, Rawiri especially levels a strong indictment against maternity perceived as a solution to life's problems and against the idea that procreation can provide some kind of security. If women choose motherhood, like Megri in *Seul le diable le savait* and Emilienne in *Fureurs et cris de femmes,* it is on their own terms. Héloïse Brière accentuates this decision in an extremely pertinent manner: "The child that will be born will be neither a trophy of fertility nor a means of assuring a husband's fidelity: Emilienne assumes responsibility for herself as a modern woman through a maternity that upsets the established order" (1994, 70; my translation). These women writers reconceptualize motherhood, introducing the idea of nonbiological motherhood and mother substitutes.[24] This idea has been particularly developed by Beyala in *Loukoum* and *Maman a un amant,* in which Mariama assumes the role of the sole legal mother. Although Mariama is sterile, she carries the names of the children of Soumana, Abdou's second wife, in her *livret de famille.* She is therefore the only one who exists as the mother, as Soumana has no legal civil identity (French law does not recognize polygamy). Brière elaborates this point in her study on maternity, remarking that "[Mariama's] identity is assured by her social role, and not by her fertility. . . . Finally judged for her human qualities and not for her fertility, Beyala's character is freed from the weight of the African past" (1994, 71; my translation). Brière thus achieves a redifinition not only of motherhood but also of the mother and the status of the child: "A devourer of children in the African context, here, the mother becomes their protector, which allows her to affirm the primacy of the child over the adult and of the future over the present" [Dévoreuse d'enfants dans le contexte africain, ici la mère en devient la protectrice, ce qui permet d'affirmer la primauté de l'enfant sur l'adulte, celle de l'avenir sur le présent] (71). Brière reevaluates woman as a participant in the construction of Africa:

> By means of a writing that problematizes motherhood, women writers have raised questions about androcentric power. Refusing the child, or trying to have it under different conditions, puts the spotlight on the failure of the post-colonial state. Behind this critique lies a desire to experience motherhood in a new form in which the child is valued for himself and in which motherhood has been freely chosen, whether it is biological or not. This is an indictment to obtain recognition for woman's contribution to the construction of Africa on new grounds. (71; my translation)

As the positions of mothers, children, and family are redefined by women writers, so is man in his status as father; these reevaluations are indispensable steps in the development of a new sexual ethic.

The Absent Father

I will use the same corpus as in a previous section (Rawiri's *G'amàrakano, au carrefour* [1983]; Beyala's *The Sun Hath Looked upon Me* [1996], *Your Name Shall Be Tanga* [1996], *Seul le diable le savait* [1990], and *Assèze l'Africaine* [1994]; and Bassek's *La tache de sang* [1990]), with the addition of *L'appel des arènes* (1982) by Sow Fall.

In *L'appel des arènes* (Sow Fall 1982), the father has a problematic role in Nalla's education and development. If we examine his role in the light of Madeleine Borgomano's structural analysis, we can see that the father belongs to the negative extreme in that he tacitly agrees with his wife's decisions. Absorbed by his work as a veterinarian, the father leaves all authority to Diattou in dealing with the child. He is symbolically absent from the family structure.[25] He is especially noteworthy for his change of orientation in this regard, becoming an active character and playing a positive role at the end of the novel. His transformation occurs thanks to the influence of his son, who has become his reeducator, reinitiating him in the joys of traditional cultural events.

In other texts, the father's absence is literal and as such, emphasized. In *G'amàrakano* (Rawiri 1983), the family's subsistence-level poverty results from the numerous times that a man has walked out on the mother. The familial structure is built as a conglomerate of substitute figures of authority. It is held together by the grandmother's authority in taking care of the two youngest boys and by the elder brother. He is a young, married man who draws a small salary as a mechanic but tries nonetheless to give a little money or a few provisions to his mother from time to time. The grandmother has a preeminent role even though the novel's development reveals a weakening of her position, since the daughter sides with her mother. In this context, the daughter represents her mother's only hope of escaping their misery. This situation explains her complaints against her daughter's initial refusal to use her sex appeal like other girls do in order to rise above this milieu. The immediate conclusion is that the daughter is useless or ungrateful if she is not willing to do this for the family. Because of the matrifocal structure in which the father is unknown, man appears as an external figure from this point on. He is considered solely as a source of money. Man has become a generic object. His looks, his ugliness, or his age make no difference. What counts is his wallet and the apparent social position that he holds.

Beyala's novels adopt this matrifocal structure with only a few differences. First, the grandmother figure, a tie to the past and a symbol of resourcefulness and wisdom, the guardian of a certain order, has disappeared. The older or younger brothers and uncles have also disappeared. There are no men left in what seems like the skeleton of a family that has been reduced to mother and daughter alone. Each novel explores a variation on this basic theme. In *The Sun Hath Looked upon Me*, Betty, the real mother, has also left, leaving her child Ateba to her Aunt Ada's care. Ada thus functions as a mother substitute. We have two maternal figures here who complement each other in the protagonist's gaze or memory. As a young adolescent, Ateba discovers man through the many lovers who pass through the house (and the bed) of her mother and her aunt. Man actually remains unknown to her, and she is apprehensive about encountering him:

> She doesn't know man. She's never had a father. Ada's lovers don't interest her except to the extent that they pass through like a note, slide by without ever impressing themselves on her memory. (Beyala 1996, 42)

In *Tanga,* the father exists in the beginning, but only as an extreme oppressor of the mother, whom he beats and cheats on, and of his daughter, whom he abuses and rapes. From childhood on, Tanga and Ateba are led to consider man as the enemy; they see man as someone who makes them suffer, as someone who fails to understand women, and as someone to get rid of. On the contrary, in *Seul le diable,* the protagonist has a plethora of official fathers. One is a Greek-Bantu and the other is a Pygmy, but neither of them is a real father, as she discovers too late. In no case do they represent figures of paternal authority. Both are described, in effect, as entirely submissive to "Lady Mother." They are both indecisive and dependent, and Megri can respond to them only with pity and a sort of protective, quasi-maternal love. Their weakness produces a fundamental difference in the protagonist's behavior. Because the man that she has seen in each of them seems weak to her, she will never feel the fear or repulsion that Tanga and Ateba feel when faced with the stranger. Megri will be ready to defend man against the entire community and to love him as well. In *Loukoum*, the father—along with three mothers, one the legal wife and the other two the official wives—is finally present. As in *L'appel des arènes,* though, he is mentally absent. Nonetheless, the relation between father and child takes on a different nature because father and child are the same sex. A new type of complicity is formed between men. Through his father, Loukoum learns or becomes aware of what he should or should not do as a man.

Like the protagonists of the previous novels, however, the child also comes to judge his father. In accordance with the adage that the truth always comes from children's mouths, Loukoum points out a number of

weaknesses in his father's behavior, for example, his wavering and his flirtations with other women:

> If this continues, I think I am going to strangle my dad. But there you
> have it, because he's my father. The Koran forbids that, it says so in black
> and white: "Thou shall honor thou father, thou mother whatever happens.
> (Beyala 1995, 41)

Loukoum also observes meaningful positive changes in his father's attitude, in particular after Soumana's death:

> My Dad changed a lot. Now he helps M'am with the children and in the
> kitchen too. You'd think he'd grown millions of years older in just two
> weeks. It's as if something has happened on earth that caused him not to
> be the same anymore. He talks to M'am with respect and, sometimes, he
> caresses her, just like that, like little kisses on the neck. I have never seen
> him do that before. He often speaks to her kindly, but you'd think that
> M'am didn't believe in it too much. So she bursts out laughing and pulls
> away. (162–163)

Through these changes in his father's attitude, the son perceives his
father's vulnerability and a shift of power from father to mother. Loukoum
still feels jealousy and rivalry when his father returns home from prison
and takes back his old position (and his armchair). Now he has to return to
his initial status, whereas during his father's absence, he got to play the
role of the man in the house (in a proper and figurative sense), sitting in
his father's chair, being served tea:

> I am the man of the house. I sit down in my dad's armchair after work.
> . . . M'am serves me the tea. She sits down next to me and tells me sto-
> ries. She talks about dad, her marriage, my sisters and me. Simple things
> of everyday life. (Beyala 1995, 168)
> It bothered me a little when he took his armchair back. It was almost
> like a shock. But he is so nice that well, after all, he's my Dad. (Beyala
> 1995, 172)

In the final pages we glimpse the hope for some happiness. The family
unit can regain its strength and well-being even though "the paths of happiness are very complicated" (177).

Some of the recent novels, however, oppose this image of the physically and mentally absent father; they emphasize the father's active participation as a parent and his investment in the family, which is greater than
the mother's. *Sous la cendre, le feu* (Mpoudi Ngolle 1990), *La tache de
sang* (Bassek 1990), and *Fureurs et cris de femmes* (Rawiri 1989) stress
this particular element, whereas the counterexample resides in pointing out

the mother's indifference or even her instability. *Sous la cendre le feu* especially develops this image of the modern, devoted father. Through the narrative voice of Mina, the protagonist, we see the societal view toward the father's unusual care for his children. Although Fanny, his first child, is not his own, Djibril still shows the greatest concern in taking care of her.

> I have to admit that Djibril was a wonderful and very affectionate father. He adored our two children, and they felt the same about him. I could see that the children were more attached to him than to me, and it wasn't hard to understand why. When I wasn't attending classes, I was doing my homework. . . . I was studying and it was convenient not having the kids pulling on my skirt. Later on I would feel jealous towards Djibril for having usurped my place, but it was ridiculous to feel this way. So I struggled to repress this stupid, childish feeling.

> *[Il fallait bien le reconnaître, Djibril était un père merveilleux et très affectueux. Il adorait nos deux enfants, ceux-ci le lui rendaient bien. Je voyais bien que les enfants lui étaient plus attachés qu'à moi, et cela se comprenait aisément: quand je n'étais pas à mes cours, je faisais mes devoirs, . . . j'étudiais et cela m'arrangeait de ne pas avoir les petits dans mes jupes. Plus tard, il m'arriva d'en éprouver un sentiment de jalousie vis-à-vis de Djibril qui s'était approprié ma place, mais je me sentais alors ridicule et je me dépêchais de refouler un sentiment aussi bête et puéril.]* (Mpoudi Ngolle 1990, 100)

Mina acknowledges her inability to take care of children and her feelings of guilt for delegating this task to her husband. She is jealous of Djibril, feeling left out and excluded from the bonding between father and child. As Mina makes progress in her therapy, another image of Djibril takes shape. He reveals himself as an inflexible man who wants to assert his virility after being ridiculed by his friends for his participation in the household chores.[26] Furthermore, when Mina manages to break free of her personal crisis, the truth breaks out: Djibril has abused his daughter Fanny. Mina had shut herself up in a state of madness as part of an attempt to bury this act deep within her memory, in order to flee reality: "I had to accept the evidence that I had thought I could escape my responsibilities by hiding behind this mental condition which, in a way, removed me from reality. I had to realize that this was not the right solution" [Je dus me rendre à l'évidence que j'avais cru échapper à mes responsabilités en me réfugiant derrière cet état mental qui me soustrayait en quelque sorte à la réalité et que ce n'était pas la bonne solution] (Mpoudi Ngolle 1990, 91). The almost perfect image of this modern father is only temporary and gradually falls apart in the course of the story. What appears at the same time is the community's resistance to seeing a man play this role. They accuse him of feminizing himself, of being submissive to his wife, and of having lost all power in his own household. Here, we find the traditional elements of derision directed at the husband-father by family or friends in order to get him to reassume the expected patriarchal role.

In *Fureurs et cris de femme,* (Rawiri 1989), Joseph also appears as an image of the modern father. He gives advice to his wife and helps her before and during her labor.

> He would change her diapers and give her the bottle. . . . Often he would leave the office early in order to be with his wives. This group of words, "my women," sounded pleasant to his ears and had an important effect on him. During the night, when Rékia would cry and her mother was exhausted, he was the one who would rock her to sleep. The child slept better in her father's arms than in her mother's, and this was a bad habit of which they had a hard time curing her. He was also the one who watched her first steps through the rooms of the house.
>
> *[Il langeait et donnait le biberon. . . . Souvent il quittait le bureau avant l'heure pour être auprès de ses femmes. Ce groupe de mots "mes femmes" avait une consonance agréable à ses oreilles et une portée considérable pour lui. La nuit , lorsque Rékia pleurait et que sa mère était exténuée, c'était lui qui la berçait. L'enfant dormait mieux dans les bras de son père que dans ceux de sa mère, une mauvaise habitude qu'ils eurent beaucoup de mal à lui enlever. Ce fut encore lui qui dirigea ses premiers pas à travers toutes les pièces de la maison.]* (34)

Similar images of a father's devotion to his children and a sharing of domestic tasks between husband and wife appear in Maïga Ka's *La voie du salut suivi de le miroir de la vie* (1985) and Philomène Bassek's *La tache de sang* (1990). Both of these novels stress the husband's initial positive willingness, then his growing reservations, and finally his refusal to be the devoted father. His refusal results from his friends' pressure; they ridicule his lack of virility.

In *La voix du salut,* point by point Racine renounces his initial attitude in favor of complete cooperation and communication with his wife. This process ends in his taking a *drianké* for a wife, which causes an immediate rupture with his first wife, Rabiatou (and indirectly contributes to the suicide of her friend, Sokhna.)

> He would come home later and later. He hardly had any meals at home anymore. If he did stay at home, he would never loosen his lips and would submerge himself in reading his newspapers. Rabiatou was suffering. Racine didn't love her anymore. . . . Maybe she was too European for him, not African enough?
>
> *[Ce dernier rentrait chez lui de plus en plus tard. Il ne prenait pratiquement plus ses repas à la maison. S'il lui arrivait de rester chez lui, il ne desserrait pas les dents et se plongeait dans la lecture de ses journaux. Rabiatou souffrait. Racine ne l'aimait plus. . . . Peut-être était-elle trop européenne, pas assez africaine?]* (Maïga Ka 1985, 96)

Again, it is the woman's turn to question or doubt her own conduct, whereas the man has been called back to order by the community (the term *to call to order* is meaningful in itself.) In *La tache de sang* (Bassek 1990), Mandika thinks that his wife, Patricia, goes too far in participating in social and political activities in women's organizations. Although he was initially open to sharing the household chores, Mandika becomes critical of this plan and refuses to continue to follow a lifestyle that comes directly from France and that therefore has no relation to him and his wife as an African couple. Once more, the husband-father has done an about-face on the controversial subject of the emancipation of women, which is so opposed to the African spirit. Mpoudi Ngolle's *Sous la cendre le feu* stresses Djibril's limitations as a modern father. The same situation has been repeated. Teased by his friends and urged on by his sister, he gradually refuses to feed and change diapers for his new son after having been so proud to do this for his daughter Fanny.

> He always thought it was normal to take care of all these chores that are usually exclusively reserved for women. Why would he suddenly feel ashamed to be seen preparing the baby bottle in front of his sister? . . . A serious change began taking place in Djibril.
>
> *[Il avait toujours trouvé normal de s'occuper de toutes ces taches exclusivement réservées chez nous à la gent féminine. Pourquoi devant sa soeur cela deviendrait-il une honte d'être vu en train de préparer un biberon? . . . Un grave changement était en train de s'opérer en Djibril.]*
> (Mpoudi Ngolle 1990, 132)

Each of these cases illustrates the ambiguity of the father's status in society, in African society in particular. Any closeness between father and child (whether son or daughter) is interpreted as proof that the man is soft, that he acts as "someone who voluntarily renounces his masculine privileges and abdicates the power and preeminence of being a man that the patriarchal order grants him" (Badinter 1992, 194; my translation). By replacing his wife in this role of mothering their children, he attracts the ridicule not only of his friends but also of his own family, including the women. As with Racine (in *La voie du salut*), Djibril's wavering behavior shows man's limitations in his efforts to share household chores and to establish a modern couple. Badinter notes that "it is often the feminine partner who imposes this new behavior that is profoundly foreign to him. The man feels as though his masculinity were under attack, his identity wavers, and, more often than not, the couple breaks up" (1992, 195). This remark is particularly fitting in the case of Racine and Rabiatou: The relation ends abruptly with the wife's suicide, which is followed by her friend's tragic death.

Through their variants, each of these cases gives cause to reexamine the question of mothering and maternity. Does a woman have the right to neglect her children or leave her responsibilities to her husband in order to study, work, or participate in a political organization? The feminist side of the question highlights the guilt-forming process that insidiously functions against women and their desires for self-realization. Why should women feel guilty for wanting to study or for wanting to succeed in a profession or career? Rabiatou (in Maïga Ka's *La voie du salut*), Patricia (in Bassek's *La tache de sang*), and Emilienne (in Rawiri's *Fureurs et cris*) feel guilty each time they choose a voice that differs from the woman's traditional prerogative and from a woman's duties in general, by which I mean the perceived duties of being a wife and a mother in the home. The narrative voice invites readers to go beyond this guilt toward a new awareness of what is nothing other than a form of emotional abuse of women. The other issue raised is that of responsible and lasting fatherhood.

Beyond all these questions, these women authors single out the dual paradox concerning woman's situation as a mother and man's as a father. Because of her biological nature—she alone can bear children—woman sees herself as limited to maternity. Faced with this condition that should demonstrate a priori women's superiority, men have turned it to their advantage by creating a dubious theory of maternal instinct and by creating patriarchal rules. Whether she refuses this role or finds that she is unable to conceive, woman is marginalized and denied a complete identity as a woman. As Badinter explains, even if man does not actually see himself excluded from playing the role of a father, he has trouble defining himself as one. This explains his general attitude and preference for appearing as an absent father rather than appearing *soft*, which would constitute a negation of his virility.

> The theory of maternal instinct postulates that the mother alone is capable of feeding and taking care of the child because she is biologically determined for this purpose. The mother/child couple would form an ideal unit that neither can nor should be disturbed. By supporting the idea of the child's exclusive attachment to its mother, and of the mother's natural predisposition for taking care of the child, the father's exclusion is justified and the mother/son symbiosis is equally reinforced.
>
> *[La théorie de l'instinct maternel postule que la mère est seule capable de s'occuper du nourrisson et de l'enfant parce qu'elle y est biologiquement déterminée. Le couple mère/enfant formerait une unité idéale que nul ne peut ni ne doit perturber. En soutenant l'idée d'un attachement exclusif de l'enfant pour la mère, et d'une prédisposition naturelle de celle-ci à s'occuper de celui-là, on légitime l'exclusion du père et on renforce d'autant la symbiose mère/fils.]* (Badinter 1992, 103)

Badinter's analysis of masculine identity and her conclusions are entirely applicable to the African man in the context of a modern couple in modern Africa. Emphasizing the connection between the status of the mother and the postulate of maternal instinct, on the one hand, and the man's difficulty with defining himself as a father, on the other, she remarks: "Once men became aware of this natural disadvantage [the fact that only women can give birth] they created a highly effective cultural buffer: the patriarchal system. Today, now that they have been compelled to get rid of the patriarch, they need to reinvent the father and the concept of virility that arises as a result" (Badinter 1992, 278; my translation).

Notes

1. This separation of mother and son is the object of numerous passages in Camara Laye's *L'enfant noir* (1953), Francis Bebey's *Le fils d'Agatha Moudio* (1967), and Mariama Bâ's *Scarlet Song*. The latter novel focuses more on the son's return home. The separation of mother and son remains to a large extent in the background.

2. The term *roman de formation* refers to the terminology utilized by Jacques Chevrier in *Littérature africaine* (1984) in his classification of the different types of African novels.

3. Other examples of romans de formation constructed along the lines of this model are Camara Laye's *L'enfant noir*, Bernard Dadié's *Un Nègre à Paris* (1957), Ake Loba's *Kocoumba l'étudiant noir* (1960), and, of course, Cheikh Hamidou Kane's *L'aventure ambigüe* (1961).

4. The following analysis of *L'appel des arènes* integrates elements from my previous article, "Gender, Age, and Reeducation: A Changing Emphasis in Recent African Novels in French," *Africa Today* 38 (1991): 54–64.

5. Borgomano also emphasizes this distancing oneself from the past in *Voix et visages de femmes* (1989), in which she develops a portrait of Diattou.

6. The image of abandoned motherhood is proof of her professional failure. African mothers withdraw their confidence in her. They accuse her of having the evil eye and causing the death of newborn babies. In the end, Diattou wanders from room to room, speechless and unkempt. This scene confirms the vision of failure and lost identity.

7. Among these women authors, Aminata Sow Fall is one of the few to portray women so negatively. Borgomano observes that "the narrator's harsh attitude towards her female character seems excessive and strange" (1989, 67). Sow Fall has often rejected the feminist label, claiming that she writes first as a citizen of Senegal and that for this reason she owes it to herself to deal with the problems affecting her country. Part of the reason she rejects the term *feminist* is its very Western connotations. She portrays women as equal to men, including in their weaknessses and greed.

8. For more on this, see the section "The Prostitute Mother" in Chapter 2. The mother-son relation is examined there in greater detail in the framework set up by the mirror image of the mother as prostitute.

9. Nafissatou Diallo's *Awa, la petite marchande* (1981) and Ken Bugul's *The Abandoned Baobab* (1991) are the most typical examples, although in the first case the departure and stay in France figure within two chapters toward the end of the story. The novel concludes with the father and daughter's return, each having gained valuable experience and prestige as a result of their travels in a foreign land.

10. Another example is Thérèse Kuoh-Moukouri's *Rencontres essentielles*. This novel describes the sufferings of a Camerounian woman after her relationship with Jo, another Camerounian, falls apart. She meets Joël in Paris when they are both students there. He returns to their native country and gradually forgets about his wife only to finally pursue his wife's friend, a French woman with whom he will have a child. In practice, the initial situation and the mother-daughter relation have been swept away in order to depict the more traditional conjugal relation (and an adulterous interracial relationship to boot).

11. This evocation emphasizes above all the disappearance of any feelings of plenitude: "Life was like a river flowing on a flat riverbed. . . . In that time, we desired nothing but our health and peace of mind. We were happy with the lives we were leading. No one asked for anything more. Any event that surpassed the usual daily grind became a cause for great dancing, singing and rejoicing. . . . But today everything is just sad. . . . People jealously keep what they have and envy what they don't possess" [La vie était comme un fleuve coulant sur un lit plat. . . . En ce temps-là, on ne désirait rien. Sinon la santé et la paix de l'âme. On se contentait de la vie qu'on menait. On n'en demandait pas plus. Tout événement qui échappait au train-train habituel était prétexte à des danses et des chants. . . . Mais aujourd'hui, tout n'est que tristesse. . . . On garde jalousement ce que l'on possède et on envie ce que l'on n'a pas] (Rawiri 1983, 27).

12. The relation between the grandmother and her own daughter develops in the same way as in *Mon mari est capable* (Boucoulon 1988) and *L'appel des arènes* (Sow Fall 1982) when the grandmother projects her bitterness and pain onto the child's mother, her own daughter, for having rejected the authority and responsibility that she is still supposed to exercise over her as a parent.

13. Here, as in *L'appel des arènes,* the mother indirectly participates in the child's destruction. She is unable to discern what is beneficial for the child's future (independent of whatever may be beneficial to herself). Her attraction to Western criteria of success, nevertheless, reveals a certain deviance: She is less interested in success obtained through education and the white man's diplomas and more in an immediate, visible success to be found in the possession of the external signs that are associated with it, for example, nice clothes, a car, money, and a villa.

14. See Mildred Mortimer's excellent analysis "Women's Flight" in *Journeys Through the French African Novel* (1990). The section on *Le baobab fou* is entitled "The Orphan's Quest: Ken Bugul," 165–177.

15. "By the light of the lamps, our two shadows touched and crossed on the ceiling like two swords. Giving in to her habit, Dame maman placed her hand on mine. Her touch was hardly heavier than a feather's" [A la lueur de nos lampes, nos deux ombres se heurtaient et se croisaient au plafond, telles deux épées. Cédant à l'habitude, Dame maman posa sa main sur la mienne. Un attouchement guère plus pesant qu'une plume] (Beyala 1996, 45).

16. For example, Megri *(Seul le diable)* watches over her mother's sleep: "When I left the room, her chest was rising and falling, rising and falling" [Quand je quittais la pièce, sa poitrine se soulevait, retombait, se soulevait, retombait] (Beyala 1990, 46).

17. The questions of the right to abortion and illegal abortion are taken up several times, as they are a new phenomenon in the African novel: "Kama's legislation prohibited any move for abortion, except in the cases where the mother's life is at risk. The risk did not have to be present, but imminent, so the husband's legal authorization thus proved necessary" [La législation du Kama prohibait toute manoeuvre d'avortement, excepté en cas de risque mortel pour la mère. Le risque

n'était pas présent, mais imminent. L'autorisation légale de l'époux s'avérait donc nécessaire] (Bassek 1990, 131); "'Don't worry Patricia, your struggle is mine.' Inside herself, Patricia was still undecided. The resolution on abortion applied to her own mother, so her opinion would count for her too" ["Ne t'alarme pas, Patricia, ton drame et ton combat sont les miens." Au fond d'elle-même, Patricia restait indécise. La résolution de l'avortement portait sur sa propre mère et son avis comptait pour elle] (131); "The lady doctor held out a prescription and a pink pill that she had carefully wrapped in some cotton. 'It has a magical power,' she said, with a tone of complicity towards her friend" [La doctoresse lui tendit une ordonnance et un comprimé rose qu'elle avait soigneusement enveloppé dans du coton. "Il a un pouvoir magique," dit-elle d'un air entendu à son amie] (132).

18. This theme already appears in Anglophone authors' works, in particular in Buchi Emecheta's *The Joys of Motherhood* (1979) and Flora Nwapa's *One Is Enough* (1981). In the novels that we will be looking at here, the question takes on another form, appearing as the question of the African woman's maternal desire.

19. This same phenomenon is treated by certain male authors, for example by Denis Boucoulon in *Mon Mari est capable*. Abandoned by his father at birth, the protagonist is rejected by his mother precisely because the child reminds her of this unhappy past. The son's relation to his mother is characterized by a mixture of frustrated passion and hatred. The traditional story of the adolescent's departure for Paris takes a new twist, since it is lived as a form of punishment and unbearable separation. He then experiments with homosexual behavior and soon turns towards male prostitution. Again, as in *L'Appel des arènes,* the grandmother holds the only position of real authority. She is the only person to give him the little love that he receives.

20. This is a good place to remind our reader of the child's ambiguous status in African society. On the one hand, children have always held a key position in African society by virtue of the fact that their number has been a sign of the father's power. This was a masculine power but also an agricultural power in the sense that children represented an important source of labor. On the other hand, they have no position of their own. Childhood is not considered a condition but is viewed instead as a transitional passage between birth and entry into adult life, which is officially marked by rites of initiation. According to this conception, children should be educated and raised in order to become morally respectable adults capable of helping their elders as quickly as possible. As an example, we must point out the fact that children do not usually eat with adults. They receive the leftovers that remain after the adults have already been served. (This contrasts with the typical Western ideal where children are treated as kings and queens, served first and given the most tender morsel or the most generous portion if there is a dessert.)

21. See Ghazi M. Farooq, Ita I. Ekanem, and Sina Ojelade, "Family Size Preferences and Fertility in South-Western Nigeria," (1987, 75–85); see also, from the same book, Wolf Bleek, "Family and Family Planning in Southern Ghana," 138–153.

22. See Philippe Ariès's *Naissance de l'enfance* (1960), an analytical historical study on the origins of the idea of childhood. Ariès demonstrates that this notion began with the development of bourgeois life and a sense of familial private life.

23. *Loukoum* represents an orientational change in this respect. This change appears in Aminata's attitude toward her child, Loukoum, as well as in the form of the story, which centers upon the child as the main narrative voice. Given the

family structure, Loukoum has an abundance of mothers, and through each of them, he discovers a different facet of the maternal image.

24. As examples, Brière cites Anna-Claude's character in Beyala's *Tanga* (1996) and Mariama's in Beyala's *Loukoum* (1992) and *Maman a un amant* (1993).

25. There are also the examples of Myriam Warner-Vieyra's first two novels, which reveal the paternal figure's ambiguity. In *Le quimboiseur l'avait dit* (1980), the father is shown in an inferior social and psychological position in relation to his wife (even if his childish attitude is actually healthy, as opposed to his wife's social ambitions acquired through contact with white people.) Thus the mother appropriates the right to make decisions for her daughter even though she has already abandoned her, and her project of bringing her daughter with her to Paris involves a hidden scheme to use her for various services. This manipulation presents another problematic aspect of the mother's role. In *Juletane* (1982), the protagonist is an orphan raised by her stepmother in the great metropolis after her parents' death. The character's development reveals that her psychological breakdown results from both her husband's emotional withdrawal and from a lack of family support, both present and past. In this case, family support also includes the transmission of traditions and Antillean roots. Because she grew up exiled from her origins and was transplanted into a new environment that was closer to her childhood experience, she crumbles psychologically and is no longer able to re-source herself.

26. In this respect, Djibril is an essential representative of the modern man. His position is defined by the fact that he plays a predominant role in taking care of the children, leaving his wife the time needed for studies or professional development. According to Badinter, this new type of man is characterized by his openness to mothering. He is "the father/mother who takes care of his daughter all by himself, because the mother cannot assume this responsibility" (1992, 196; my translation).

5

The Body and Sexuality

Difference reduced to sexual identity is [thus] posited to justify and conceal exploitation. The Body, the most visible difference between man and woman, the only one to offer a secure ground for those who seek the permanent, the feminine "nature" and "essence" remains thereby the safest basis for racist and sexist ideologies.
— Trinh T. Minh-ha (*Woman, Native, Other*, 100)

There are dangers in reducing a person's identity to a sexual representation and, consequently, of reducing woman to a representation of her body. Woman runs the risk of being confined to a binary opposition where woman and body are paired in opposition to man and soul.

Furthermore, in most cultures this opposition has been recurrently applied to sexual politics:[1] (1) Heterosexual relationships have been institutionalized according to what is presented as a regulating principle of binary hierarchical opposition between a male and a female. In this relationship, woman's identity is derived from man's. She is the other (representing a lack of), and her desire is necessarily heterosexual. (2) Power in its different forms reinforces this notion of heterosexuality and male oppression. (3) The human body is defined not as a signifying entity but as "a set of boundaries, individual and social, politically signified and maintained" (Butler 1990, 33).

Although it falls directly in the category of Western feminist theory, Judith Butler's *Gender Trouble, Feminism and the Subversion of Identity* offers relevant observations on the social envelope surrounding the question of sexuality. Butler demonstrates that gender is "a reality created through sustained social performances [that] means that the very notions of an essential sex and a true or abiding masculinity or femininity are also constituted as part of the strategy that conceals gender's performative character and the performative possibilities for proliferating gender configurations outside the restricting frames of masculinist definitions and compulsory heterosexuality" (1990, 140). As a result, any representation that falls outside the norms, in the margins of patriarchal laws, obviously constitutes a potential danger for the center, as it calls its balance into question. This possibility explains the efforts of society to keep the physical and social body intact.[2] It also explains the regulations and constraints imposed on the female body and the strict confinement of woman's sexual desire. I am thinking especially of the Islamic religious discourse aimed at confining woman spatially and psychologically within a restricted frame in order to limit what is considered her dangerous insatiable sexual appetite.[3]

Isolating the female body in its representation runs the risk of falling back on another binary opposition that is entirely linguistic, thus siding with the patriarchal law that wants to define woman in opposition to man. It is necessary to disrupt and break the silence imposed by man—who has always had the right to decide what could be shown and in what conditions—on anything that addresses desire and sexuality. To speak about her body and her desires therefore represents a daring act for a woman writer, particularly for the African woman.

My objective here is to show how and to what extent women writers have broken the silence regarding all sexual representation in African literature, whether their works are part of the canon or not, and how they have attempted to reconquer a body that has been taken away from them. On this point, in "De l'aliénation à la réappropriation du corps chez les romancières de l'Afrique noire francophone," Béatrice Rangira Gallimore shows that "the female body is constantly subjected to manipulations of social pressure" (1994, 54; my translation). The female body is an object from the start.

> In Africa, she says, it is through the body that society stabilizes and perpetuates itself. Thus, this body must be shaped, controlled and branded. The control of the body is translated through the verbal injunctions regarding the way to maintain one's body, which is regulated by a code that determines good and bad behavior. The traditional female education teaches a woman that she should keep her eyes lowered, says Mina, the heroine in Evelyne Mpoudi Ngolle's *Sous la cendre le feu.* (55)

Béatrice Rangira Gallimore's examples stress the different types of objectification to which the female body is submitted: "a body that is looked at," a body that is bought in exchange for dowry, or else a body that is submitted to genital operations. Rangira Gallimore remarks:

> This notion of the female body as a consumer good clearly appears in the form of the body marks that most girls in African societies bear. . . . Society, and more precisely a patriarchal society, brands the female body in order to ensure total control over woman and to prepare her for her role as passive receiver. The female sexual organ is often considered as a tool-organ that produces pleasure. The females' testimonies collected by

Thiam show that the female's body cannot seek sexual pleasure for herself. (1994, 56)

Reproduction is another role attributed to the female body, which Rangira Gallimore sums up in the following lapidary formula: "Under this double role that is conferred upon her with marriage, the female body as product leaves the market in order to become a producing body." From this standpoint, the body assumes a new value with respect to its "integrity," in other words, its "virginity."[4] When the same woman who was valued for her virginity proves unable to bear children, she is looked down on by society, no longer respected. We thus end up with two types of contrary images in women's literature, one as frequent as the other, "[either] women whose bodies suffer deeply from the agony of being infertile, [or] women whose bodies fall apart because of their numerous pregnancies" (Rangira Gallimore 1994, 56).

Fureurs et cris de femmes (Rawiri 1989) is a perfect illustration of the first situation. *La tache de sang* (Bassek 1990) gives an excellent portrayal of the second.

Inscriptions of the Female Body

With the increased visibility of Francophone African women writers on the literary scene in the 1980s, the body took on a more important dimension. Its writing renews the traditional frame of the body as object; it can also be a manifestation of psychosomatic troubles, an expression of female desire, and the creation of a specific space for woman. Echoing Awa Thiam's precepts of self-representation, and Luce Irigaray's on a more theoretical level, women writers demonstrate that "the female body does not remain an object of men's discourse, nor of their many arts, but it becomes the principle for a female subjectivity that is experienced and chosen by women [le corps féminin ne reste pas objet de discours des hommes ni de leurs divers arts mais (devient) enjeu d'une subjectivité féminine s'éprouvant et s'identifiant elle-même] (Irigaray 1987, 68).

Both the description and the function of the body in women's texts have undergone a progression. The body first had to be introduced in the texts. Unlike Maghrebin literature, where there has been a long tradition of writing and a poetic of the body and sexuality, writers from sub-Saharan Africa have been rather reserved about it.[5] Essentially, the body was first used as a sign of woman's psychological suffering. This representation occurs, for instance, in Mariama Bâ's *Scarlet Song* (1986) and Myriam Warner-Vieyra's *Juletane* (1987). As victims of madness or depression, both protagonists (Mireille, Juletane) undergo bodily changes. These changes translate into a further negative evolution due to their position at the margins of society. The emphasis is mainly on the loss of an initial physical beauty or glow and the concomitant appearance of multiple psychosomatic troubles: loss of sleep, loss of appetite, aphasia, nightmares, and all kinds of other anxieties. The physical deterioration is continuous and occurs as the outer manifestation of an unresolved internal conflict. However, in all these examples, the body remains peripheral to the novel, appearing only as an element of the female character's suffering. There is not a separate discourse on the body per se.[6] Angèle Rawiri truly innovates in this respect, as she explores the body mainly along three lines: the transformed body, the body as discovery, and the body as suffering.

The Body Transformed in Rawiri's Texts

Toward the end of the 1970s, a new tendency appeared in West African societies: social success through appearance. In this context, the female body took on greater value as a sign of self-affirmation and as a sign not only of one's own financial and social success but of the companion's.

G'amàrakono, au carrefour (Rawiri 1983) opens with Toula's financial difficulties and her frustrations about her secretarial work. She is uncomfortable because she feels her body is obese and unattractive, because of her cheap-looking clothes and the humble origins of her family.[7] Opposite this situation and character stands another female character, Ekata. She embodies all the new principles that lead young women to social success. As Toula's friend, she plays the role of guide and initiator, pushing her to follow the same path of success and to escape from Igewa's unambitious and stifling milieu:

> I don't understand your obstinacy to keep living among these poor and boring people. . . . They have a dumbing effect on you. Why don't you try to free yourself from this spider web that eats a little bit more of you up every day?
>
> *[Je ne comprends pas ton entêtement à vouloir vivre au milieu de ces gens pauvres et ennuyeux. . . . Ils t'abrutissent. Pourquoi n'essaies-tu pas de sortir de cette toile d'arraignée qui te dévore chaque jour un peu plus?]* (58)

The first part of the novel describes Igewa's milieu and Toula's frustrations but also her scruples about changing. She hesitates to aspire to a position that is not her own and to be among people who rely on these new principles, "'a world that only has eyes for instruction, money and appearance,' a world where 'women are no longer the same. They have a job. They have more freedom and they try to be attractive to men.'" ["un monde qui n'a d'yeux que pour l'instruction, l'argent et même l'apparence," un monde où "les femmes ne sont plus les mêmes. Elles travaillent. Elles deviennent plus libres et elles cherchent à plairent aux hommes"] (Rawiri 1983, 18).

Toula's body "craves all the delights of this world" (Rawiri 1983, 25). Her decision to enter this world is the result of her mother's pressure. Her mother encourages her to change, to be physically attractive, and to attract men in order to help her family financially.

Her attempts to lose weight and to take care of her body are all efforts to not resemble her mother (see Chapter 4). Her attitude becomes the sign of the extreme importance of social success, in which she denigrates her social and biological roots. This aspect of the story is central to its development, as the chapter titles "La métamorphose" (Metamorphosis) and "Vivre son corps" (To live one's body) clearly indicate. The narration proceeds to describe Toula's transformation. Step by step, it exposes her subjection to a notion of success through physical appearances.

The first step is to realize that women's search for beauty can be explained by men's domination: "Men are still ruling over women. That forces us to make every possible effort and to use all our charms to be attractive and submit ourselves to their whims." [Les hommes commandent encore aux femmes. Et ça nous oblige à faire tous nos efforts, à déployer tous nos charmes pour leur être attirantes et nous soumettre à leurs caprices] (Rawiri 1983, 19). The second step is to succeed in seducing men. The woman must follow two elementary rules: (1) be seen in the "in" places; (2) demand the largest possible amount of money from men and make them pay for everything. Ekata says: "I am happy with their money and I try to enjoy life as much as I can" [Je me contente de leur argent et de jouir de la vie tant que je peux] (47).

Rawiri also analyzes man and woman in their paradoxical and demanding behavior. For instance, "[men's] pride pushes them to manifest their affection in incredible expenses even if this means great sacrifices" [leur orgueil les pousse à manifester leur affection par des dépenses incroyables au prix parfois de grandes privations] [(Rawiri 1983, 47). Conversely, women are more and more demanding of men: "They are no longer content with a man who walks and eats bread at lunchtime. They are looking for a man who has money and a name" [Elles ne se contentent plus d'hommes qui marchent à pied et se nourrissent de tartines de pain aux heures des repas. Elles cherchent un homme qui a un nom et de l'argent] (48). The obvious conclusion to the first lesson is that "unselfish love no longer exists" [l'amour désintéressé n'existe plus]. "Unconsciously, woman thinks of her lover's or husband's wallet" [Unconciemment, la femme songe au portefeuille de son ami ou de son mari] (48). This passage exposes a new condition, that the race for appearances and seduction creates a vicious circle insofar as men expect a certain appearance of women, and women expect gifts that match the demand.

The second lesson involves becoming aware of the fact that beauty can be purchased: "This beauty and this charm that fascinate you can be acquired through clothing and make-up. In a word, it can be obtained with money. Any man or woman who has money can become more beautiful." [Cette beauté et ce charme qui te fascinent s'acquièrent par l'habillement et le maquillage en ce qui concerne les femmes. En un mot par l'argent. Tout homme ou toute femme qui a de l'argent s'embellit] (Rawiri 1983, 61). In this context, being obese is an absolute barrier to social success; Toula is rejected for not taking care of her body.

The reader finds something unheard of in an African text—detailed dietetic advice as well as advice about makeup and exercise. In particular, Ekata gives Toula a magazine with all kinds of advice on these points: "You'll find a list of tempting low-calorie foods there" [Tu y trouveras aussi une liste de mets appétissants à basse calorie] (Rawiri 1983, 63). Advice and comments about weight loss are spread throughout the text, signaling Toula's success as well as her disappointments and relapses. For example, her clumsiness after a few exercises is described. We are told about her first lost kilos, about her ideal weight, about her diet of grapefruit to make up for some sweets that she ate when she was feeling lightheaded. In the end, her abrupt failure and her psychological helplessness are depicted when she gorges on sweets and other foods and gains back all the weight she had painstakingly lost.

Her dark complexion appears to be another barrier. Through Ekata's voice, Rawiri describes skin bleaching, particularly popular in the beginning of the 1980s, as light skin was said to be judged more attractive by men:

> I find you too dark, too. Light skin is better these days. If you look carefully around you, you'll see that single girls prefer to have kids with white or *métisse* men. They know that *métisse* girls are sought after at every level of society. If you travel on African airlines, you'll notice that light-complexioned *métisse* stewardesses are the ones who serve in the first-class cabin. They are also the ones you find at receptions.
>
> *[Je trouve aussi que tu es trop noire. La couleur claire passe mieux aujourd'hui. Si tu regardes bien autour de toi, tu constateras que nombres de filles célibataires préfèrent avoir des enfants avec des blancs ou des métis. Ces femmes n'ont pas tort. Elles savent que les métisses sont recherchées à tous les niveaux de la société. Si tu voyages sur certaines compagnies aériennes africaines, tu remarqueras que ce sont les hôtesses de l'air métisses ou brunes qui servent en première. Ce sont celles aussi que l'on trouve dans les salons d'honneur.]* (63)

Such language immediately recalls Fanon's (1952) remarks in *Peau noire, masques blancs* about the white woman's fascination for the black man and for her white skin on his black skin. But the question here takes on quite a different perspective, as the consequences of such fascination are reflected back onto the African woman. In *La voie du salut*, Maïga Ka also attacks African women for wanting to look like white women and for using bleaching creams such as Xessal:

> Most Senegalese women, regardless of interdictions and police checkups at the market, decided one day that "white" or at least a light color was better than their natural dark complexion. We now see an indiscriminate use of pharmaceutical products and all kinds of creams for a bleaching effect.
>
> *[La plupart des femmes sénégalaises, faisant fi des décrets et des descentes de police sur les lieux de vente de ces produits, ont décidé un jour que la couleur <<blanche>> ou à défaut claire est plus belle que leur couleur noire naturelle. On assiste alors à un usage effréné de produits pharmaceutiques, de pommades de tout sorte, tendant à décolorer.]* (1985, 111–112)

Maïga Ka particularly addresses the negative effects of these creams. In *G'amàrakono*, on the contrary, Toula's mother and Ekata compliment Toula on her new complexion; she had been the only one to resist this change: "We are first and foremost black women. How can we give up our color?" [Nous sommes avant tout des noires. Comment pouvons-nous avant tout renoncer à la couleur de notre peau?] (Rawiri 1983, 63). Here, an initially veiled criticism operates in two stages. The narrative voice, reinforced by the grandmother's, dwells almost silently on Toula's physical and psychological changes. It merely notes the changes until the ending retrospectively sheds light on the global criticism of the whole enterprise. Another important difference between this novel and Maïga Ka's *La voie du salut* is that Ekata realizes the aberration in changing her complexion and denying her blackness; yet she feels that she must comply if she wants to participate in the social phenomenon, if she wants to succeed. In order to seduce and attract men, one submits to certain essentials: "I know that this is not normal. But go and make men understand that. The facts are there. If you are light-skinned or a *métisse*, men see you from a distance and come closer to get a better look at you" [Je sais que ce n'est pas normal. Va le faire comprendre aux hommes. Ce sont eux qui nous influencent. Les faits sont là. Lorsque tu es claire ou métisse, les hommes t'aperçoivent de loin et s'approchent pour mieux te voir] (Rawiri 1985, 63). So Toula looks for the creams that will lighten her complexion. The narrative voice gives a detailed description of the possible options and prices: exfoliating creams, cleansing creams, purifying masks, and so on. Calixthe Beyala's *Assèze l'Africaine* also gives an account of the success of light skin with African men and of women's attempts to conform. When Assèze arrives in France, she gets advice from her three new friends as to what she should do to improve her physical appearance, to arouse men's interest, or to find a husband. The advice here is similar to what Ekata tells Toula:

> "Your skin is too dark," says Yvette.
> "Men prefer women who are the color of a ripe banana," says Fathia.
> The first rule was the cleanliness of the skin. It had to be bleached, disinfected, smoothened. She recommended everything to me that bleaches, cleanses, lightens, everything that exfoliates and erases. ...
> "Don't forget to apply the *ambi* to soften your skin and accentuate the whitening," says Fathia.
>
> *["Ta peau est trop noire," dit Yvette.*
> *"Les hommes préfèrent les femmes couleur banane mûre," dit Fathia.*
> *La première règle était la propreté de la peau. Elle devait être javelisée, désinfectée, râpée. Elle me recommanda tout ce qui décolore, nettoie, blanchit, tout ce qui gomme et efface. ...*
> *"Sans oublier de mettre l'ambi pour adoucir la peau et accentuer le blanchissage," dit Fathia.]* (1994, 243)

Here, too, the priority is to be beautiful and to be seen.[8]

The second part of Rawiri's *G'amàrakano* underlines the extent of Toula's changes, giving us her starting point and the intermediate steps:

The starting point. She displays a total rejection of her body, betraying an obsession with it:

> Unconsciously, she puts her thick hands on her voluminous neck. Fiddles with her big tits spread flat over her chest, kneads the rolls of fat of her belly and thighs. Is it possible to get rid of all this fat?
>
> *[Elle passe machinalement ses mains épaisses sur son cou volumineux. Tripote ses gros seins étalés sur sa poitrine, pétrit comme une pâte les bourrelets de son ventre et de ses cuisses. Est-il possible d'éliminer cette masse de graisse?]* (Rawiri 1983, 65)

The negative connotation of the adjectives (thick, large, voluminous, big, fat)—and the pejorative verbs (fiddles with, kneads), underscore Toula's loathing for her own body. In this obsession with thinness, fat and chubby body parts seem utterly repulsive to her, and she regards them as the very cause of her social failure. She can see only one solution to this problem. She has to resort to cosmetic surgery, to be massaged and have her body cared for all day long, since her ultimate goal is "to please, to please all these men" [plaire, plaire à tous ces hommes] (Rawiri 1983, 65).[9]

The intermediate step. The diet does not seem to work, as her body becomes flabby: "After the first two weeks, the cellulite is still there. Instead of melting away, the fat seems to spread and make little pools on her body" [Après les deux premières semaines, la cellulite est toujours là. Au lieu de fondre, les bourrelets s'amassent et forment des îlots sur tout le corps] (Rawiri 1983, 85). Toula's progress is closely scrutinized. If she does not lose weight easily, it must be due to a lack of exercise. The social and dietary restrictions that Toula imposes on herself cause real psychological suffering. For example, she refuses to go out because she is afraid she will be unable to resist the temptations of food. Toula goes through a phase of discouragement and mental emptiness, reaching the point where she almost swallows a bottle of detergent without noticing. Her predicament comes very close to the problems of anorexia that were discussed earlier, although anorexia is examined differently in this novel as an essentially Western phenomenon. She must fast to the point of dying in order to please. She must be thin like a model on the cover of the magazines she reads, and she must lose more and more weight and invest totally in what she thinks is the path to success.

The third step. Psychological changes result from Toula's physical changes. In particular, she looks strikingly more self-confident (in her way of walking, in her ease with speaking and with starting conversations). She is also remarkably successful with men, which entitles her to ask for anything she wants from them. She receives gifts from Eléwagnè, the director of a bank, while saving her real love for Angwé, Eléwagnè's employee, who casts a blind eye on the relationship between Toula and his boss. The narrative voice thus describes a period of illusions when Toula thinks she has reached the top: She has mastered her body; buys all the dresses she wants; receives a villa, a car, and money from Eléwagnè. Elated by her success, she is also delighted to discover desire and sexual pleasure with Angwé. Like Beyala, Rawiri gives the reader access to the female psyche and sexuality. I will come back to these two points later in this section.

The narrative voice also emphasizes Toula's naiveté about keeping her two relationships—one that is real love, the other more businesslike but somehow pleasurable. Toula's failure, which was already foreshadowed by the grandmother's bad omen and Mebalé's death, comes abruptly. Toula loses everything at once. Angwé commits suicide because he can no longer bear the thought of Toula in his boss's arms. On discovering that Toula had a relationship with one of his employees, Eléwagnè refuses to see her. Mebalé's death resurfaces. Because Ozoumet was jealous of her old friend's success, she could not simply be happy with the money she had extorted from Toula but told Eléwagnè about Angwé. Toula has returned to square one. She has no love and no financial or maternal support. She wanders alone in her villa, the cruel symbol of an artificial life. Worse off than before, Toula feels completely empty. She has no hope and no remaining illusions. In the last scene, she is shown going back into the street, trying to attract men one more time, but this effort is brought on by her failure and her fall. Her body looks dull and ugly. She feels sad. As she is totally ignored by the passing cars, she keeps walking alone in the rain. Her grandmother's prophecy has come to pass; Toula has become "the laughable plaything of a whirl of envies" [jouet dérisoire d'illusions] (Rawiri 1983, 27).

The negative effects of Western society on African women is denounced through a dramatic ending and the author's ideological stance. Ultimately, the novel raises the issue of appearances as a new form of slavery. The text is an exploration of the problem not only through Toula's unfortunate example but also through the simultaneous analysis done by the extradiagetic (third person) narrative voice and the collective gazes of the grandmother, the mother, and Ekata as they perceive her changes. The protagonist's ideas extend beyond her own thoughts to recount what appears in women's magazines, for instance, the role of clothing or designer names. The obvious dictatorship of appearance in regard to identity is emphasized.

The reader can see two parallel discourses here. One appears in magazines. This is the one adopted by Ekata, Toula, and all the women of her age who share the same ambitions for success. The other discourse is more subtle: The third-person narrative depicts the dangers of such changes for African youth. The first discourse is presented in detail, from simple advice to the arguments meant to convince women of the advantages of changing their bodies, for instance, "an overfull belly weighs the body down and makes your thoughts sluggish" [un ventre exagérément plein alourdit le corps et ralentit la réflexion] (Rawiri 1983, 72).

The second discourse enables the reader to grasp the gravity of the problem; it also raises the question of the criteria of beauty.[10] How can we explain the fact that Western criteria of beauty may override African criteria of beauty? Why would African men want African women to emulate Western ideals? What makes African men say that an African woman is beautiful? Her slender form, light skin, and fine features? Or a plump form, a dark complexion, and full features? Do the Western criteria of beauty necessarily mean that the men (and the women who follow them) are under a strict Western influence? And in this respect, should the second criteria be considered as closer to African roots? Does it even make sense to speak of such criteria? What does the use of the qualifier "more African" mean or imply?

Could it be that the hyperbolic importance of appearances and the adoption of new criteria of beauty are no less than the result of the extreme influence of the Western model? In their desire to imitate the Western model, are African women led to adopt the Western woman's obsessions as well, in particular the obsession with the body?

To this day, not a single sociological study on African women has explored this issue. What becomes clear, however, is that African women are prisoners, trapped between two choices that are equally limiting. On the one hand, they are supposed to be the keepers of tradition. They are even supposed to embody it, preferring a "more African" lifestyle even in their way of dressing. On the other hand, young women trying to find financial support through men are supposed to follow Western fashions and trends, so that in men's eyes, their companions look better and more important. Either option implies a restriction of African women's freedom.

Francophone authors' focus on these issues is meaningful in itself, and I will examine this focus in more depth in Part 3. This phenomenon, the importance of fashion and appearance, can be traced back to colonization. For example, Francophone African countries are more likely to follow the Western criteria for clothing and makeup found in France than the ones that can be found in England. The social origin of these women writers must also be taken into consideration. Most of them are from the middle class, or even the upper class, and logically, they deal with issues and events that may be more developed or more important in the urban population and in their class. This focus on appearance is not necessarily representative of all African women. However, novels from the second part of the 1980s, especially Beyala's works, are innovatative in this respect. These later authors introduce us to a new, less privileged milieu and thus to a new series of class-related problems.

The Body as Suffering in Rawiri's Texts

I will refer here to the same corpus of texts used in Chapters 1 and 3 as a starting point for my analysis of Rawiri's *Fureurs et cris de femmes*. In both cases, we observed the same physical and psychological changes as signs of the character's negative transformation. In the case of the foreign wives (Mireille in *Scarlet Song* and Juletane in *Juletane*), their beauty fades and they concomitantly experience psychosomatic troubles such as loss of sleep and appetite, aphasia, and nightmares and all forms of anxieties; at times they even refuse to eat or drink.[11] As I mentioned earlier, their continuous physical deterioration is an external manifestation of an unresolved internal conflict. It is the sign of their loss of power over their husbands and, as a result, a loss of power over themselves and their bodies. The next step in their negative transformation is the onset of anorexia and general aphasia. The protagonist withdraws from reality and the outside world, closing herself up in her suffering. In *Juletane*, this withdrawal begins with Juletane's keeping a diary, in which she will retrace her suffering until she dies. She also signals her breaking point in her refusal to eat, her desire for revenge, and her progressive loss of sanity. The presence of anorexia in African literature represents a completely new phenomenon, especially since it is not part of the culture. It is, or has been, essentially a Western phenomenon, dangerously spreading in today's society. Individuals, primarily adolescents and young women, starve themselves in order to reach an illusory ideal weight, continuing to the point of physical and mental exhaustion. One cannot imagine this illness as part of African society. Yet although anorexia is rarely directly named, it has been largely alluded to and represented in several novels in the 1980s.[12]

The description of woman's suffering is nothing new in the Francophone African novel, but in women's works it assumes new proportions in its nature and intensity. In contrast to men's writings, where women's suffering is mostly physical and limited to a specific domain—maternity and delivery or illnesses—Emilienne's suffering in *Fureurs et cris de femmes* can be defined by the absence of what she desires and the absence of anyone to share her pain. Emilienne experiences an intensification of suffering because she is left to confront it alone.

> Her suffering is not that of delivery which, once it is gone, gives extreme joy to the mother holding her newborn in her arms. Her suffering is dry and leaves a feeling of insurmountable guilt. It is the type of pain that makes a woman ugly, that makes her mean and bitter for having failed where others have succeeded.
>
> *[Sa souffrance n'est pas celle de l'accouchement qui, une fois disparue, procure une joie extrême à la mère qui tient son enfant dans ses bras. Sa souffrance à elle est aride et laisse un sentiment de culpabilité insurmontable. C'est le genre de douleur qui enlaidit et fait faner une femme, qui la rend méchante et aigrie pour avoir échoué là où d'autres réussissent.]* (Rawiri 1989, 24)

Fureurs et cris de femmes reveals a semantic network of suffering that focuses on the body and the belly in particular. As the matrix par excellence, Emilienne's belly refuses to be empty and barren, symbolically enacting her struggle with consciousness and the unconscious. Emilienne is described from the very first pages through her body parts, her worries, her pain, and the cause of this pain (her inability to remain pregnant). She has "dry and scorching lips," her nails are bitten, she is "all hunched up." She "nervously kneads her lower-part," her suffering undoubtedly announces "the flow of big blood clots," she "lets her hand feel the part where her husband usually sleeps," she listens to "that part of her body." She thinks about "the little girl she would like to become again." There are a night of nightmares, damp sheets, rainy mornings, bitter cold. Her belly is like "a haunted place."

She experiences a range of feelings from worry to panic to horror to sadness to pain, both physical and psychological. Emilienne's failure is given from the beginning of the novel as irremediable; she displays "the resignation of someone who has been sentenced to death" [la résignation d'une personne condamnée à mourir] (Rawiri 1989, 100). Her body becomes a space of fright and despair. Her infertility pushes her over the edge.

> She puts her hand to her belly. The pain intensifies around her belly button; it feels like a sharp razor, cutting from inside. "By tonight, it will disintegrate completely," she grumbles, "only a useless uterus will remain."

> *[Elle porte derechef la main à son ventre. La douleur s'intensifie au niveau du nombril, elle est plus aiguë, on dirait une lame de rasoir incisant son intérieur. "D'ici ce soir, il sera complètement désintégré," maugrée-t-elle, "il ne restera qu'un utérus inutile."]* (13)

The descriptive detail recalls a medical exam, introducing a new perspective through which the female body is represented. Using words such as *uterus, cervix, vagina, anus, embryo,* the author gives an account of female matters that have been hitherto silenced: hemorrhage, nausea, vomiting, miscarriage:

> She is brutally drawn back to her body by a violent tearing; is it the uterus or the cervix? She cannot know. Whatever, she thinks, biting her lips to stifle her oncoming scream. She now feels a sort of heaviness in her arm. Before she has even had time to get into a comfortable position to be ready for this expulsion that she has been dreading since morning, the warm slimy liquid oozes imperceptibly between her slightly opened thighs.

> *[Elle est brutalement ramenée à son corps par un déchirement violent; est-ce l'utérus ou le col? Elle ne peut le savoir. Peu importe, pense-t-elle en se mordant les lèvres pour étouffer le cri qui déjà monte à la gorge. Une sorte de lourdeur se déplace à présent vers le bas. Avant même qu'elle n'ait adopté une position confortable pour ce rejet qu'elle appréhende depuis le matin, le liquide gluant et chaud coule sournoisement entre ses cuissses raides légèrement écartées.]* (Rawiri 1989, 25)

> The viscous fluid continues to ooze around her vagina, her anus and on the sheets. Panicked, she fights, kneads this belly that will betray her to the very end. Nothing can stop the flow. Reaching her breaking point, with no strength left, she finally relaxes and lets herself go empty.

> *[Le liquide poisseux ne continue pas moins de se répandre autour du vagin, de l'anus et sur les draps. Affolée, elle se débat, pétrit ce ventre qui la trahira jusqu'au bout. Rien ne peut plus cependant arrêter l'écoulement. A bout de forces et de nerfs, elle se décontracte finalement et se laisse vider.]* (25)

A second network of terms evoking the abject and the repulsive is superimposed onto the first semantic field. Words such as *vomiting, slimy and viscous liquid, fetid smells,* convey Emilienne's feelings about being ill and her loss of consciousness in their most minute details. The repulsive spreads systematically, seeping in everywhere, invading every description, including those taken from the medical field: "Emilienne lets her genitalia be examined and her discharge taken for lab tests . . . a little uneasy at being fiddled with by a man" [Emilienne se laisse fureter son appareil génital et prélever ses pertes vaginales . . . un peu mal à l'aise de s'être laissé tripatouiller par un homme] (Rawiri 1989, 110–111).

Suffering explodes in this situation: Emilienne not only screams, cries, and sobs but literally witnesses her own disintegration when she views *"her own waste"* [déchets . . . en décomposition] (Rawiri 1989, 27; my emphasis). Emilienne is nothing but a woman rotting away: "A big black clot splats down on the tiles, leaving an empty feeling in her gut" [Un gros caillot de sang noirâtre s'abat comme une claque sur le carrelage, laissant dans son ventre une impression de vide] (Rawiri 1989, 27).

By throwing the soiled sheets into a garbage bag, thus getting rid of her cumbersome "wastes," Emilienne signifies her feelings of shame, loneliness, and pain. A woman truly in the margins, she also symbolizes by her act the disintegration of her character, and beyond that, the character of a modern Africa that is drifting away.[13]

> What will become of this Africa incapable of governing itself, a victim of natural catastrophes and attacked from the outside by economic and financial crisis? The least we can say is that the future looks frightening. The belly of Africa will soon become as sterile as mine.
>
> *[Que deviendra cette Afrique incapable de se gouverner, victime des calamités naturelles, attaquée de l'extérieur par la crise économique et financière? Le moins que l'on puisse dire, c'est que l'avenir paraît effrayant. Le ventre de l'Afrique deviendra bientôt aussi stérile que le mien.]* (Rawiri 1989, 124)

Rawiri now describes an increased awareness that leads to a phase of rebellion and finally to physical and psychological liberation. Emilienne's evolution begins with her new respect for her body and her perceptions. She analyzes her feelings (and her lack of feelings for her husband) and thereby frees herself to overcome her sterility. She proves that "each individual, woman or man, can and must reinvent her/his personal and collective history" (Irigaray 1990, 29; my translation). We can now grasp the difference between Emilienne and Toula (in *G'amàrakano*). Toula remained a prisoner because she was manipulated by men and deprived of her own body. Symbolically, Toula's final failure illustrates the need to "kill the artificial woman that prevents the real one from breathing"

(Cixous 1975, 43; my translation). In contrast, Emilienne indicates the possibility of a woman's rewriting herself completely and overcoming silence and woman's age-old victimization. Through her protagonist's liberation, Rawiri indicates that we all have the ability to reinvent ourselves, to reinvent our his/story and find a way out of the confinement of social pressure.

The ending does not point to Emilienne's failure but to the failure of her husband and mother-in-law; she asks both to leave her house. This eviction occurs at a time when she is finally pregnant and therefore, theoretically, if we follow their logic, a real woman. By slipping free from her yoke as a spouse, the protagonist reveals a new path for the Francophone African woman. This alternative also appears in Anglophone women's texts, particularly in Flora Nwapa's *One Is Enough* (1981) and *Women Are Different* (1986). Rather than cope with an unhappy marriage and suffer from her husband's infidelities and her mother-in-law's interference, the young woman decides to start anew, alone, without any marital constraints, so that she can focus on her professional and personal development.

Depicting extreme individual suffering, Rawiri attacks the dictatorship of beauty and of the body, the notion of mandatory motherhood for woman, the pressure from mothers and mothers-in-law, and the burden of traditions. In doing so, she confronts her African readers with the situation of modern African women. She shows that these readers, both women and men, are directly responsible for the perpetuation of certain limitations placed on their well-being.

The author's strategy represents a specific characteristic of the evolution of female Francophone writing: More than an illustration of woman's hitherto silenced suffering, more than a call for empathy, the text has the vigor of a sociopolitical pamphlet addressed to us. Like Calixthe Beyala and other women writers of the same generation, Rawiri systematically creates an environment of suffering where abjection and horror figure as integral components in the search for an alternative for woman or for the woman-child. The representation of violence inflicted on the body, the discovery of the female body, and an exploration of sexuality are combined to form a radical provocation aimed at liberating us through catharsis.

More important, the inclusion of new linguistic fields and especially of medical terms are key steps toward inscribing woman's difference and acknowledging woman as a writer. Echoing Cixous, the African woman writes herself, makes herself multiple, puts herself in opposition to sexist language; she introduces us to her own new areas of exploration, in particular the writing of her body: "In writing herself, woman will become reacquainted with the body that she has been deprived of, that has been turned into a threatening foreigner in her place and the cause and the site of inhibitions" (Cixous 1975, 43).

Like Rawiri's, other women writers' approaches to the body follow a progression: Women writers have moved from the periphery of literature to the center, where they describe woman in all her circumstances and responses. They describe her happiness, sadness, and pleasure but also her suffering as a locus of exploitation and social pressure. Blaise-Romuald Fonkua, in "Ecritures romanesques féminines: L'art et la loi des pères," examines the body and what is at stake here. He concludes, "The question raised by every woman novelist looking at woman's uneasy relationship to her body is that of dealing with the external gaze that conditions woman's happiness or her identity. For them, it is more specifically a matter of reflecting on the search for whatever justifies a woman's existence and allows her to truly experience the feeling of happiness" (1994, 115; my translation). However, taking Leti's wandering in *Une vie de crabe* (Boni 1990) as an example, Fonkua goes on to claim that woman translates her feeling of malaise through an ailing body into a feeling of emptiness, a sense of dissatisfaction: "Female existence can only be conjugated in the mode of 'a non-life, a non-sense'" (1994, 115).

By denouncing the female body as object, by exploring the body as an erotic zone, a zone of pleasure, but also as a zone of suffering and a privileged site for self-knowledge, women writers have broken the silence to create a new space. This space is no longer in the margins but has become central to African literature. From this space, women writers from now on are in a position to explore sociopolitical questions and to enter an area that has been regarded until recently as man's privileged domain.

Sexuality and Desire in the Feminine Mode

I imagine a sinusoidal desire
A desire that undulates through successive approaches
And finds its eternity in rhythm
Like the ocean: it is never hard and will never be flaccid
. . . I love you and survive through this love
Through this love, I create and regenerate
I always survive and engender love
. . . I am speaking of a desire that would enrich you
without depriving me
A desire that could fill me without making you empty. (my translation)

[J'imagine un désir sinusoïde
Un désir qui ondule par approches successives et trouve son éternité
dans le rythme
Tel l'océan: il n'est jamais bandé et ne sera jamais flasque

. . . Je t'aime et survis par cet amour
Par cet amour je crée et revis
Je survis et engendre toujours l'amour
. . . Je parle d'un désir qui t'enrichirait sans m'appauvrir
D'un désir qui pourrait me remplir sans te
vider.] (Liking 1983, 69)

Until the 1980s, all questions of sexuality were truly expunged from the text. They were approached solely from the perspective of the love relationship between two young people of the opposite sex (and sometimes from different cultures and races). On the one hand, the novel described external difficulties affecting the couple (the parents and/or the community's opposition, their marital relationship); on the other hand, it described the couple's attraction for one another as well as the evolution of their relationship. The most frequent scenario was either a complication—for instance, the wife's infertility or a miscarriage—or a deterioration of the relationship because of the husband's decision to take a second wife. In fact, women writers in the beginning of the 1980s largely directed their gaze at women's frustrations caused by the arrival of a cowife. This thematic thread appears, for instance, in *So Long a Letter* and *Scarlet Song* by Mariama Bâ, *La voie du salut suivi de le miroir de la vie* by Maïga Ka, *Juletane* and "Sidonie" (in *Femmes échouées*) by Myriam Warner-Vieyra, to mention only a few.

These texts, however, never directly deal with the question of woman's desire and female sexuality. These notions were still buried in a traditional idea of romantic love, heterosexual of course, and conceived along the lines of the European model. Following in the footsteps of Werewere Liking and Ken Bugul, Angèle Rawiri, Véronique Tadjo, and Calixthe Beyala introduce true innovations in their treatment of these questions. They implement new perspectives (examined in the next section). These authors do not merely evoke woman's desire for love; they go beyond that, describing and exploring love in its most minute nuances and implications, introducing the possibility of a relation outside the usual norms.

Woman's Awakening: *G'amàrakano and* Fureurs et cris de femmes

The title of the third part of *G'amàrakano*—"Vivre son corps" (To live one's body)—explicitly refers to the implications of Toula's physical and psychological transformations. Beyond mere changes in her body, Toula discovers an active sexuality through her new success with men. Two types of scenes appear. Some resemble the typical scene of violence or rape as found in *O pays, mon beau peuple!* by Ousmane Sembène (1957) or in *La vie et demie* by Sony Labou Tansi (1979) or in *Les deux mères de Guillaume Ismaël Dzewatama* by Mongo Beti (1983). All of these offer many illustrations of man exerting his power over woman. The other type of scene is an expression of love in all its sensuality while still stressing man's violence:

> All of a sudden, Eléwagnè falls on her, bearing down on her with all his weight. He presses his lips violently against hers. Short of breath, Toula opens her mouth slightly. A warm nervous tongue probes her reticent mouth. Her legs are violently splayed apart. She tries to resist, but Eléwagnè holds her in this position, and after a few brutal attempts, he inserts his sex in her with the aid of his hand. Toula's body and heart are split with an acute flash. He wriggles around, carried away. His breathing gets faster.
>
> *[Brusquement, Eléwagnè s'abat de toute la hauteur sur elle, l'écrasant de tout son poids. Il presse avec violence sa bouche contre la sienne. La respiration coupée, Toula desserre les dents et entrebaille les lèvres. Une langue chaude et nerveuse fouille sa bouche réticente. Ses jambes sont violemment écartées. Elle essaie de se débattre. Mais Eléwagnè la maintient dans cette position, et non sans tâtonnements brutaux, introduit, à l'aide de sa main droite, son sexe en elle. Le corps et le coeur de Toula sont transpercés d'une douleur fulgurante. . . . Celui-ci s'agite, s'emporte. Sa respiration s'accélère.]* (Rawiri 1983, 175)

The text remains perfectly traditional in the sense that the initiative is given to the man; he is profiled as the male conqueror and she is captured in a clichéd female passivity. The narration, however, gradually introduces the discovery of pleasure in love and reciprocal exchange in Toula's relationship with Angwé:

> With her body becoming completely relaxed, she abandoned herself to the young man's soft insisting caresses. She was moaning, rearing up, leaping, shivering, screaming, yelling. Finally, she went stiff. She was dead. When Angwé took her back into his arms in the morning she was panting from the desire to relive a pleasure that she had never known before.
>
> *[Son corps devenant tout mou, elle s'était abandonnée aux tendres et insistantes caresses du jeune homme. Elle gémissait, se cabrait, bondissait, frissonnait, criait, hurlait. Finalement, elle s'était raidie. Morte. Lorsqu'Angwé la reprit dans ses bras le matin, elle haletait du désir de retrouver un plaisir jamais connu jusque là.]* (Rawiri 1983, 142)
>
> The two bodies unite in a ferocious thrust. Their lips are already searching each other out. Toula's hands softly touch, then boldly caress the body of her friend. She licks the sweat dripping along his muscles. Angwé balls himself up and then thrusts forward. All of his muscles harden. He delicately spreads her legs. Toula keeps still, but her eyes go wide and dart about. Her body twists around, carrying Angwé with it.

Stifled moans accompany their rhythmic motions. Then suddenly two screams rise up in the room and pierce the night. They spend a long time looking at each other and burst out laughing.

[Les deux corps s'unissent dans un élan farouche. Déjà leurs bouches se cherchent. Les mains de Toula effleurent puis caressent franchement tout le corps de son ami. Elle lèche la sueur qui coule de son corps. Angwé se ramasse sur lui-même puis bondit. Tous ses muscles durcissent. Il lui écarte délicatement les jambes. Toula reste figée, mais son regard s'anime. Son corps ondule entra înant celui d'Angwé. Des gémissements étouffés accompagnent leurs mouvements rythmés. Tout à coup deux cris s'élèvent dans la chambre perçant la nuit. Ils se contemplent un long moment et éclatent de rire.] (187)

The difference between the first and second scene suggests Toula's sexual awakening. From being a passive participant, Toula has become active, more self-confident, and more daring. She takes the initiative. In the wake of Rawiri's work, sexual descriptions have been more detailed and have become integral parts of women's texts. For example, we can find similar images in Véronique Tadjo's *A vol d'oiseau* (1986) and *Le royaume aveugle* (1990) or in Tanella Boni's *Une vie de crabe* (1990).

Their bodies became two iron bars being forged on the anvil of desire. The bodies were heating up to a thousand degrees. A thousand degrees in the rain. Accompanied by tears of joy. And the bodies fused together. Clumsily. Skillfully. Marvelously. Then burnt and burnt forever.

[Les corps devinrent deux barres de fer qui se forgeaient sur l'enclume du désir. Les corps chauffaient à mille degrés. Mille degrés de chaleur sous la pluie. Avec la complicité des larmes de joie. Et les corps se soudèrent l'un à l'autre gauchement. Adroitement. Merveilleusement. Puis brûlèrent, brûlèrent sans fin.] (Boni 1990, 97)

In both texts, desire is proclaimed in all its force: "The man and the woman were waiting for the rain to end. But the rain was never-ending . . . like desire. The end of desire means the death of love. The end of the rain means the death of life" [L'homme et la femme attendaient la fin de la pluie. Mais la pluie n'avait pas de fin . . . comme le désir. La fin du désir c'est la mort de l'amour. La fin de la pluie c'est la mort de la vie] (Boni 1990, 97). Desire is recognized for its purely sexual pleasure, in its desire of the body, of the other, but also in its longing for oneself:

A pleasant feeling beginning in her sex spreads throughout her body and hardens her breasts. Toula remains immobile on the bed. The inside of her belly shivers. A burning desire to make love curls inside her belly and bites at her sex. Her body is covered with drops of sweat. She feels a terrible urge to caress herself, but she is holding back. She is scared: "this can't be my body, unwinding like this." She is afraid to move. This body that is getting so wildly excited cannot be mine. No, this can't be my own flesh speaking this new language.

[Une sensation agréable part de son sexe, parcourt tout son corps et vient se durcir ses seins. Toula resta inerte sur le lit. Le creux de son ventre frémit. Un ardent désir de l'acte d'amour habite son ventre et mord son sexe. Son corps se couvre de gouttelettes de sueur. Elle a une envie terrible de se caresser, mais se retient. Effrayée. Ça ne peut pas être mon corps qui se déchaîne ainsi!" Elle a peur de bouger. Ce corps qui s'exalte aussi sauvagement ne peut être le mien. Non, ce n'est pas ma chair qui, subitement, parle ce langage nouveau.] (Rawiri 1983, 175)

Toula fears this new sexual power that drives her to seek pleasure with Eléwagnè, for whom she otherwise has no deep feelings: "I love Angwé and here is my body getting completely out of control over someone else's body" [J'aime Angwé et voilà que mon corps s'affole grâce à un autre!] (Rawiri 1983, 175). In *Une vie de crabe,* Léti experiences the same type of dilemma as she has to decide between father and son:

All of a sudden, she felt sandwiched between an ex-husband and a friend, a father and his son, two men in fact. She was wondering. . . . She was wondering which of these two men was more in her skin, in her heart, in her senses. . . . She would have to choose. It was difficult to share herself, to share her night with one man, and even more with two men.

[Elle se retrouva soudain, ..., prise en sandwich entre un ex-mari et un ami, un père et son fils, deux hommes en somme. Elle se demandait. Elle se demandait lequel de ces hommes lui collait à présent le plus à la peau, au coeur, aux sens. . . . Il lui faudrait choisir. Difficile de se partager, de partager sa nuit avec quelqu'un, encore plus difficile avec deux hommes.] (Boni 1990, 67)

Through a combination of free indirect discourse and extradiagetic voices, African women writers explore new questions about womanhood, about her pleasure, about listening to her body in its most intimate parts, about her expectations of sex. The question of marriage and love relationships is recast. Even though the contextual framework remains completely normative, women are offering some new explanations for their hesitations to get married because they are now thinking about the problem in terms of pleasure and sexual freedom: "She wanted both to belong to one man and to be with all the others" [Elle voudrait à la fois appartenir à un seul homme et être à tous les autres] (Rawiri 1983, 151).

Fureurs et cris de femmes innovates in its presentation of the traditional theme of deteriorating marital relationships and husbands who lose interest in their wives. Indeed, Emilienne responds by experiencing a number of psychosomatic troubles, for instance, bulimia. However, she also responds to the situation by seeking sexual pleasure through her new feeling of attraction to her secretary, Dominique.

Emilienne has refused to analyze the new needs of her flesh. For all she knows, her senses are awakening to a strange desire that was sparked by the first shiver she felt from touching this other woman.

[Emilienne s'est refusée à analyser les nouveaux besoins de sa chair. Tout ce qu'elle sait, c'est que ses sens s'éveillent à un désir étrange suscité par ce premier frisson ressenti au contact de cette autre femme.] (Rawiri 1989, 113)

Emilienne discovers a new interest in being well dressed and taking care of her body, and a new pleasure in being caressed by a woman.

She stretches out before placing her head on the thighs of her new friend. Smiling, Dominique pulls off her shirt and delicately, with her long polished nails, touches her breasts as she removes them from her bra. Emilienne feels paralyzed, but lets her continue.

[Elle s'étire avant de poser sa tête sur les cuisses de sa nouvelle amie. Souriante, Dominique lui relève le chemisier et fait parcourir délicatement ses longs ongles vernis sur ses seins qu'elle sort de leur soutien-gorge. Emilienne se paralyse, mais se laisse faire.] (Rawiri 1989, 115)

Even though Emilienne is blossoming, the lesbian relationship remains considerably limited in its representation. Emilienne considers it a mere substitute for the relationship with her husband, even though she questions her dependence on him, on men: "Could her existence depend only on a few drops of sperm?" [Son existence ne tiendrait-elle qu'à quelques gouttes de sperme?] (Rawiri 1989, 117). In addition, the narrative voice underlines the state of "emotional weakness" [faiblesse émotionnelle] that drives Emilienne to have a relationship with a woman. Once again, the emphasis is on the exceptional circumstances of the situation, on somehow justifying and explaining it. During all this time, although Emilienne opens up to Dominique and discovers new areas of sensuality for her body, she remains ashamed of their relationship, and, despite Dominique's efforts to dissuade her, she is determined to reconquer her husband, Joseph. In fact, it turns out that Dominique is none other than Joseph's lover and that she seduced Emilienne on his recommendation. The love relation between women is denigrated, reduced to a conniving scheme. Irène d'Almeida pertinently comments on this point:

Rawiri portrays a lesbian relationship—a daring undertaking in African fiction—only to make a mockery of it in the novel's finale. Dominique begins as a figure to free Emilienne and then is reduced to an almost stock "other woman," a creation of melodrama. Emilienne seems to break out of her prison of cultural expectations, to become the liberated modern woman of the new class, only to be at the last moment redefined yet again by her pregnancy. I believe that the contradictions that run throughout the novel can be completely resolved. Rawiri's novel, intentionally or not, reflects somewhat realistically an actual confusion that exists in many African cultures attempting to find a new harmony between the old and the new. (1994b, 98; my translation)

I must add that if Emilienne defines herself once again through pregnancy, she does so on her own terms and within a nonnormative context, since she asks her husband and mother-in-law to leave her house. In doing so, she declares both her emotional independence and her professional success and financial power. Furthermore, that a lesbian relationship is part of the plot, however clumsily represented, is still indicative of a new tone of voice in women's texts. This leads us to believe that female writing will come to progressively include and overtly approach this other dimension of love. I thus completely second d'Almeida in her conclusion: The novel gives an account of transformations in progress in African cultures as they search for a more stable balance.

Corps-à-corps with Love: Tadjo's Le Royaume Aveugle

His body was smooth like a lagoon in the sun and her shapes were round, similar to those rocks that can be found around the shore.
     . . . She was made of arabesques and of flesh, fragile, her chest swinging slightly, her belly ready to welcome life.

[Il avait le corps lisse comme une lagune au soleil et elle avait des formes rondes, un peu comme ces rochers qui bordent le littoral.
     . . . Elle était faite d'arabesques et de chairs en volume, fragile, la poitrine se balançant légèrement, son ventre prêt à accueillir la vie.]
(Tadjo 1990, 49)

Through a suggestive depiction of the sensuality and aesthetic beauty of body, through a feeling of perfection and serenity, *Le royaume aveugle* offers a primordial space for love and renders the exploration of the body and of the other as dynamic elements in self-discovery.

The novel further develops certain themes of *A vol d'oiseau* (Tadjo 1986). A collection of continuous and discontinuous fragments and vignettes, this long poem is a journey among different spaces and cultures and signals the importance of love in the transformation of societies for a better humanity. For Akissi in *Le royaume aveugle,* experiencing love means leaving the world of blindness to face the reality of a corrupted kingdom that is doomed to perish.

Chapter 10, entitled "L'amour" (Love), is composed of two indirect discourses, both introduced in an elliptical way: A man speaks; *then* a woman speaks. To male desire expressed in all its virile magnitude, the woman responds with her need for fusion with the other. These are classic expressions of love and desire.

Give me your thighs and let's make love astride. Your body is a storm, a tornado in which I sink to die and to be reborn as many times as you want. Deep inside you, I dig a fertile tunnel where my seeds will germinate. . . . Give me your sex and let it join with mine, let them fight and tumble and embrace and exhaust each other.

Give me your deep slit one more time.

[Donne-moi tes cuisses et faisons l'amour à cheval. Ton corps est une tempête, un raz de marée dans lequel je me noie pour mourir et renaître autant que tu voudras. Je creuse au fond de toi un tunnel fertile où ma semence germera. . . . Donne-moi ton sexe et qu'il rejoigne le mien, qu'ils luttent et culbutent et s'enlacent et s'épuisent.

Fais-moi encore le don de ta fente profonde.] (Tadjo 1990, 51)

Come, I want to love you beneath the open sky. My skin quivers when you touch it.

Come, sail as far as you wish on the waves of my desire that has no name and that flows inside me like a powerful stream.

Come, so that we can forget that tomorrow we may part.

. . . Come, I give myself to you just as I am. And I call you and call you.

[Viens, je veux t'aimer à la face du ciel. Ma peau tremble quand tu la touches.

Viens, vogue aussi loin que tu veux sur les flots de mon désir qui n'a pas de nom et qui coule en moi comme un fleuve puissant.

Viens, pour oublier que peut-être demain nous serons séparés.

. . . Viens, je me donne à toi telle que je suis. Et je t'appelle et je t'appelle.] (52)

The same sensuous force appeared in *A vol d'oiseau*, especially in the two following passages:

I wrap myself in his scent, wet my face with his perspiration, touch his skin, bite his shoulder, swallow his desire, close my eyes, stretch my body, call him and expel him.

[Je m'enveloppe de son odeur, mouille mon visage de sa sueur, touche sa peau, mords son épaule, avale son désir, ferme les yeux, tends mon corps, l'appelle et le rejette.] (Tajdo 1986, 80)

I remember. His scent was in my nostrils. His perspiration tasted salty in my mouth. My saliva was enjoying its strength and energy, and I was discovering the hunger of my desire.

[Je m'en souviens. Son odeur emplissait mes narines. Sa sueur salait ma bouche. Ma salive se gavait de sa force et de son énergie, et je découvrais la famine de mon désir.] (1986, 80)

The descriptions stand out in the immediacy of their suggested images. Desire is intensified with the recurrence of commands and the use of the imperative mode. Love, moreover, is revealed in the reciprocity of desire and the strength of the lovers' passion. The only danger comes from the outside world. An incredible strength surges forth during this interlude in a world of blindness without hope; hence the title of the following chapter: "L'amour les yeux fermés" (Love with your eyes closed).

> She would give herself to him and it was her soul that she was offering, her heart, it was her life. She would have wanted to melt and be mixed with his flesh to form a single being, to be sure that he would never leave her and that they would never be strangers to one another.
>
> *[Elle se donnait à lui et c'était son âme, qu'elle offrait, son coeur, c'était sa vie. Elle aurait aimé fondre et se mêler à sa chair pour ne faire qu'un, être sûre qu'il ne la quitterait pas; qu'ils ne seraient plus jamais étrangers l'un pour l'autre.]* (Tadjo 1990, 54)

Similarities in feelings and needs can be found between the female characters Akissi in *Le royaume aveugle* and Tanga and Anna-Claude in *Tanga* (Beyala 1988, 1996). In *Tanga,* love appears like a refuge for the protagonist; it is a response to her desire to lose herself in the other protagonist, to hide and make up for a fundamental lack. As in *Seul le diable le savait* (Beyala 1990), where the Foreigner acts as a catalyst for Megri when she discovers her inner self and matures, Karim plays the role of initiator and guide for Akissi in the growth of her awareness not only as a woman but also, perhaps more crucially, as a member of her community. Love drives her to a higher political awareness. Metaphorically, love opens her eyes and frees her from the kingdom of blindness while forcing her to take sides. She can no longer be content with her status as the king's daughter. Akissi must confront reality. To do so, she goes through an initiation in the village. There, "the old woman" teaches her real life, real values, and the possibility of being authentic:

> My girl, do not forget the image that you have of yourself. . . . Don't waste your soul, and if you should die some day, do it after you lived to stop the end of the world.
>
> *[Ma fille, ne perds jamais l'image que tu te fais de toi-même. . . . Ne gaspille pas ton âme et si tu dois mourir un jour, fais-le après avoir vécu pour empêcher la fin du monde.]* (Tadjo 1990, 101)

Through her love for Karim and her initiation, Akissi is encouraged to take action and revolt against the epitome of patriarchy embodied by her father and his corrupt kingdom:

> Reality appeared that day for the daughter of the king in all its horror. The filth and the stench of those places made her turn her head in disgust. Akissi laid eyes on her father for the first time in her life. Her heart trembled. He was finished.

[Mais pour la fille du roi, la réalité apparut, ce jour là, dans toute son horreur. La saleté, la puanteur des lieux lui firent tourner la tête. Akissi posa les yeux sur son père pour la première fois de sa vie. Elle eut un coup au coeur. C'était un homme fini.] (Tadjo 1990, 121–122)

Just as in *Seul le diable,* love lasts barely an instant, doomed to destruction because of external forces. Like "l'Etranger" (the Foreigner), Karim is arrested and declared a threat to the community because of his revolutionary ideas. Forbidden, passionate, fleeting love is central to women's more recent novels. Tanella Boni's *Une vie de crabe* (1990) offers another example. Here, the relationship between Léti and Niyous is declared taboo even though their relationship cannot really be considered incestuous—Léti is Niyous's stepmother.[14]

I was waiting for you, but you're not the kind of man that people wait for. You run, you fly, you disappear. You are the air we breath. . . . You are leaves of *nim.* You are the bitter taste of life. That is why we are both alike. You—an enigma. I don't even know your name anymore. Bridge of vines, rat, mosquito, tortoise, toad, crab, cockroach?

[Je t'attendais. Mais tu n'es pas l'homme que l'on atttend. Tu cours, tu voles, tu t'évanouis. Tu es l'air que l'on respire. . . . Tu es les feuilles de nim. Tu es l'amertume de la vie. C'est pour ça qu'on se ressemble tous les deux. Toi l'énigme. Je ne sais plus comment tu t'appelles. Pont de lianes, rat, moustique, tortue, crapaud, crabe, cancrelat?] (Boni 1990, 77)

In spite of this love that makes Léti feel as if she is committing an offense, and all the more so since she will see Niyous's father, Djamane, again for a one-night stand, Léti has been won over and decides to live this love, although she fears it will last only an instant.

To speak with one's sex. Here is where life's barriers begin or end. Alpha and/or Omega. You who are nameless—allow me to call you love. You will be mine for a time. I don't know when you will fly away aboard a supersonic jet or on some space shuttle, leaving for other planets or the clouds. We have left the regions lit by day. But there is nothing to fear. You and I together—it is simply wondrous. We are fighters, aren't we? Remember, we are combatants for life!

[Dire avec le sexe. C'est ici que les barrages de la vie commencent ou prennent fin. Alpha ou/et Oméga. Toi sans nom, accepte que je t'appelle amour. Tu seras mien pour un temps. Je ne sais pas quand tu t'envoleras à bord d'un supersonique ou d'un astronef, pour les nuages ou d'autres planètes. Nous avons quitté les zones éclairées par la lumière du jour. Mais il n'y a rien à craindre. Toi et moi ensemble, c'est tout simplement merveilleux. Nous sommes des battants n'est-ce pas? Des lutteurs pour la vie souviens-toi!] (Boni 1990, 99)

Just as she feared, one morning the soldiers come by: "Happiness had lasted but a fleeting instant. It was gone" [Le bonheur n'avait duré que le temps d'une hirondelle. Envolé] (Boni 1990, 107). Unlike Léti—or Megri (in *Seul le diable*) or Madjo (in *L'amour cent-vies*)—Akissi in Tadjo's *Le royaume aveugle* lacks courage and obstinacy in opposing the patriarchal order. She remains paralyzed, passive, and inactive.

> Maybe you should have loved another woman. As for myself, I have no convictions. I tire of everything so quickly. I don't know how to suffer. I retreat every step of the way. I let myself live. My greatest passions come from love. In you, I saw another flame and I wanted to approach it, but my wings are already burning from contact with your ardor. I already know that I will never have your strength and endurance.
>
> *[Tu aurais peut-être dû aimer une autre femme. Moi, je n'ai aucune conviction. Je me lasse très vite de tout. Je ne sais pas souffrir. Je recule à chaque pas. Je me laisse vivre. Mes plus grandes passions me viennent de l'amour. En toi, j'ai vu une autre flamme et j'ai voulu m'en approcher. Mais déjà, mes ailes brûlents au contact de ton ardeur. Déjà, je sais que je n'aurai jamais ta force et ton endurance.]* (Tadjo 1990, 124–125)

If Akissi's love is doomed to end, it nevertheless remains "the only truth that they still possessed" [la seule vérité qu'ils possédaient encore] (Tadjo 1990, 126). Véronique Tadjo portrays the limits of authentic love in its different phases: from hope to the promise of a future and then, when the limits have been reached, simply the possibility of remembering what love was. Akissi refuses to follow Karim's path and sacrifice her own life. Their love will survive in Akissi even if she must live without Karim. Left alone to face his own destiny, a destiny that he has accepted by refusing any compromise, Karim assesses his lover's behavior. Unlike Akissi, he could not keep living with his eyes closed. It was because Akissi could not face reality, because she could not find an independent self outside of him—in other words, because she saw love as a refuge rather than as a reciprocal force—that she lacked confidence and did not have faith in their union. Karim tells Akissi,

> You know perfectly well that it would be crazy for us to expect anything from one another. You can't hide anything from me. I know why you came to me. You are lonely too. You want me to help you live, but can't you tell that my solitude is my most faithful companion? Don't you understand that I will never be able to live your life for you?
>
> *[Pourtant ce serait folie, tu le sais bien de tout attendre l'un de l'autre. Tu ne peux rien me cacher. Je sais pourquoi tu es venue à moi. Toi aussi, tu es seule. Tu veux que je t'aide à vivre. Mais ne sens-tu pas que ma solitude est ma compagne la plus fidèle? Ne comprends-tu pas que je ne pourrai jamais vivre ta vie pour toi?]* (Tadjo 1990, 128)

In the same monologue, Karim admits that he is guided by a force beyond his own control, a force that comes first before any other passion, including their love. Under these conditions, Akissi was running to her own destruction.

> You aren't safe with me. I am possessed by a passion that is stronger than the others. If you stay with me, I will send you to the bottom. I will subject your body to a trial by fire and I will crush your illusions to a pulp.
>
> *[Avec moi, tu es en danger. Je suis habité par une passion plus forte que les autres. Si tu restes avec moi, je te ferai toucher le fond de l'eau. Je mettrai ton corps à l'épreuve du feu et j'écraserai tes illusions pour en faire de la chair à pâté.]* (Tadjo 1990, 128)

Akissi's and Karim's love, both a "chant-roman" and a legend, becomes a metaphor for the new generation and the need to sacrifice in the process of building a new Africa. Love, however strong it may be, is not enough: "One can really feel that this is a sterile century. Even love finds it hard to be fruitful" [On sent bien que c'est un siècle stérile. Même l'amour a du mal à féconder] (Tadjo 1990, 29). Men and women must face reality and stand up for the conditions and the consequences of a different future.

Beyala goes further in this exploration. Her first three novels broach the questions of sexuality and female desire. She treats these questions by scrupulously examining the responsibilities of each party engaged in the love relation and, beyond that, their participation in society.[15]

Pleasure, Climax, and Suffering in Beyala's Texts

Love and woman. By exploring relationships between mothers and daughters, between daughters and fathers, and between women, Beyala exposes the principles of commodification that control relations between individuals. She denounces the falsification of love in all its manifestations, whether it is the basis of erotic or family relationships or of friendships.[16]

Tanga is particularly symbolic of the revolt against the reduction of the body and of feelings. It is because Tanga is rejected by her mother and forced by her into prostitution that she becomes disappointed with filial love. Likewise, it is because she is disappointed in her love for men that Tanga starts searching for real love, which she thinks she can find in motherhood. Her feelings for Pieds-Gâtés, who was abandoned in the street by his parents and whom she wants to adopt, ends up being only a pale substitute for real love. Pieds-Gâtés is disoriented by her approach and her gestures of love because these are unknown to him. When Tanga is deprived of her notion of love as (free!) self-denial, the commodification of the body develops further. This commodification extends beyond usual prostitution; it constitutes the actual basis of relations between men and women.

Within this context, Beyala depicts the primary relationship between a man and a woman, which is a relationship of inequality based on woman's humiliation and submission.[17] There are many scenes of rape, violence, and submission:

> As he caresses her, he tries to hurt her tightly closed lips. A deep disgust overwhelms her and she gives such a start that he lets go of her. . . . He forces her down, forces her to crouch. (*The Sun,* Beyala 1996, 24)

The war of the sexes has been declared. In response to man's initial violence, woman expresses a fierce desire to break the chain, to "find the woman again and destroy the chaos." [(re)trouver la femme . . . et anéantir le chaos] (Beyala 1996, 102). She responds by expressing an unequaled violence in her desires and fantasies:

> And if she were to stop the flow of history by tearing his sex organ with her teeth? And if, with the sharp edges of her nails, she were to shred his lower belly? She'd make stew with his hair, a stew, black and sweet like the shade that pacifies her senses after the light has attacked them. (24)

The violence of the language and the daring and extremeness of the protagonist's thoughts become recurrent obsessive images in Beyala's first two novels; in *The Sun Hath Looked upon Me* these thoughts are of castration and ultimate revenge on man. Man is represented in his most vile aspects, as a repulsive animal. He is reduced to mere body parts, generic items: "The pile of grease is sleeping, a hairy arm dangling off the bed" (Beyala 1996, 104). Man is shown incapable of feelings or of any refinement; he is obnoxious and vulgar. Woman appears more subtle, more clear-sighted, not "buying" his words: "She listens to him and agrees with all the idiocies that he utters" (100).

The thorough examination of man's body marks a new step, as it anticipates the introspection of the male voice in *Loukoum.* Essentially, two types of men appear in Beyala's texts. In their profiles and behaviors, they embody the two sides of masculine identity. One is a cruel, violent man who thinks he can prove his virility and identity by using his strength and by dominating women with violence in sexual and nonsexual relations. This is the man who appears in *The Sun* and *Tanga* as a temporary, passing lover who is never in the position of the father or even the impregnator. In her study on masculine identity, *XY*, Elisabeth Badinter characterizes this man as "the cruel man" [l'homme dur], a catalog of the worst male stereotypes: obsessed with competition, driven by intellectual and sexual performance, self-content and self-confident, aggressive, alcoholic, incapable of committing to anyone else" (1992, 194; my translation). She nonetheless makes a distinction between *le macho* pure and simple ("who first of all represents man's superiority over woman") and *l'homme dur* (the cruel man) who "offers more information about man himself: he is a machine who represses his feelings and treats his body like a tool" (194). He proves to be only a mutilated man, inadequate. At the far end of the spectrum is *l'homme mou* (the soft man), who is weak and dominated by women. Badinter defines him as follows: "the one who willingly renounces his male privileges, who abdicates the power and male preeminence that are usually bestowed on him by patriarchy" (194).

This last portrayal corresponds to the profile of Megri's two fathers in *Seul le diable,* "Papa bon Blanc" and "Le Pygmée." Both live under Bertha's (Dame maman's) power in a complete inversion of patriarchy where the woman enjoys polyandry and exercises a sort of male power over her husbands. The two images of *l'homme dur* and *l'homme mou* fuse to become one in the mutilated man in *Loukoum*: Indeed, Abdou is a combination of all man's negative facets, displaying his fickleness, his need to seduce, and the outer machismo that enables him to veil his feelings; he also displays a childlike fragility and vulnerability when he begs woman to guide him in the path of love.

In contrast, each novel reveals a lucid woman who is aware of man's weaknesses in his words and deeds. In her "terrible and total understanding of men," [terrible et totale compréhension des hommes] lies woman's obvious superiority: "She wanted to speak like this in order that man would expose himself within the limited form of his limitations" (*The Sun,* Beyala 1996, 7). Women's responsibility is equally emphasized. Because of their knowledge, their desire for men is a weakness; they are responsible for their own misfortune:

> These last few nights her own thoughts have abandoned her for a man. She has to pay for her misdeeds. . . . On her knees, her face raised to the sky . . . the position of the offending woman since time immemorial . . . seated. Crouched. On her knees. (24)

Woman is thus denounced for her vampiric relation to man and her nihilism;[18] she feeds on man because she lives and acts for man alone, in other words, because she cannot exist without him.

> They chewed on her. She submitted to their caresses, their kisses. For them to swell, she murmured obscenities. She forced hoarse screams and Ateba was never able to decide whether these were screams of pleasure or of pain. (Beyala 1996, 96)

In this examination of woman's responsibilities for maintaining the status quo of relations and keeping herself in the position of an object, Beyala demonstrates that this objectification is just as much the woman's fault as the man's. The woman is responsible for her own slavery to the extent that she abides by patriarchal values that dictate her status, including her appearance.[19] In looking for the authentic, woman must also embrace her own body and her own criteria of beauty, rejecting criteria that have been dictated by men and society, whether African or European. This search for the authentic woman is expressed symbolically when Ateba offers her body to the rain.

> Ateba gets undressed and rushes out in the rain. She holds her body out to the water, she gives herself, she takes herself, she spreads her buttocks and offers her belly. (*The Sun,* Beyala 1996, 91)

This is a scene of climax, of pleasure,[20] but it also represents the desire to find purity again, to wash oneself of all impurities: "She is under the impression that each drop of water is making her immaculately clean and taking her out of the QG [the slums] and the black filth of its sewers" (Beyala 1996, 91). In the same spirit, she must dance for herself without attracting man's attention, unlike her mother, Betty, whose moves were calculated to attract men. The narrative voice thus accentuates the similarities in the attitudes and behavior of the prostitutes in the story—Betty, Ada, and Ekassi. The dance scene shows the seductive play of men and women. From there, Beyala points out the primordial anomaly, the discrepancy between being and looking, between what the woman is and the role she plays:

> That's it. Ateba Leocadie remembers—she is woman, mistress, man's woman. She has found her role, she almost feels better. Suddenly, she becomes two Atebas. The woman and the actress. The ordinary and the extraordinary. (99)

In a world that resembles the theater, the female prostitute is the only one to play her cards openly, since she presents herself from the beginning as a sort of actress. The others, men and women, are playing an unacknowledged game of seduction. In *Le deuxieme sexe,* de Beauvoir mentions the similarity between married women and prostitutes, although she stresses a fundamental difference: "The legitimate woman, oppressed as a wife, is respected as a human being . . . whereas the prostitute does not have the rights of a person, for she embodies all the figures of female slavery" [La femme légitime, opprimée en tant que femme mariée, est respectée en tant que personne humaine. . . . Tandis que la prostituée n'a pas les droits d'une personne, en elle se résument toutes les figures de l'esclavage féminin] (1949, 247–248). Beyala demonstrates that this difference is nullified, that in reality each woman is dominated by man and is oppressed unless she reacts with radical rebellion, in other words, unless she can "find the woman in her and destroy the chaos."

Seul le diable le savait further illustrates the ambiguous association between seduction and oppression. This association is actually Megri's guiding principle, as she intends to create "the ideal mask of seduction that would enable her to conquer the Foreigner" [le masque idéal de séduction qui (lui) permettrait de conquérir l'Etranger] (Beyala 1990, 67). However, after she tries for a while to seduce the Foreigner and make herself beautiful as other women do, Megri discovers the pleasure of being beautiful for her own sake within a love relationship. Megri's attraction to the Foreigner and their love come to compose one of the main arguments in the novel—that real love does exist. Beyala elaborates on the notion of real love, of love as passion. This love first manifests for Megri in fantasies and dreams.

> Terrified and ravished at the same time, I submitted to his desires, to his devouring sensuality, to his erotic fantasies. At times his progress was rapid and brutal. At others, on the contrary, his long preliminary strokes had me plunging in the troubled waters of passion.
>
> *[A la fois terrifiée et ravie, je me soumettais à ses désirs, à sa sensualité dévorante, à ses fantasmes érotiques. Par moments, sa progression était brêve et brutale. A d'autres au contraire, ses longues caresses préliminaires me faisaient plonger dans les eaux troubles du plaisir.]* (Beyala 1990, 66)

This love later appears in the opposition between her pale sexual life with her lover in Paris, Jean-Pierre, and the sensuousness and the eroticism of her relation with the Foreigner.

> His lips slowly descend, drawing arabesques on my breasts and my belly. Encouraged by my tension, he grabs my legs, one after the other, brings them to his shoulders and thrusts into me. . . . Slowly, he teaches me, takes me apart, reinvents me. . . . Our hips bear down, rise up, synchronized, languorous, floating, as if to stop time and space. Time disappears. Space too.
>
> *[Lentement, ses lèvres descendent, dessinent des arabesques sur mes seins, sur mon ventre. Encouragé par mon trouble, il saisit mes jambes, l'une après l'autre, les porte sur ses épaules et s'enfonce en moi. . . . Lentement, il m'éduque, me disloque, me réinvente. . . . Nos hanches s'épuisent, s'élèvent, synchronisées, langoureuses, flottantes comme pour arrêter l'espace et le temps. Le temps qui s'efface. L'espace aussi.]* (Beyala 1990, 90)

For an instant, love is acknowledged in all its purity and absolute power: "And I understood, without him having to explain, that he loved me from the start, that I loved him and that we were anchored in this certainty. Who says this kind of love cannot exist?" [Et je compris sans qu'il ait besoin de me l'expliquer que, depuis toujours, il m'aimait, que je l'aimais et que nous étions ancrés dans cette certitude. Qui a dit qu'un tel amour n'existait pas?] (Beyala 1990, 87–88).[21] The following lines imply that her feelings for the Foreigner are ambiguous: "I wanted the Foreigner. The need for possession in love took over" [Je voulais l'Etranger. La nécessité de la possession amoureuse s'empara de moi] (89). The word *possession* falls at the intersection of love and magic. Insofar as the Foreigner's identity is surrounded by mystery and doubts, Megri's possession may be the result of magic—perhaps he is the devil in person. Perhaps a love with such strength cannot exist naturally.

Power and sexuality. This love's limitations are described in terms of freedom and once more in terms of domination, albeit emotional. For the Foreigner, Megri is ready to annihilate herself, to be the submissive woman: "I had become the shadow of his steps, although he did not seem to want to make love again" [J'étais devenue l'ombre de ses pas sans qu'il semblât manifester l'envie de renouer notre étreinte] (Beyala 1990, 112); "But I tried to be a docile woman that he could have used as he wished" [Pourtant, je m'étais *efforcée* d'être une femme docile dont il aurait pu user à sa guise] (113).

Beyala describes sexual relations, female desire, and the act of seduction between men and women with a finesse and an acuity that are revolutionary in themselves. But she goes even further, exploring delicate zones that may be difficult to accept even for the woman herself. She denounces the ramifications for woman of a relationship that she is ready to give herself to so completely that her feelings border on masochism:

> I would have wanted him to hit me, to grab me by my hair and drag me through nettles and mud, for him to punish me for the wrong that I had not done. I would have accepted anything as long as this dreadful indifference that he was showing me would stop.
>
> *[J'aurais souhaité qu'il me frappe, qu'il m'attrape les cheveux et m'entraîne entre boue et épines, qu'il me punisse de la faute que je n'avais pas commise. J'aurais tout accepté, pourvu que cessât cette abominable indifférence qu'il me témoignait.]* (Beyala 1990, 114)

This passage brings us back to the initial question of power and domination. Michel Cornaton, in *Pouvoir et sexualité dans le roman africain* (1990), defines the relation between the two:

> Power and sexuality are two intricate realities. Where there is production and reproduction, there is sex, even if it is imagined, as psychoanalysis clearly shows. Power is also a place for pleasure, and sexuality is the domain of power over the other and over oneself. To convince oneself of this, one need only compare the numerous expressions and imagery about

the conquest of power and of a sexual partner (most often, a woman). (50; my translation)

Cornaton explains the position of authority in love: "Authority is male. . . . It is an attribute" (1990, 40). In contrast, the woman, of course, "has no specific authority: she only has what the man lets her have as long as he exercises his sexual power" (40).

From this point, understandably, the description and the analysis of female sexuality, of woman's sexual behavior, are limited to mere speculations (evidenced in the following passage in the conditional mode and the adverbs expressing doubt) derived from Freudian and Lacanian theories about lack:

> Woman merely takes part in power and strength, although *according to common knowledge she must possess* an enormous power of seduction and an unrestrained sexual power, a sort of animal sexuality. (Cornaton 1990, 40; my emphasis)
>
> To make love. . . . *This would be different* for woman. Her sense of being is not as dependent on one organ alone, but on the totality of her body. This lesser specification of orgasm enables her to better dissociate eroticism and sex and *no doubt* explains her greater capacity for making love. (41; my emphasis)

We end up with a series of hypotheses—not to mention assumptions—about woman with no attempt to explore female sexuality and desire any further. In the light of such assumptions, the reduction of woman to a mere commodity, to an object of desire, of male desire, to something at stake between men and between communities, appears almost to be expected.

I should also emphasize the remarkable absence of women writers' texts in Cornaton's critical analysis. Female sexuality remains ignored, even by critics. Could this silence be meant to mask all the last remaining taboos about women? Beyala's approach opposes the canonical norms and codes of *bienséance* (decorum) on a cultural as well as on a linguistic level. Beyala introduces the body in the text and makes it systematically visible, whether it is male or female. Moreover, she represents men and women in their most private intimacy, deconstructing the implications of body language for her readers along with what it means in terms of passion, violence, submission, or lack. Furthermore, she inscribes difference in the text, substituting new female paradigms for a sexist language.

However, whether in *The Sun Hath Looked upon Me, Your Name Shall Be Tanga,* or *Seul le diable le savait,* love appears as a fleeting moment, everything else being suffering and *decrescendo,* becoming something like the Pygmy's love for Dame maman, "a thread that has been strung beyond its breaking point" [un fil tendu au-delà du supportable] (*The Sun,* Beyala

1996, 39). In this context, the alternation between passionate love scenes and scenes of abuse and rape, such as the ones described by Ateba or Tanga, are designed to be a series of shock-therapy treatments that force readers to reassess their own notions of love and relationships.

From desire to suffering. The writing of the body and the representation of sexuality appear somewhat more provocative in Beyala's works than in those by the other female writers. In Rawiri's *G'amàrakano* (1983) and *Fureurs et cris de femmes* (1989), the scenes of sexuality are limited to just a few, and their function is almost incidental. They are there simply as elements of the protagonist's transformation of body and mind and are thus symbolic of the African woman's change in the beginning of the 1980s and of her quest for freedom, including sexual freedom.

In Beyala's works, these scenes become integral parts of the text and of her examination of society. They provide us with access to the profound mechanisms and operations on which society is based: inequality between men and women; male domination, including male sexual demands; the commodification of relationships; woman's dependence; the desire for revenge; the search for a place of total harmony; and love between women. The exploration of the female psyche and feminine sexuality carries a political agenda—to deconstruct the hidden mechanisms of society that produce a nonchalance tinged with resignation as well as the current stagnation.

Generally, three types of scenes appear: (1) Scenes of rape and violence express man's brutal, domineering power (male bodies, as we saw, are presented in their most repulsive aspects, virtually bestialized). (2) Scenes of total harmony depict bodies fusing in the passion of love; this is especially true of love scenes with the Foreigner in *Seul le diable*. (3) Some scenes depict a mere substitute for, a bland version of, love, a kind of living death of love. These appear, for instance, in the account of Megri's sexual experience with Jean-Pierre in *Seul le diable:*

> And Jean-Pierre. Elected to the stature of my dreams. . . . Pitiful in bed. Whatever limits the time of our duets on the fold-out bed to two minutes forty-five seconds on work days and three minutes ten seconds on the weekends. He fucks me like a rooster or a duck—with short, dry, rapid strokes. The way he lets himself fall off the side of the bed is no doubt responsible for this association. Once he has spat out his little desire, he gratifies me with a peck on the lips, rolls over on his side and falls asleep, happy to have made love.
>
> *[Et Jean-Pierre. Elu à la dimension de mes rêves . . . Pitoyable au lit. Ce qui cantonne le temps de nos duos sur couchette à deux minutes et quarante-cinq secondes les jours ouvrables et à trois minutes dix secondes les week-ends. Il me baise à la manière d'un coq ou d'un canard. A petits coups secs et rapides. Sans doute sa façon de se laisser tomber sur le*

côté est-elle responsable de cette association d'idées. Toujours est-il qu'une fois son désir craché il me gratifie d'un baiser sur les lèvres, il roule sur le côté et s'endort, heureux de s'être fait l'amour.] (Beyala 1990, 9–10)

Ateba and Tanga (in *The Sun* and *Tanga,* respectively) evoke their relations with Jean and Hassan, both described as pale, unsatisfactory versions of love under the sign of lack. Against this general feeling of lack, woman now demands her right to pleasure, to orgasm, refusing to be only man's plaything in the satisfaction of his pleasure.

> And what Pleasure is there for me? The act of possessing a man without having the least feeling, there is my condition, the justification for my existence, which is already more than enough to satisfy me!
>
> *[Et moi, quel Plaisir? L'acte de posséder un homme sans éprouver le moindre sentiment, voilà ma condition, la justification de mon existence, ce qui est déjà plus que suffisant pour me combler!]* (*Seul le diable,* Beyala 1990, 10)

Because the encounter with man produces only lies and disappointment, woman is left with two options: to retreat further into herself, to shape her own dream and close her eyes, or to use sex in its function of providing contact with men. Otherwise, she can refuse to lie and marginalize herself. She can become the mad woman that people gawk at in the street, as described in *Tanga.* This last option becomes the protagonist's choice, as she would rather inflict suffering on herself than have it inflicted on her by a man and have to confront the disillusionment of nothingness. The narrative voice betrays both her feeling of extreme despair (as in *The Sun* and *Tanga*) and, in contrast, her resignation when confronted with emptiness (in *Seul le diable*). The conclusion to the three novels, however, is the same: There is no pleasure for the woman, only physical and psychological suffering. In fact, sexual scenes are intimately mixed with violence and horror. True love, love as passion, is reduced to a fugitive instant; everything else is abjection.

How shall we interpret this apocalyptic vision of love if not as a hermeneutic approach to a catharsis that will free men and women from their imprisonment? Indeed, this is a literature of horror and abjection in the sense that Kristeva uses in her analysis *Pouvoirs de l'horreur: Essai sur l'abjection.* I will return to this element of catharsis in Part 3, where I analyze women writers' depictions of violence and horror.

Like Rawiri, Calixthe Beyala systematically creates a universe full of suffering, abjection, and horror in her search for an alternative life for woman, for the woman-child. Violence inflicted on the body, the discovery of the female body, and an exploration of sexuality all converge to form a radical provocation geared to liberate us through catharsis. Following Luce Irigaray's precepts on self-representation, Beyala proves that "the female body does not remain an object of male discourse nor of male arts, but it becomes the pole of a female subjectivity that can be experienced and self-identified" (1990, 68; my translation).

To speak of the female body but also of the male body, to speak of sexuality and represent it, to evoke desire and states of lack, are all so many steps toward writing woman's difference. To echo Hélène Cixous, the African woman introduces areas of exploration that are specific to her body and sexuality: "By writing herself, woman will recapture the body that has been taken away from her, that was made into a troubling foreign entity in her place . . . the cause and site of inhibitions" (Cixous 1975, 43). The approach to the body in its interactions has undergone a profound evolution. From a peripheral presence, the body has become primordial in order to describe woman in all her different states: happiness, pleasure, but also suffering, which is a site for exploitation and social pressures. By denouncing the body as an object and exploring it as an affirmation of the female being and of the self through the discovery of erotic zones, but also as a "geography of pain" (Lionnet 1995, 109), the female writer breaks the silence and creates a new space, a space that is no longer marginal but central to African literature. From this space, she can now explore sociopolitical questions and enter an area that previously was man's privileged domain. Through the systematic provocation of representing the forbidden, Beyala moves her readers, forcing them to confront their responsibilities. Above all, she suggests the possibility of a new ethic for relations between the sexes, one that is based on dialogue rather than on violence and domination, a discourse in which woman guides man, as M'am does in *Loukoum:*

> "I am learning to appreciate better the joy of having a wife like you and of having our children too. I love them. I love you." "Well, if you love us, everybody will love you the way you deserve to be loved." . . .
>
> "Yeah, but tell me, woman, one day will you forgive me for all the pain I've caused you?"
>
> Then I heard M'am weep. (Beyala 1995, 174–175)

In order to reach this point, a maturation process was needed; it was achieved through the previous novels, through a series of symbolic deaths and murders. In Beyala's first novel, the woman killed the man; in her second, the daughter killed the mother; in her third, the woman killed her misguided dreams. A new woman was finally born, and as a result, a new society was formed. Thus *Loukoum* marks a new step in the construction of a new sexual ethic between men and women, because a dialogue has opened up between them; the words *smile, happiness,* and *joy* find true meaning in the universe that Beyala has created.

Behind a somewhat racy title, *Loukoum*'s sequel, *Maman a un amant* (1993), calls this balance into question once again; it reopens the debate about woman's possibilities for experiencing other than temporary happiness.

Notes

1. By sexual politics, I mean the set of laws, practices, and taboos that regulate sexual behavior and impose a restrictive frame on male and female desire.

2. In this respect, Butler quotes Mary Douglas, who suggests that "the naturalized notion of 'the' body is itself a consequence of taboos that render the body discrete by virtue of its stable boundaries. Further the rites of passage that govern various bodily orifices presuppose a heterosexual construction of gendered exchange, positions, and erotic possibilities. The deregulations of such exchanges accordingly disrupt the very boundaries that determine what is to be a body at all" (Butler 1990, 132–133, quoting Douglas 1969).

3. See Fatna Aït Sabbah (1986).

4. See, for example, *C'est le soleil qui m'a brûlée,* where Ateba is subjected to the *test de l'oeuf* (the egg test) (Beyala 1987). Rangira Gallimore comments on this passage by observing that Ateba loses control over her own body, noting that the egg is cold.

5. On the representation of the body in Maghrebin and Caribbean literature, see Odile Cazenave, "Le corps-langage dans le roman maghrebin et antillais," *Nouvelles Ecritures Féminines, 1: La Parole aux Femmes,* special issue, *Notre Librairie* 117 (April-June 1994): 61–65.

6. Rawiri's first novel, *Elonga* (1980), remains within this initial framework: The body is still merely the place for serious suffering. This suffering is testimony to the power of black magic, which affects the protagonist and his family: Abscesses cover his whole body, which is completely deformed by the illness. His wife has a sudden accident. Finally, an infected abscess grows and spreads in his daughter's body, and she later dies from it.

7. Male writers have treated this type of desire, but in a somewhat different context. They criticize the African woman in her desire to look like the white woman. See, for instance, Cyprien Ekwensi's *Jagua Nana* (1961) and Okot p' Bitek's *Song of Lawino* (1966). *Jagua Nana,* as we saw in Chapter 2, describes the evils of urban society through its heroine's life of debauchery. Mineke Schipper de Leeuw, in *Unheard Words,* remarks that the character is used by the older generation to criticize youth: "The older generation is increasingly troubled by this development, wondering where it will end: everyone knows that white women are the embodiment of immorality. Traditions and morals can no longer be upheld when girls start identifying with that kind of pattern. Literature does indeed provide a stereotype image of the 'modern' woman, and authors with traditional views are critical of the changing times, not least where women are concerned. The African woman who adopts 'Western' dress and asserts her independence proves the undoing of the male character and of society itself. She is the antithesis of the conventional mother, virtuous and devoted" (1985, 32).

As Schipper de Leeuw analyzes it, p'Bitek's *Song of Lawino* shows Lawino's similar failure compared to her rival, Clementine. "Clementine is modern, she uses make-up, lightens her skin, and tries to lose weight like a white woman. She impresses Ocol, who has had a Western upbringing and loves city life. Lawino, repudiated by her husband, incarnates African traditions in the East Africa of the sixties. By contrast, Clementine wants to look like a Western woman and she indiscriminately copies everything that is considered part of the image. She thinks that this will make her more attractive and more interesting, but from a traditional point of view the opposite is true. Modern is equal with shameless" (1985, 33). Now, *G'amàrakano* differs in the narrative voice's attitude toward the protagonist and her empathy for what she identifies as true suffering imposed on African women in modern society.

8. Like Toula, Assèze experiences anxiety in dealing with her physical changes: "I had the annoying impression of being in the hands of Ava Gardner's designer, Greta's makeup artist, and Audrey Hepburn's maid. To listen to them discuss their beautician's program was hellish and I measured the handicap of being African in Paris by its complexity. Big clouds passed before my eyes and expressed the fatality of my being a black woman" [J'avais l'impression angoissante d'être dans les mains de la couturière d'Ava Gardner, de la maquilleuse de Greta et de la chambrière d'Audrey Hepburn. A les écouter parler de programme de mise en beauté etait infernal et je mesurais par sa complexité le handicap d'être africaine à Paris. De gros nuages passaient devant mes yeux et exprimaient ma fatalité d'être une femme noire] (Beyala 1994, 244).

9. We find the same preoccupation with appearance and the body in *Tanga* (Beyala 1988, 1996). Tanga's relation to her body, however, is more ambiguous insofar as she is conscious of the slavery that it implies; she is aware that her body is simply a commodity, and she therefore hates it.

10. We can ask about the specificity of such phenomena; if we think of American and European women, we can find certain similarities in body and mind. See Hansen and Reed's *Cosmetics, Fashion, and the Exploitation of Women* (1986), a political analysis of women's manipulation by men as they are submitted to another form of slavery through their bodies and a series of criteria imposed on the workplace. See also the more recent *Beauty Myth* (Wolf 1991), in which Naomi Wolf addresses the problem of women's obsession with the body and thinness. Both analyses bring an interesting perspective to the matter, pointing out the constraints imposed on women in Western societies. They argue that beyond these constraints lies the intention of controlling women. When they are obsessed about their shapes, women forget other aspects of daily life, particularly what is of feminist concern. Social and political questions thus come second, enabling men to have power for themselves alone. In other words, this well-planned intoxication prevents women from speaking and therefore from becoming fully emancipated.

11. In Isabelle's and Marie-Pierre's cases (the characters are in *O pays, mon bon peuple!* [Sembène 1957] and *Les deux mères de Guillaume Ismaël Dzewatama* [Mongo Beti 1983], respectively), the transformation is generally positive. The description, however, emphasizes abrupt upheavals and sudden changes: fatigue, dark circles under the eyes, "bad" hair; these are all marks of their phase of discouragement. On the contrary, in their phase of integration, they are characterized as having an African look; their initial glow has been replaced by a suntanned complexion and a natural strength of the body.

12. Besides *Scarlet Song* and *Juletane*, I can also cite *Le quimboiseur l'avait dit* (Warner-Vieyra 1979), *La voie du salut* (Maïga Ka 1985), *Etrange héritage* (Ami 1985), *G'amàrakano* (Rawiri 1983), and *Fureurs et cris de femmes* (Rawiri 1989).

13. The same association between the protagonist's failure and the impasse of African society exists in *G'amàrakano:* "Toula is a victim of this world of mirrors

that creates desires and jealously keeps what it owns. She cries because she is no longer content with what she has, because she has seen what a sensitive person in her condition is not supposed to see" [Toula est victime de ce monde de miroirs qui crée des désirs et garde jalousement ce qu'il possède. Elle pleure parce qu'elle ne se contente plus de ce qu'elle a. Car elle a vu ce qu'une personne sensible de sa condition ne devait pas voir] (Rawiri 1983, 27).

14. For another example of impossible, fleeting love, see Werewere Liking's *L'amour-cent-vies* (1988). The relationship between Lem and Madjo embodies all the mythical forbidden forms of incestuous love. Looking for his original half, Lem pursues Madjo, who is actually his grandmother as well as the reincarnation of the buffalo-woman.

15. Some elements of my analysis on Beyala are part of my article "Provocation et sexualité comme agenda politique dans le roman africain au féminin: L'exemple de Calixthe Beyala," in *The French Novel from Lafayette to Desvignes,* ed. P. Brady (Knoxville, TN: P. Brady, 1997).

16. *Seul le diable* in particular exposes the mercantile transactions between men and women, especially within the family, where Dame maman uses her body as a commodity—"Just this evening I was laid by the chief of the village" [pas plus tard que ce soir, j'ai été la chose du chef]—and accepts the "semi-deaf Pygmy" [Pygmée dur d'oreille] because he had "a thick wallet" [le portefeuille bien rempli] (Beyala 1990, 38). The mercantile approach also appears in the two husbands' attitudes. More specifically, Papa bon Blanc's proposal to marry Megri's mother and to officially acknowledge Megri as his daughter in the world of the whites reduces her mother to a mere object of exchange (not to mention the obvious latent racist connotations concerning the other and colonialist domination): "And I am ready to have you recognized as the wife of a white man, when even you know just what you are worth." [Et je suis prêt à te faire considérer comme la femme d'un blanc quand toi-même, tu sais ce que tu vaux] (40).

17. Bjornson defines man's position as follows: "In *SLM [The Sun],* men are portrayed as having produced this ugliness by their selfish pursuit of their own gratification. All the men she encounters attempt to dominate her and to force themselves on her. And their corrupt mentalities have produced the ugliness in which she feels entrapped" (1991, 417).

18. Compare Megri's definition of her mother: "a femme fatale who had grown up on this earth and drunk to her full content the desires of men" [une femme fatale qui avait grandi sur cette terre et bu jusqu'à satiété le désir des hommes] (*Seul le diable,* Beyala 1990, 114).

19. This point serves as the central argument of Rawiri's *G'amàrakano, au carrefour* (1983).

20. I am using the word *pleasure* in the Freudian sense, that is, extreme relaxation and an absence of any tension, which is synonymous with nonpleasure.

21. Tadjo asks a similar question about the existence of love: "How could he have felt such a desire, if the nerves along his spine that speak of love did not exist?" [Comment aurait-il senti un tel désir, si le long de sa colonne vertébrale, les nerfs qui disent l'amour n'avaient pas existé?] (*A vol d'oiseau,* Tadjo 1986, 81).

6

Toward a New Sexual Ethic: The (Re)Presentation of Man

It was not too long ago when woman was the dark continent of humanity and that no one ever thought of questioning man's identity. Masculinity seemed self-evident: bright, natural and the opposite of femininity. The last three decades have blown apart these millenial proofs. Because women have sought to redefine themselves, they have forced men to do the same. XY remains a constant, but masculine identity is no longer what it used to be. (my translation)
—Elisabeth Badinter (*XY: De l'identité masculine*, 10)

As Awa Thiam suggested in *La parole aux Négresses* in 1978 and Carole Boyce Davies reiterated in her introduction to *Ngambika* (Boyce Davies and Adams Graves 1986), women writers have taken control of speech in order to reestablish an accurate image of the African woman. This image has been excessively deformed and stereotyped in the eyes of both European and African men. These women writers have tried to produce an accurate image of the African woman in order to give voice to her hopes and frustrations in a form that affirms her identity.

The search for the authentic woman is not to be considered as an end in itself. Instead, it represents a stage in the formation of an equitable structure and a new ethic governing relations between the sexes. One consequence of this progression is that the attempt to build a new society requires not only a reevaluation of woman in her desires and responsibilities but also an exploration of the other so as to better understand him and thus to achieve a change in his ideas and behavior toward woman.

With *Elle sera de jaspe et de corail: Journal d'une misovire*, Werewere Liking ushers in a woman's discourse on man. The "misovire" assumes the function of observing men in order to guide them and give them strength and dignity—"these men who come and go with their tail between their legs, accepting themselves as inferior, with nothing beautiful or powerful to teach or to offer" [qui s'en vont la queue devant basse s'acceptant inférieurs sans rien de beau, de puissant à enseigner, à offrir] (1983, 12).[1]

In this context, Angèle Rawiri and Calixthe Beyala merit special attention not only for representing man in a new light through an honest attempt to understand the motives that guide his behavior but also for their daring study of his desires and expectations in matters of love, marriage, and family. Their studies are composed in either direct or indirect homodiegetic discourse.

Masculine Empathy in Rawiri's Texts

Angèle Rawiri gives voice to masculine discourse in an extensive manner that parallels her exploration of the feminine psyche. Her first novel, *Elonga*, has as narrator the male offspring of an interracial couple. His mother died giving birth to him, and he lived in Portugal until his father's death. He is treated like a foreigner by the members of his own family. Because he is an outsider whose financial and social advantages annoy them, he faces difficulties similar to those of the foreign woman or white wife. Caught between two worlds, his privileged gaze filters each impression for the novel's readers. Africa, instances of witchcraft, his family including his wife and daughter, are all presented through his voice. Rawiri has introduced a new strategy that will crop up again twelve years later in Beyala's *Loukoum*. Rawiri adopts a masculine voice as the main narrative voice and uses it almost exclusively to deal with the underlying elements of an Africa in decline.[2] In particular, *Elonga* deals with the problems resulting from a preoccupation with appearance and the craze for European clothes. The novel especially raises the problem of witchcraft, which weighs on a younger generation that can manage only limited resistance to this traditional outlook.

G'amàrakano takes up one of these thematic strands—the race to emulate Western appearances—in order to emphasize its dangers. In addition to the protagonist's development and her access to differing social circles, the author presents certain aspects of women's circumstances as well as the masculine perspective on this subject. Through the exchanges that take place between Toula and Angwé, Toula and Elangwa, and Tabassou and Onanga, a dialogue is developed between man and woman on their respective roles and their conceptions of love.

> "I just ask myself why women absolutely insist on proving to men that they are worth something. Why don't they stay in their place? . . .
>
> "The African woman's evolution is upsetting. If only she didn't identify with the desires of Western women, things would be all right."
>
> "You don't understand a thing," Onanga violently retorts. "Believe me, it is disappointing. You should know that we aren't claiming the right to have whims, but rights themselves."

"Je me demande pourquoi les femmes veulent absolument prouver aux hommes qu'elles valent quelque chose. Pourquoi ne restent-elles pas à leur place? . . .

"L'évolution de la femme africaine est déroutante. Si encore elle n'i-dentifiait pas ses désirs à ceux des Occidentales, Ça irait."

"Vous ne comprenez rien," rétorque violemment Onanga. "Croyez-moi, c'est décevant. Sachez bien que nous ne revendiquons pas des caprices mais des droits." (Rawiri 1983, 120)

This dialogue is above all an occasion for women to develop their position and an explanation of man's resistance to their achieving emancipation. Rembeyo demonstrates that the male refusal arises in part from the disintegration of traditional social structures as a result of colonization. This disintegration has also led to the disappearance of certain positions for women in traditional society (as storytellers, for example) and thus necessitates a redefinition of woman's position in modern society. The masculine objection also, paradoxically, arises from men's insistence on idealizing woman and associating her with a much stronger figure—precolonial Africa's keeper of traditions. This idealized role is a stifling mold in which woman has been contained. Even if the discussion creates an opening for a wider dialogue, it is limited to an oratorical joust as proof of each character's spirit. Without questioning either character's behavior or personal conceptions, the discussion still represents significant progress in the woman's gesture of offering the man a hand, in her desire to know the other, and in her ideas about the social structure.

Fureurs et cris de femmes takes an enormous literary step forward. It is no longer a superficial gaze at man's interests but a profound exploration of who or what this other is. Through the selections of narrative voice and a series of flashbacks, Rawiri grants the reader access to Joseph's internal discourse and memories. At the same time as Emilienne, he tries to retrace the moment when their relationship began to fall apart, the moment when he began to lose interest in his wife.

It is quite likely that my lack of interest goes back to Emilienne's first series of spontaneous miscarriages. Life as a couple is so strange! Every passing day can help reinforce the feelings and ties that bring a couple together or that pull them apart. You never realize when it's going on. Then one morning you wake up and realize that you have spent the whole night on opposite sides of the bed and that this has been going on for a number of weeks.

[Il est fort probable que mon désintéressement remonte à la première série d'avortements spontanés d'Emilienne. Comme c'est bizarre la vie d'un couple! Chaque jour qui passe peut contribuer à renforcer les sentiments et les liens qui consolident un couple ou à les éloigner l'un de l'autre. On ne s'en rend jamais compte sur le moment. Un matin, on

réalise qu'on a passé toute la nuit chacun de son côté et que cela se produit depuis plusieurs semaines.] (Rawiri 1989, 35)

Joseph scours his memories, looking for any details that might indicate when this change began. He becomes aware of all the power games, of the silence used as a weapon for wearing the opponent down, of the tactic of not communicating with the other, and of preferring contact with his friends. The masculine intradiagetic discourse also explains the husband's views on the difficulties of reconciliation caused by his and his wife's diverging feelings and attitudes:

> After several days of atrocious suffering brought on by the frightening discovery that your love was slipping away, after conducting a minute analysis of all the degrading relations, you seriously decide to pick up the missing pieces and repair the broken chords. Then something else comes up! The other is in a bad mood that day or simply hasn't prepared for reconciliation at the same time as you. Then, as if to discourage you, she comes out with some diatribe that paralyzes you. As for your good intentions, you keep them filed away in your heart, so that if she ever reproaches you for your indifference, you will be able to whip them out. When you are hurt, you fall back on your pride. And some people say that making up takes two. . . . Well, yes, but she would have only needed to be a little sharper that day in order to read into your eyes and find that glimmer that swore you would begin anew.

> *[Après plusieurs jours de souffrance atroce à la suite de la découverte effrayante de l'effritement de l'amour, après une analyse minutieuse des rapports dégradants, on décide avec gravité de rassembler les pièces manquantes et de ressouder les cordes cassées. Mais voilà! Ce jour-là, l'autre est de mauvaise humeur ou tout simplement ne s'est pas préparé en même temps que vous à la réconciliation. Comme pour vous décourager, elle sort un pavé qui vous paralyse. Vos bonnes intentions, vous les classez dans votre coeur pour les ressortir brutalement si elle vous reproche un jour votre indifférence. Blessé, on se replie dans son orgueil. Et on se dit qu'une réconciliation se fait à deux . . . pourtant . . . oui, pourtant il aurait suffi qu'elle soit ce jour-là plus perspicace pour lire dans vos yeux et y déceler cette lueur qui jurait de tout recommencer.]* (Rawiri 1989, 35)

In contrast with previous male discourses in women's novels,[3] Rawiri offers a positive interior monologue. In his ideas about love, the man feels a sincere will and desire to strengthen and preserve his conjugal bond. The adjectives *atroce* (atrocious) and *effrayante* (frightening) reveal not only Joseph's awareness about his new situation but also his genuine suffering as he experiences the deterioration of his conjugal relations. The verbs *décide,* (decide) *rassembler,* (pick up) and *ressouder* (repair) indicate the man's decision to take action and improve the situation. Portraying man in this light breaks with the tone of previous women's novels. The narrative

voice indirectly raises the question of woman's responsibility in her refusal to cooperate, her lack of intuition, and her clumsiness in accepting
excuses that have been made as attempts at reconciliation.

The interaction between Joseph and Emilienne constitutes both a representation of masculine thought and a search for some interpretation that
makes sense of man's behavior in a given situation. In particular, we have
a study of the man's reasons for pursuing relationships elsewhere. The first
explanation is that masculine pride has been wounded by an inferior professional situation. In other words, Joseph feels humiliated because he
earns less than his wife and, finally, because his wife has shown her
mother-in-law their respective pay stubs. This proves beyond a doubt who
makes more money and who supports the mother-in-law, which, for the
son, represents the ultimate humiliation.

> Isn't it enough that the entire town knows that your work puts a roof over
> my head? Did you still have to humiliate me in front of my mother? If
> you want a divorce, there is no reason to wait. Your superior attitude is
> really getting on my nerves. I can tell you right now that I will never let
> myself be dominated by a woman, not even one who claims to participate
> in a movement for emancipation. . . . I've had enough of this crap.
>
> [*Ne t'est-il pas suffisant que toute la ville sache que ton entreprise me
> loge? Te fallait-il encore me dévaloriser auprès de ma mère? Si tu veux
> divorcer, alors ne tardons pas. Tes airs de supériorité me deviennent in-
> supportables. Apprends que je ne me laisserai jamais dominer par une
> femme, même se réclamant d'un mouvement d'émancipation . . . J'en ai
> ma claque.*] (Rawiri 1989, 70)

Once more, the exchange between husband and wife suggests that Emilienne is at least partly responsible for her husband's anger and frustration.
Immediately following the previous passage, the text returns to a feminine
discourse in order to show the reader the other side of the coin.

> As a result of this typically male revolt, Joseph became crude, vulgar and
> easily angered. He started drinking excessively and refused to bring his
> wife to the official receptions. He even stopped answering invitations
> from their friends. The mood in their relationship very quickly became
> intolerable.
>
> [*Suite à cette révolte typiquement masculine, Joseph devint irascible,
> grossier et vulgaire. Il se mit à boire avec excès et refusa d'emmener son
> épouse aux cérémonies officielles, et même de répondre aux invitations
> que leur adressaient leurs amis. Très vite, l'atmosphère conjugale devint
> insoutenable.*] (Rawiri 1989, 71)

In order to put a stop to all this, Emilienne starts a conversation in
which she takes responsibility for her ridiculous behavior and asks Joseph

to forgive her for trying to play power games with her money: "I need you and it certainly isn't my social standing that will fill the void you will leave if we ever split up" [J'ai besoin de toi et ce n'est certainement pas ma condition sociale qui comblera le vide que tu laisseras si jamais nous nous séparons] (Rawiri 1989, 71). The discussion allows them to take stock of the situation: Joseph suffers the barbed comments of his friends and his financial inability to support his wife; basically he is jealous of his wife's success. He rejects the idea of taking a second wife and then reaffirms his love for Emilienne in words and in action, promising never to leave her no matter what happens (although he makes no promise to be faithful.) The discussion marks the beginning of a new warming in their relations, which lasts for about a year. The end of the analepsis (flashback) allows the reader to assess the situation and to extrapolate some judgment of masculine behavior in general or of man's "genetic" infidelity.[4]

Rawiri introduces another striking innovation in character relations, that of the reconciliation between the husband's wife and mother, which bothers and confuses the man. The extradiagetic narrative voice interprets Joseph's feelings as something like jealousy toward his wife because she receives more attention from Eyang than he does. The result is that Joseph begins to come home earlier to watch the development of this new relationship. He feels that he is being spied on and observed by the two women and believes that they are always talking about him. This development sparks a new narrative and has the paradoxical effect of making the husband disappear from the house for a time.

Emilienne's reflections on her personal experience constitute a didactic assessment of love relationships between men and women. Certain stages are deemed inevitable: seduction, possession, and pleasure; boredom and distancing:

> In her arms, he becomes a lover, a friend, a child and a father, one after the other. Curled up in his strong arms, she trembles, shakes and swoons with desire. She is the cause of all this sensual excitement. She is the desirable woman. Alas, this is an eternity that does not last very long. . . . She refuses to believe for a single second that the distant look of the loved one slumped between her breasts may denote some kind of boredom.
>
> The moment soon arrives when she is just another presence. Of course, she is still desired, but no longer as the center of the world. Through him, she can see her various flaws appear and gradually turn into cumbersome monuments.

> *[Dans ses bras, il devient tour à tour l'amant, l'ami, l'enfant et le père. Lovée dans ses bras vigoureux, elle palpite, s'extasie et se pâme de plaisir. Elle est la cause de tous ses chavirements sensuels, elle est la femme désirable. . . . Une éternité qui, hélas, ne durera pas longtemps. (. . .) Elle ne veut pas croire une seule seconde que le regard lointain de l'être aimé, vautré entre ses deux seins, dénote d'une certaine lassitude.*

Arrive le moment où elle devient une présence tout court. Certes encore désirée, mais non plus le point central du monde. A travers lui, elle peut voir surgir ses défauts et devenir progressivement des monuments encombrants.] (Rawiri 1989, 112)

According to Emilienne, when two people have become bored with each other and failed to have children, there are two possible scenarios. If they are not married, they can either separate and remain friends or fail to overcome their loss and survive together somehow. From the woman's perspective, the fundamental difference between their two reactions is that the man will rush to find another companion, preferably someone younger than he.

When Joseph takes Emilienne out to dinner to announce his project to start a new company, we see another example of the distance between husband and wife. For Joseph, this occasion is an opportunity to share his pleasure and pride with his wife and to publically display her as his official companion. Emilienne, on the contrary, feels bitter about having been kept in the dark and used in an official capacity. She thus becomes aware of the distance in their relationship and the difference between her former joy and her present indifference. Although her indifference actually rekindles Joseph's interest and love, it is also another point of contention and an opportunity to point out the contradictions in Emilienne's behavior. She appreciates this evening out, as it reminds her of their first dates, yet she does not know how to share his joys.

> For the man she thinks she still loves, she feels nothing. His successes—from which she knows that she has been excluded no matter what he says—no longer interest her.
>
> *[Pour l'homme qu'elle croit encore aimer, elle ne ressent rien. Ses succès dont elle se sait exclue, quoi qu'il en dise, ne l'intéressent plus.]* (Rawiri 1989, 131)

Two discourses have been superimposed here: the discourse of the irremediable situation in which something has definitively been broken and the discourse on the illusion of loving someone. The female character also expresses a loss of confidence in herself. Emilienne feels guilty and withdraws into what she thinks of as her only responsibility—to have children.

> Seated next to her husband, Emilienne feels pathetic. She feels like she has betrayed him. If only she had the courage and the wisdom to step outside of herself and turn to him so as to better understand him, in order to be better understood and to seek forgiveness. She remains resolutely silent, as if paralyzed by her feelings of guilt.
>
> *[Assise à côté de son mari, Emilienne se sent minable et a le sentiment de l'avoir trahi. Si seulement elle avait le courage et la sagesse de sortir*

d' elle-même et de se tourner vers lui pour mieux comprendre, mieux se faire comprendre, et se faire pardonner. Elle reste toutefois résolument silencieuse, comme paralysée par sa culpabilité.] (Rawiri 1989, 132)

The question of sterility allows two other differences in men's and women's behavior to appear. Joseph's anger at Emilienne's attempt to make him shoulder the blame for her sterility pushes him to admit to his double life and the existence of an extramarital relation from which he has two sons. His confession of this situation exposes their completely opposed concepts of love. Joseph imagines that he can bring his children into their house to be raised by Emilienne. For him, such an arrangement would be a perfect compromise and proves his love for his wife, for it is with Emilienne that he wants to live, and she is the one who should have the honor of raising his children. For Emilienne, Joseph's affair is a humiliating betrayal and a definitive sign of her partner's lack of love for her. She feels that her body and her wifely love have been shunned. She is also jealous that her husband has sighed in another's arms, that he has known sexual pleasure with someone else.[5] There is something new, however. The narrative voice still stresses Joseph's awareness of the pain that he has inflicted on his wife by making this revelation and the fact that he can no longer bear her silence.

> He falls silent, conscious of the wound in his wife's heart that he has been opening up with a scalpel, but he doesn't want to stop; nor can he stop. He will keep going to the end of the story. He cringes when he hears the muffled cry in Emilienne's throat as it is stifled in her twisted mouth. At this point in his story, this cry and this pain are also his own.
>
> *[Il se tait, conscient de la plaie au coeur de sa femme qu'il est en train d'agrandir au scalpel, mais il ne veut pas et ne peut pas s'arrêter. Il ira jusqu'au bout du récit. Il souffre du cri intérieur qu'il entend monter à la gorge d'Emilienne, puis s'étouffer dans sa bouche pincée. A ce point de son récit, ce cri et cette douleur sont aussi les siens.]* (Rawiri 1989, 133–134)

Joseph's effort to empathize with the woman is presented as something new in his development. The masculine concept of love also appears in Joseph's feeling that he has betrayed his wife. This feeling spurs a desire to break up with his mistress, but he uses his blood relations, his sons by her, as justification for acting otherwise.

The representation of man and his internal discourse operates in two ways. The homodiagetic discourse gives a direct voice to the man. The feminine discourse is an attempt to figure out man's needs, to understand and to analyze the motives that influence male behavior. In the end, both of these discourses alternate. They run together and apart in order to explain the difference in both of their fundamental conceptions of love. This distanciation translates their mutual inability to find any more than temporary grounds for understanding.

The Masculine Voice in *Loukoum*

Beyala's texts simultaneously expose man's body and masculine sexuality. African male writers have been largely reticent about describing sexuality and the body; African female authors of the second generation have put the body, both woman's and man's, at center stage.

Man's behavior, attitudes, and physical being are observed and described in detail by the protagonists. Man is represented in terms of his limitations, his beliefs about strategies for dealing with women, and his brutality, particularly in sexual relationships. Especially in *Seul le diable* and *Tanga*, man is ridiculed, animalized, and metonymically reduced to his genitalia or some other body part.

With *Loukoum*, man discovers himself and his weaknesses, his vulnerability, and his fragility in contrast to woman's strength. Man appears to be at a loss in relation to the evolution of his brothers, the world, African women, and his own children. He is distraught about his inability to adapt to a new culture and to standards different from his own. Both in his letters and in his final exchange with M'am, Abdou expresses a need for feminine guidance in the language of love and dialogue with woman.

For the first time, Beyala utilizes a combination of alternating masculine voices, that of Loukoum, a seven-year-old boy, and his father, Abdou, a municipal worker for the city of Paris. The father's voice offers an overall view of the immigrant Malian community in Belleville, a heavily populated neighborhood in Paris. With this narrative choice, Beyala puts a new slant on the traditional theme of African literature of independence that presents the shock of two cultures in the form of an African character who comes to France or Paris in order to study and who has trouble maintaining his own identity. Beyala modifies this situation in several ways. The African man does not come to France alone but with his family. He does not come to study but to find work, and he no longer is there on a temporary basis but as an immigrant: "I came to this country in the grip of material gain, expelled from my own land by need" (Beyala 1995, 11). The opening letters show the disillusionment resulting from immigrant status and the women's role in adapting to life in a country that is not their own.

By placing the African man in the position of an exile and by giving him the immigrant's marginal status, Beyala can illustrate man's fragility anew. Through his own marginality, the man is brought closer to woman's place in society; he thus finds himself in a better position to understand her. Empathy becomes possible because there has been a similar experience of suffering and weakening from the beginning. Man is exposed in his complete vulnerability and in his need for woman as a guide. It is through her and in her alone that he exists and is able to survive. He asks the question about the origin(s) of woman, of women, choosing the language of poetry, dreams, and legends to describe her and the calming effect that she has on him:

> She lays her clothes on the fingers of the stars. Her body leans over, she takes my hand. "You are the pearl, the human pearl. Who sends you? God or the devil? No. Don't answer me. Let me be. Let me reinforce that tower you wanted to construct and which exile is crucifying. Don't be afraid any more. I shall build the nest of your dreams' shore for you." (Beyala 1995, 35)

The first sentence recalls Ateba's *(The Sun)* legend about the origin of women and the celestial position that they abandoned so that they could descend to earth and help men. (In the story, men are called "human pearls.") Man reestablishes woman in her position as his savior, as the only anchoring point in this unknown world of change and wandering. In *The Sun* man follows the woman's lead, adhering to the myth of the celestial woman.

> A heavy sob sits on the edge of my eye. I clasp on to her breast, her belly, the warm fleece of her sex, as if on to a new land, a new dawn. And for me these images reinvent the legends of before in a mystical farandole. (*The Sun,* Beyala 1996, 35)

In *Loukoum,* Abdou's poetic letters reinforce the same motif of woman as a savior. Thanks to the woman, "exile serves as a truce" (Beyala 1995, 35). When Loukoum feels bewildered, he grabs hold of woman in search of a little warmth. He needs contact and M'am's embraces. With each new expression, man betrays the depth of his pain and his vulnerability as a nonbeing, as the eternal immigrant. The image of the strong, domineering man who masters woman has disappeared.

> I lost my soul over an ocean.
> . . .
> I am a noise, barely a breath.
> . . .
> I am transparent. (Beyala 1995, 51)

Man has actually adopted the language of the victim, a language typically associated with woman. In contrast to her previous texts, Beyala attempts to restore the African man's textual voice here and thus to change stereotypical views of him. For example, by comparing black men's and white men's behavior in sex and love, Abdou destroys the typical stereotypes about the African man's sexuality. Woman has returned to her customary place in the masculine utopia as a "natural and necessary monster" [monstre naturel et nécessaire] as guide, legend, and wisdom.

> Why a woman, you'll say to me? Why women? The love of women guides me through my memories. They are my legends. I have married this legend. And in my madness, woman shines like a lantern. A small exiled moon. She is my only wisdom. (Beyala 1995, 65)

Woman is defined here as a peaceful island, a figure of strength, the protector of Africa and of roots. Because it is a masculine discourse, we are almost not surprised to find textual images reminiscent of those that appear in Senghor's "Femme noire."

> So I curl up in those magical sheets in which woman weaves me thousands of dreams, on the other side of the wounds. She teaches me the legends anew and I ejaculate my tenderness in the wind.
> Woman is my drug. I will never be tired of it.
> Fragile hours resounding with hope,
> From which I hollow out my frenzy so I can coil up inside it. (*Loukoum*, Beyala 1995, 65)

Elsewhere, however, love and sexuality assume a new dimension; they are an indispensible condition for existence. Without them, man would feel excluded from society. Women's wisdom appears in its obvious strength: it is by women and in women that man exists. Woman creates man, gives him life, and enables him to go on living.

> They. Women. They know how to invent me, they also know how to adopt me, to reinvent me. I, who am only a breath, madness anchored inside the skulls of idiots. . . . And in a flight of mumbled words, the women recreate me. . . . I travel on their bodies which open up to my tenderness and I fall asleep, inside the open arms of heaven. Exile moves away. (Beyala 1995, 78)

Woman's value and image evolve from the rescuer and comforter to the person who disturbs the status quo through her own transformation. Woman is presented through the typical clichés of her ambiguity and her strength, as a buoy and an anchor, but also as a threatening force in her ambiguity as an intermediary point of contact with the French culture: "Woman, You know, is an ambiguous creature. Her magnificent vagina opens at our song and her lips of sun cause the promises of morning to raise straight up to the horizon" (Beyala 1995, 20). The guiding metaphor of woman as celestial guide has been replaced with the metaphor of woman as ambiguity and danger in order to emphasize the distance between man and woman in relation to their exile. The man accuses the woman of seeking out some insignificant freedom and of discovering different ways of being and doing things as a woman and as a wife. He especially concentrates on her physical changes. The masculine voice becomes bitter, if not angry. Whereas the man expresses a certain nostalgia for the past as he turns his attention toward the African continent, the woman seems to fully embrace this new space and to adopt the new society's way of life. Lost in this world, the man admits that he cannot communicate his anguish: The women do not listen to him anymore.

> Oh my friend, disaster has rung my doorbell.
> The women have gutted themselves behind my back. They have removed the hair from under their armpits and shaved in the pubic area. Nothing is named by its name anymore. I no longer recognize the geography of the land drawn in MY OWN HOUSE. The pity of it all. . . . Leave the buttocks as they are, strong and muscular. Let the flesh flow over. They're fat but not ugly at all. Dye the hairs with clay, but let the sexual organs live freely and the sun, reflecting itself there, will indicate the seasons to me. (Beyala 1995, 91)

The changes described in *Loukoum* recall the transformations of body and mind that appear in Rawiri's *G'amàrakano*. The important difference is that Abdou complains about this new condition, particularly about the intitiative that the women have taken in the sexual domain: "They make love to me and I'm ashamed. They're impaling this little tortured body with love and pleasure. Since when, friend, and in what country, do women govern?" (Beyala 1995, 91). The man's perspective is that women no longer respect his nostalgia. He has become nothing more than a pest to them.

> I become an embarrassment, a blind thing that understands nothing at all. The women think that I've gone mad. Maybe I am crazy. Threatened, humiliated, ridiculed, I must not proclaim my bad temper. (91)

Abdou's exchange with his white, male interlocutor assumes a new tone. His questions cease to be rhetorical in order to ask a practical question. He asks a man-to-man question about the attitude he should adopt to deal with woman's emancipation. The other men in the story—Kouam and Ndongala—ask this question at the same time. The man experiences genuine distress when confronted with the disintegration of his usual cultural points of reference, all the more so since woman represented his last possible safe haven in the midst of a foreign environment: "In my House, the giraffe of anguish is whirling around. . . . The dawn of perdition is bathing my house in a wounding light" (Beyala 1995, 102). For the first time, man recognizes his and woman's irreducible interdependence. The narrative voice thus describes a before and an after in relation to woman:

> You know, before, my voice would sing beautifully.
>   Womankind would adorn herself in love,
>   She would abolish emptiness, and without hesitation she would make the springs of hope flow.
>   Woman has changed. . . . My destiny is toppling. (102)

The masculine anguish that this new woman allows the author to introduce provokes a dialogue between an African concept of masculinity and a concept of Western feminism. This African concept of masculinity is presented as directly responsible for the changes that the African woman undergoes. Disoriented, man has to question his own existence as he searches for a "scrap of understanding" (Beyala 1995, 102). He thus reaches the point where he can begin to bare his soul. The things that he has done were for woman and her affection. The usual position of strength in the relationship has been inverted. (The position of strength is specified in the Koran in the claim that man has a right to expect respect and love from woman, since he is the [financial] provider.) If man works, it is so that he can obtain a bit of woman's affection or love.

> Why? I have done what was necessary. I sold my life to work for a little bit of bread, so that the brightness of women's eyes would be full of affection. From this coffin, my House, I demand only laughter, the drunkenness of dance. And tenderness placed there a well-deserved reward. (102)

Because man no longer recognizes this new woman and her new needs, he feels anguish in the face of the unknown, as well as his own sexual inadequacy. Beyala gives a voice to man's fears in confronting the new woman. Because she has already closely examined woman's position in the figures of the mother, the daughter, and the prostitute, she is now prepared to begin a new analysis of society and to explore the questions—and the anguish—of the other sex. The discourse does, however, contain echoes of the past in the form of a representation of stereotypically anti-women discourses. For instance, man's desire is to see woman respect the old traditions and to act as a guardian of the African past (in a precolonial African utopia).

> One of them daubed herself with lipstick, the other painted her eyes like two enormous black holes. I no longer recognize them. What is happening? Nothing has a name any longer! I don't know anything any more. I am nothing any more. And every day, the women hack away a little of my dreams, these dreams constructed for them. I am afraid. (Beyala 1995, 103)

With this new refrain, with this complaint about the changes in women, the man appeals to the past as a last resort. The image of the past is naturally the symbolic image of woman as a black goddess. He wants to "recuperate" woman and to stick her back into her protective box as a woman-object who has been idealized as the protector of all virtues:

> My eyes shut and behind my closed eyelids there is a woman's gaze that shines more brightly than the sun. From head to toe, she is like ebony. Her cheeks are like heaven and her waist like an ear of corn. Nightly, on her shoulders, there are two silver braids that are finished off with rings of gold. . . .
> Her name is Star.
> She holds out her naked and strong arms to me. She calls me, she calls out to me. She claims that she is able to put me at the threshold of paradise. (Beyala 1995, 108)

But this call for the image of a strong, imposing, reassuring woman, a chthonic maternal image, an image of woman as sorceress, fails. Man finds his nonexistence confirmed. He is now exiled twice over, first from his country and now from his wives.

> Since the women have started serving glasses full of independence in my house, since they have been drinking that sap, I am learning how not to be a man any longer. Who am I? An immigrant. A burdensome mouth. An airstream passing through. I have no landmark any more. (Beyala 1995, 111)

Man is exposed in all his humility; he is naked, distraught, and alone, his virility mutilated. The power relation has changed, disrupting the traditional stability. For the man this change can only be a mistake. The women must have headed down the wrong path.

This analysis refers us to current studies on man and man's place in and in relation to feminism. In particular, there are echoes here of Elisabeth Badinter's study *XY: De l'identité masculine,* in which she pursues the question of modern man's new vulnerability as woman's companion. Badinter directly relates man's new fragility to woman's recent advances. As woman gains freedom and new rights, man feels disoriented and destabilized in the present context of sexual relations. Contrary to the common assumptions about woman's difficulty in becoming and man's facility for being, Badinter demonstrates that man actually experiences greater difficulty than woman in becoming and in developing himself. She introduces the theme of the enigma of man and his present identity:

> XY is man's chromosomal formula. . . . There is a long, treacherous path from XY to the sense of masculine identity which marks the outcome of

man's evolution. This path is a little longer and a little more complicated than woman's, contrary to what people believed for a long time.

. . . XY remains a constant, but masculine identity is no longer what it used to be. (Badinter 1992, 9–10; my translation)

Extending the terms of Simone de Beauvoir's famous phrase "On ne naît pas femme, on le devient," Badinter responds in the present context: "One is not born a man, one becomes one" (1992, 50). Badinter introduces certain distinctions between man's different faces, all of which have been combined in Abdou's character. From one moment to the next, he is what Badinter defines as *l'homme dur* (the hard man), a man who is incapable of expressing his feelings, locked up in his own aggression, obsessed with performance and competition, self-satisfied, and unable to express a commitment to anyone else; and *l'homme mou* (the soft man), who is weak, dominated by women, and characterized by his renunciation of the powers and privileges that are generally granted to him by the patriarchal order.

Loukoum reveals a new kind of relation between men and women by emphasizing women's strengths. Through the characters of M'am and Aminata, we see women's courage, their determination, and especially their patience in dealing with man's whims. Whether it be in the person of Abdou or Uncle Kouam, man is represented as an inconsiderate, spoiled child, used to having his least fantasies catered to. Furthermore, as the mutilated man, the full extent of his fragility is exposed.

This same image of the disoriented man in search of a sense of direction that only a woman can give also appears in Tanella Boni's *Une vie de crabe* (1990). Young Niyous is involved in a conflict with his father, a wealthy businessman and an important figure in the town. He is uncertain about his future and degenerates from minor trades to petty thefts. He revolves between his mother and Léti, his father's former wife, who has become Niyous's lover. Both of these women support him. The mother lends him money, and Léti tries to give him some self-confidence. She encourages him to continue his studies and acts as a go-between with his father.

Here, as in Beyala's novels, the woman appears as a strong figure who is capable of surviving a lot of inner strife. Madeleine Borgomano (1994) emphasizes this in her analysis of the novel, identifying the successive points at which Léti shows her willpower. First, Léti chooses the man that she really wants, but she also leaves him when she wants to. She then chooses Niyous even though he seems to have no future and cannot support himself financially. Borgomano also cites the example of Kémin, Niyous's sister. Kémin feeds her entire family and "remains completely detached from this family that she escapes in her hairdresser's salon where she doesn't even see them anymore" (Borgomano 1994, 92; my translation). Borgomano concludes, "Women seem to have achieved greater autonomy, and their fate and their misery have been mixed up with everyone else's" (92). Through the conjunction of masculine and feminine narrative voices, the woman emerges with greater inner strength than the man; he seems lost at a difficult juncture in a social and moral world that is falling apart. This narrative structure also occurs in *Une vie de crabe,* in which Léti, Niyous, and Dramane all take turns speaking with the narrative voice.

Through Abdou's epistolary interventions, Beyala offers a new access to man's consciousness. These epistolary moments introduce a new phase in Beyala's search for a new ethical standard for relations between the sexes that is applicable to "the essence of the human male."[6] This leads to Beyala's necessary questions: Who is wrong? Who is headed in the wrong direction?

> The women have understood nothing at all. Under exile from the sun their skin has cracked. Something has become unhinged. Your wife's theories have infiltrated without their knowledge, behind my back. They are turning my life into a nightmare. They accuse me saying: "You are the executioner of our soul. You think you are charitable, but you're as cold as a blade."
>
> And what are they making of the warmth of my hands? (Beyala 1995, 111–112)

By superimposing the discourses of the man and the woman, the author allows us to examine each one's truthfulness. Through the masculine narrative voice, Beyala gives the man a chance to explain his vision of the division of responsibilities in the couple and his conception of the good (Muslim) husband and the good wife.

> On this earth where I shall be a stranger for ever, I have tried to be a good Muslim husband. I have balanced my preferences. I have two wives, but I have done everything to make one as much favourite as the other. Veiled, protected from the outside world, withdrawn on their knees, I freed them from the evil of men. Minor unkindness, exclusion, even self-centredness were of no concern to them any more. A kind of immunity. (Beyala 1995, 130)

The extradiagetic narrator's irony becomes ferocious in the masculine interpretation of the veil and the Muslim husband's duties, as in the limited male perspective on the Western woman and feminism in general. By deploying a third extradiagetic narrative voice in the background and through dialogues between men and between father and son, Beyala simultaneously presents all of the stereotypical phallocentric discourses on woman. The exchanges that take place between Abdou and Uncle Kouam in particular are a direct illustration of (African) man's stereotypical discourse on feminist Western women. These exchanges also demonstrate the masculine prejudices toward any type of feminine emancipation or contestation of masculine power.

> Nobody listens to [what] those kind of women have to say. They just chatter like magpies. There is not a man around who wants anything to do with them. Which is why they're into revolutions.
> . . . Listen, Loukoum, you're my heir. That sort of woman is bad news, spreads her legs for anyone. Never listen to them. Never. (Beyala 1995, 58)

The author's discourse appears superimposed in the wink of an eye. Beyala raises the question of the pseudofeminist discourse while displaying a caustic irony toward men who fail to perceive that real changes have occurred. The child already feels comfortable in his masculine identity and reinforces the discourse of the adult male:

> What does she want to be prophesizing that grand women's revolution? It has done a lot of good here in France, but it is a natural disaster among the immigrants. Say what you like, but in France women have suffered sexual racism. They have their reasons! But Soumana and Ma'm have never had to complain of being badly treated sexually. There has never been a tragedy or a corpse. So I don't quite see what Madame Sadock is waiting for. Finally, as my dad says, with women you can never know. (Beyala 1995, 79)

The dialogue is built around the superimposition of two discourses. One consists of the reported speech of the men. The other is the implicit discourse of the author as she points to the first. There is also the third discourse of the child who adds to the first discourse's logical meaning. In its observations and reported words, the pseudochildish voice provides a framework in which the antifeminist discourse is reproduced.

> She explains to the women what rights they have, and the great tale-for-women-who-don't-get-laid-enough. When she talks, she gestures, gets upset, and even ends up by becoming seriously angry. Not because she's furious, but because she wants to say even more, and my mothers with their limited means up top can't always understand what she's talking about. . . .
> If you want my opinion, this woman has no feeling. (Beyala 1995, 79)

Through Loukoum, Beyala indirectly comments on sociology and Western feminist discourse and its flaws: This discourse has not been adapted to the immigrant woman's situation. It does not really concern her because the stakes are different.

> In your place, I'd go there, I'd do this, I'd do that. That's just it, she isn't in their place, she has no business sticking her nose in what's theirs.

> African marriages, she doesn't have a clue what they're about. She doesn't
> understand the first thing about the way we live. (Beyala 1995, 80)

Whether in the already masculine child's discourse or in the discourse
of the father, the man shows a degree of bad faith when it comes to his
ability to accept his female companion's changes. Once again, the sincerity of the masculine discourse is singled out and thrown in doubt through
a series of winks and nods to the readers.

Loukoum introduces a second key element of change in man's behavior—his commitment to being a responsible father. In contrast to the previous novels that showed a father physically or psychologically absent,
Abdou is preoccupied with his son's future. He tries unsuccessfully to initiate him and to speak with him of Africa and his origins. The generational
conflict is similar to that described for the 1960s and 1970s in that the
child has acquired a form of knowledge considered superior to his parents'
because it leads to financial success. The difference is that both the parents
and the child live in this same foreign environment that the child prefers to
the symbols of Africa.

> You know, friend, a ridiculed father is like a jealous husband. I learn
> about my misfortune from new indecencies. . . . My son has rounded a
> headland. In the wrong direction. He is reluctant to put on his *djellaba*.
> He wants clothes like of Stallone's, exactly the same, for fear he'll feel
> lost. The crudeness of his dances astounds me, just like the contortions of
> the stars on television, and that's not all.
>   I have been invaded, friend, I am losing myself. (Beyala 1995,
> 137–138)

Abdou's reflections on Western clothes and the younger generation's
fascination with music, dances, and distractions that he cannot understand
point us to bell hooks's analysis of the dress and dances of young African
Americans. She has written on the brutality of their music and dance and
on the meaning of the dress code and the violence displayed in all of
these.[7] The gravity of the situation prompts Abdou's longest letter in the
entire story. This letter marks the acceleration of the process of alienation
for the man who has been exiled from society and for his family members
in their relations with him. The record of his experience and loss of bear-
ings shows a collective preoccupation. The question of the future of
African children and of what kind of education is to be adopted by African
parents assumes its full import and becomes explicit for the first time in
Beyala's novels. *Loukoum* contains a decisive transition in its presentation
of man learning to love and be a responsible father. No longer do we have
a father who is absent by definition; now we have a father preccoupied
with his own incompetence and who insists on playing an active part in the

child's future. The family in Beyala's novels does not collapse because of some internal structural flaw but from external circumstances. The father has done everything within his power. In complete contrast to Beyala's previous novels, the father has reached the point where he can introduce his son to Africa (Mali in this case). He describes the countryside, the customs, the smells, and the religion for him. However, he is finally forced to acknowledge his failure:

> Little by little my son was no longer listening to me. . . .
> He has acquired the vocabulary of Paris. Words scratched in by wind and weather.
> He has acquired other manners of saying hello. He knows rituals that throw me.
> He finds repugnance eating with his hands.
> He imposes other conformities.
> He imports tastes, preoccupations.
> He passes from one universe to the other without worrying about it.
> He judges ours, feels contempt. (Beyala 1995, 144)

This discourse exceeds any possible application to his son, who cannot be held responsible for most of these habits. Loukoum has become a hyperbolic representation of the younger generation. Most of these comments recall those made by the elders about the young student who returns to his country in the 1960s or 1970s. Here, however, the danger is even more serious in that Africa exists only in its evocation. If the son or the child stops listening to it, Africa disappears from the household and, with it, a stable identity for the child and the family.[8] The father finds himself at a dead end: "I don't know how to renegotiate the constraints and adjust myself. I believe I'm going mad" (Beyala 1995, 144).

The running metaphor of madness is a throwback to the character who falls prey to madness, although madness is exemplified by a man. The will to fight has been reduced to simple fantasy: We uncover a network of terms that are not common to man. These are synonyms for weakness, impotence, resignation, male madness, and extreme fatigue. Even man's will to write and act is an illusion. He will be misunderstood, and his message applies only to the past. The father's written interventions constitute a slice of life that occupies very little space in relation to the entire novel. In the end, we have to ask which of the two parts remains more important today.

The final intervention mimics her discourse of madness, of an attempt to reason, to calm oneself, and to once again be the master of one's thoughts. The character has to make himself empty, to not think, to show enough strength and peace of mind to wait for the realization of what he desires. The mind of the vagabond father hallucinates and reasons with itself. The discourse of madness is inscribed within the narration. However, the author slips an essential element of political critique into this unrestrained discourse. The man is not actually responsible for the situation. It is French law that is responsible because it did not anticipate polygamy and as many as four wives. The white man's fear of everything that appears mysterious in the culture of the other is translated into legislative and political power applied to matters of immigration and assimilation.

Loukoum represents a definitive evolution in the portrayal of man and in the representation of relationships between men and women. From now on in Beyala's fiction, love is present, but it is poorly expressed, misunderstood, composed of injustices and injuries. It exists, nevertheless, without being reduced to either simple mercantile relations or to the war between the sexes.

Beyala gives us the parallel development of the internal feminine discourse as it reacts directly to the masculine discourse or behavior. It becomes apparent through the superpositioning of the two discourses that although open hostilities may have ceased in the war between the sexes, they are still there, common and repressed, along with a male attitude that remains atavistic. The life of the women in Loukoum's family is suffused with a strong fatalism: Man may leave or play the field at any time, and woman should wait for his return and smile (without, of course, showing any resentment). But there is an important difference between the thoughts and actions of the two women. La Soumana's behavior can be explained by the fact that she loves her husband. In her eyes, M'am's behavior belongs to a different generation. Like her mother, this generation says amen to everything that the man says or does. For M'am, it is very important to observe the religious commandments and to respect Allah. She has chosen her place and explains to La Soumana that it is only a matter of time before La Soumana will adjust. Experience has taught her that Abdou will always come home. For La Soumana, accepting Abdou's behavior is out of the question. She loses her appetite over his absence and risks losing her life. In her mind, Abdou has to choose between her and the other woman. M'am believes that La Soumana response is a mistake. They must not do anything to push the man away. Is this wisdom or resignation? Should one be tolerant (in order to have peace) or tempestuous (and lose one's illusions)? In this context, La Soumana's death is symbolic of the inevitable suffering of the woman who puts all her hope in love.

Through the alternation of the two male narrators who comment on the two women's dialogues, the text offers both two male and two female perspectives on the same question. Through the dialogue conducted by the men (Abdou and Uncle Kouam), we are introduced to the question of the transfer of authority and power from the men to the women. The interracial couple of Mathilde and Uncle Kouam, moreover, exemplifies the different conceptions of marriage and man-woman relationships in the French and African cultures. The interracial context serves to introduce the spouses' differing ideas about their development as a couple and about the relation between sexuality and marriage. Unlike La Soumana or M'am, Mathilde wants a separation or a divorce. Although she admits that she still loves her husband, she clearly states that she has reached her limits. Through the example of this couple, Beyala shows part of the masculine discourse about women, including men's "simplistic" ideas about what women expect from them. They often assume that women's needs are as simple as sexual satisfaction: "As for the fucking, I've got to say that she couldn't complain about it." [Faut dire que pour la baise, elle pouvait pas se plaindre] (Beyala 1995, 208). Nevertheless, this conversation still forces Kouam to recognize that he has not always treated his wife in the best possible way. Once again, man's honesty in admitting and becoming aware of his mistakes breaks with the typical discourse of the past. Man's conception of his relation to woman is highlighted by this example. Finally, Uncle Kouam and Mathilde's relationship deals with the subject of power, which affects how both the woman and the man should proceed in order to excite the other's self-love so that each will react and desire the other anew.

Beyala adds a new element to the description of marital relations—the woman who confronts and disagrees with her husband, as exemplified in Mam's conversation with Abdou:

> "But I believe a child needs his mother, his real mother, I mean. And as for your dead body, I actually need a doormat by the front door."
> "What? What's that you're saying?" . . .
> "That you are self-centred, a washout, and that it's high time you paid attention to what's happening around you, that's what I'm saying."
> Father splutters. "But . . . "
> "No buts. Aminata can take the kid over for a few days." (Beyala 1995, 147)

Beyala explains woman's concepts of love, her attraction for man, and her distinction between love, passion, and sex through the characters of Aminata and M'am. In fact, the first sequence of events ends with a reversal of the original situation. The father's departure (when he is arrested by the authorities) and subsequent return bring about a radical change in their lives. M'am subsequently runs the house and holds the power, and so she is also in charge in the game of love.

> It doesn't interest M'am at all. You'd think that it is she who no longer sees him. He does everything. M'am has no longer the same appearance. She wears trousers, blue, yellow, red ones with matching sandals. She looks younger, more carefree. My dad, he's looking for something. Monsieur Guillaume says that he is searching for God in woman. He buys

plenty of jewelry for M'am and never lets a chance go by of paying her a compliment as if he thinks she's very beautiful. M'am doesn't listen to him. . . . So then my dad gets worried. I heard my dad say to Monsieur Guillaume that he doesn't know what to do next. That he really loves her. (Beyala 1995, 172–173)

Beyala lets us see that a certain balance of power between man and woman has been reestablished, as she goes even deeper into the question of power and reciprocity. She shows us the possibility that man can be reconciled (with woman, with his family, with himself) as the result of a profound love. This development occurs in man learning about love and life:

"I am learning to appreciate better the joy of having a wife like you and of having our children, too. I love them. I love you."

"Well, if you love, everybody will love you the way you deserve to be loved. That's the very principle of life."

"Yeah. But tell me, woman, one day will you forgive me for all the pain I've caused you?"

Then I heard M'am weep. (Beyala 1995, 174–175)

This development is the opening of a new dialogue wherein it is still the woman who guides the man on the path of apprenticeship in love. By transforming his state of mind—"making room to recognize his vulnerability" [faisant place à la reconnaissance de sa vulnérabilité] (Badinter 1992, 216)—Abdou is proof of the possibility of a new model of masculine identity. Badinter explains men's task in these terms: "[They] need to learn to express their emotions, to ask for help, to be maternal and cooperative, and to resolve conflicts in a non-violent way" [Ils doivent apprendre à exprimer leurs émotions, à demander de l'aide, à être maternels, coopératifs et à résoudre les conflits de façon non-violente] (1992, 216). The last page of the novel also mentions the new love that has arisen between Aminata and Kouam; a wind of joy blows over the entire family. Smiling and feeling happy finally appear as possibilities in Beyala's world.

Maman a un amant, the sequel to *Loukoum,* reopens the debate on the possibility of happiness for M'am and Abdou. The novel asks whether this happiness can exist between men and women in general. If M'am seems to be in control in the first part of the novel, she winds up being obliged to sacrifice her desire for change, her well-being, and her love for the good of the community. The narration describes the changes that have affected M'am's body and mind in the first part of the story. She makes all the decisions, and she decides that the family should go on vacation. She chooses the spot, and she is also the one who changes, discovering new feelings in a relationship with Mr. Tichit. Finally, she is the one who leaves the house. She does not choose to leave but is chased away by Abdou, who cannot tolerate the situation. The message of the two novels hinges on the point that Abdou cannot tolerate the same situation in which he had placed La Soumana and M'am. Jealousy, emotional blackmail, manipulation of the children's well-being, and bad blood all erupt here. Man's weakness appears, but so does his bad faith in his appeal to the African community. M'am seems like a loose woman in the eyes of the group, so her actions shame the entire family.

Through the dialogical interaction between female exchanges and male responses (the husband's and the lover's), we see that M'am was being used all along. The man who seemed to love her, who would show her another way of life, was thinking only of his own satisfaction and sexual pleasure. Mr. Tichit's selfishness proves every bit as strong as Abdou's. He cannot stand it when a woman stands up to him, and he blames M'am for ruining their "marvelous" relationship for the sake of seeing her children. The narrative voice (of Loukoum and the extradiagetic narrator) derides the relation as a watered-down Bellevillean version of love. The reader discovers that behind the triumphant title *Maman a un amant,* the woman is still only an object and a victim of man, ridiculed for her words and her acts of kindness. Beyala shows that in the eyes of the community it is unacceptable that she enjoy a little happiness, an adventure in love that is not even love with a capital L, without producing negative results. We are far from the principles invoked by Ateba, Tanga, and Megri in their search for a new authentic woman who is capable of confronting and understanding man and his limitations. The narration allows us to run back over the entire gamut of rationalizations and false excuses that have been used generically by the man against the woman. For instance, one of the lover's strategies is to change the subject in order to avoid dealing with M'am's needs. In this case, he avoids her need to see her children. Better still, he uses emotional blackmail:

> I wonder what you want. To destroy our love? I am warning you now, you won't be able to find one better than ours. We have everything we need to be happy. We get along well together, without even mentioning that we perform pretty well together in bed.

> *[Je me demande ce que tu veux. Briser notre amour? Je t'avertis: un amour comme le nôtre, tu ne peux pas trouver mieux dans le genre. On a tout pour être heureux. On s'entend bien, sans compter qu'au lit on fonctionne pas mal.]* (Beyala 1993, 287)

These phrases echo Ateba's reproaches to Hassan in *The Sun* when she realizes that he has not been listening to her and that he does not have the same need to communicate.

> All of a sudden, there was a great silence. And then I heard Mister Tichit, who was asking in a nice little voice:

"Why are you like that, huh? Why do you always want to be the boss? A woman is a fragile thing made for crying, but not for imposing her will. What on earth is going on in your little head?"

[*D'un coup, il y eut un grand silence. Et puis j'ai entendu Monsieur Tichit qui demandait d'une voix toute gentille:*
"Pourquoi tu es comme ça, hein? Pourquoi veux-tu toujours en faire à ta tête? Une femme, c'est fragile, c'est fait pour pleurer, mais pas pour s'imposer. Qu'est-ce qui peut bien se passer dans ta petite tête?"]
(Beyala 1993, 287)

This change in tactics may remind us of the first refrain about man's domination of woman as a normal situation according to the masculine point of view. Tichit's words here remind us of Abdou's, Kouam's, and others'. The man feels the need to hold the power whether he is a husband or a lover. The legend of the origin of the earth and man and woman introduced in *The Sun* resurfaces in order to be revised. The new version confirms man's traditional domination. The man, however, was not happy enough with having woman. He had to keep her in a state of slavery and imprisonment. He pretended that he always made her happy and fulfilled his duties as a man. The interaction between narrative voices emphasizes the repetition of this reality and the validity of the origin myth. Beneath the somewhat racy title *Maman a un amant,* the fact emerges that woman has failed in her attempt to escape reification once and for all. She is still a prisoner of the masculine discourse, blurred by its duality. The extradiagetic voice resurfaces in order to question the nature of the couple's reconciliation and M'am's actual happiness. M'am has sacrificed her love in order to return to the conjugal home with an empty heart. In reality, the community's final exhultation sanctions the woman's docility and the reestablishment of the hierarchical, patriarchal order. This is a return to square one. With his wife's reassurances, the man can now leave the house again whenever he wants. Stability has been restored to the couple. M'am has returned. Abdou is happy and has work, although he will soon return to his former habit of running around with other women. His straying is foreshadowed for the reader by the announcement of Marguerite's arrival:

"The poor girl, someone should really help her." . . .
She held the plates in her hands for several seconds, then she dropped everything and it crashed to the ground with a catastrophic noise.
I am not worried. The proverbial good humor of Negroes is there, and everything always works out in the end.

[*"La pauvre petite, il faut vraiment qu'on l'aide."* . . .
Elle a tenu les assiettes dans ses mains quelques secondes, ensuite elle a tout lâché et ça s'est écrasé sur le sol avec un bruit de catastrophe.

*Je ne m'inquiète pas, la bonne humeur proverbiale des Nègres est là
et tout finit toujours par s'arranger.]* (Beyala 1993, 299)

So the man goes back to philandering, and M'am submits to the destiny
of the woman-who-is-better-than-man and who is therefore supposed to
keep her dignity and not lower herself to his level. She is sacrificed on the
altar of the community. The moral of the story: If the man is happy, everyone is happy.

The indirect irony of the extradiagetic narrative voice breaks out in its
full ferocity. As a boy, Loukoum has already been wedded to the masculine
perspective that upholds the law and authority of man over woman. What,
then, is left for the woman other than the memory of a few furtive caresses
and the fact that she has learned to read and write? Her life continues just
as before.

Meanwhile, the question remains the same: When will man have a sincere attitude that lasts? The second part of *Loukoum* leads us to believe
that there can be only temporary stability, a moment of transition, and that
woman is still a prisoner of the masculine structure in her thoughts and actions. *Maman a un amant* thus represents a certain progress, but it stresses
the limitations and constraints that are involved. In this sense, both of
these novels constitute a decisive stage in Beyala's development of her vision of the couple and the woman-man relation. By transporting the action
to the African immigrant neighborhoods of Paris, *Loukoum* and *Maman a
un amant* fix the story in real life and point to the attempts to achieve objectives identified in Beyala's previous novels: the (re)discovery of an authentic woman, the getting rid of false dreams of success, and the creation
of a new balance of power between men and women by opening a dialogue
between them. Although in the first section these objectives seem to be realized, the second part moves in the opposite direction and, although
everything seems to be better on the surface, reveals a regression. The
woman remains a prisoner for having subscribed once more to the notion
of love and the conventional definition of relations between men and
women. Certainly, M'am has taken the intitiative and proven herself capable of making decisions, but only against the man from whom she has
distanced herself emotionally. Her love for Mr. Tichit is ultimately only a
response to her original attitude toward Abdou; it is a form of compliance
with Abdou's desires.

Beyala gives us an opportunity to assess the significance of a certain
amount of progress. Man has in fact become more open to changes in his
ideas and behavior. He has also expressed a new desire to cooperate and
work with the other. But this foundation still appears very temporary. The
comforts of daily life draw the man back to his habitual behavior. For

woman, progress has occurred in the form of her physical and psychological transformations. These changes have opened her up to listening to the needs of her heart and her body, although she still has to free herself from the linguistic and social constructions that perpetuate the image of the good wife who puts the good of the community before her own well-being.

Beyala thus invites us to assess the actual strength of the resistance of the claims and assumptions that govern every love relation and the difficulty of living one's love or one's relationship according to different principles. To achieve this, she has guided us in her novels along the paths of Ateba, Tanga, Megri, Aminata, La Soumana, and M'am as well as those of Jean-François, Hassan, Uncle Kouam, Abdou, and Loukoum. No progress has been made, but through the characters' struggles we have discovered the strength of the limitations that still need to be overcome, and because of this new awareness, we are compelled to participate directly in the development of Beyala's vision of a new sexual ethic.

Notes

1. The term *misovire* is a neologism formed from *misogyne* (misogynist). Liking, however, grants it a broad meaning. In an interview with Bernard Magnier ("La rencontre de Werewere Liking," *Notre Librairie* 79 [1985]), Liking explains that by *misovire* she means "a woman who does not manage to find an admirable man" [une femme qui n'arrive pas à trouver un homme admirable] (21). For a discussion of the terms *feminist, woman,* and *misovire,* see Irène d'Almeida (1994a).

2. Masculine narrative voices are also used by Elizabeth Delaygue (1986) in *Mestizo.* (In fact, she uses multiple male and female narrators to give a rendering of the problem in its geographical and historical scope.) Like Elonga (Rawiri 1980), *Mestizo* deals with mixed-race characters who live in a space where two different worlds overlap and who are therefore thoroughly marginalized.

3. In *Scarlet Song,* the masculine discourse appears in the form of grievances. Ousmane compares his white wife to Ouleymatou, an African woman and childhood playmate. The comparison is not flattering to Mireille. Renouncing his love for her, Ousmane insinuates that it was only a matter of infatuation and curiosity arising from their racial difference.

4. Emilienne ponders Joseph's infidelity: "Joseph is no different from other men who cheat on their partners in order to forget their problems or to size up their powers of seduction with women, or, if they are happy, just out of capriciousness or some lack of awareness. I wonder at what moment they are actually capable of being faithful? Aren't they all just made to constantly slip through our fingers? As for us, Joseph and me, we have been separated by a chasm that we may never be able to fill" [Joseph n'est pas différent des autres hommes qui trompent leur partenaire pour oublier leurs problèmes ou pour mesurer leur séduction auprès des femmes, ou tout bonnement, lorsqu'ils sont heureux, par caprice ou inconscience. A quel moment peuvent-ils donc être fidèles? Ne sont-ils pas tous fait pour constamment nous glisser entre les doigts? En ce qui nous concerne, Joseph et moi, nous sommes séparés par un gouffre que nous ne pourrons peut-être plus jamais combler] (Rawiri 1989, 73).

5. An additional difference shows up in their reactions to the situation. Emilienne's grief is more than a moral suffering; it has a number of effects on her body: "Emilienne is having trouble breathing. She breathes through her hands and the soles of her feet. She desperately clings to the window in order to support her weakening body" [Emilienne respire avec peine. Elle transpire des mains et de la plante des pieds. Elle s'agrippe désespérément à la fenêtre pour retenir son corps qui s'affaiblit] (Rawiri 1989, 133); "Sweat is flowing from Emilienne's thighs and armpits" [La sueur coule des cuisses et des aisselles d'Emilienne] (134). *Juletane* and *Scarlet Song* depict the same kind of suffering that is described in *Fureurs et cris de femmes:* "Dressed in a transparent nightgown, barefoot and disheveled, Emilienne leaves the house running" [Vêtue d'une chemise de nuit transparente, échevelée et pieds nus, Emilienne sort en courant] (*Fureurs et cris de femmes,* Rawiri 1989, 134).

6. The question of the "essence of the human male" (the words are Badinter's) can be found in the section entitled "Qu'est-ce qu'un homme?" of the prologue in *XY* (Badinter 1994). In relation to this question, Badinter recalls Rousseau's remark in *Emile* (Paris: La Pléiade Gallimard, 1969, Book 5, 697): "The male is male only at certain times, the female is female all her life, or at least for her entire youth."

7. See bell hooks, "My 'Style' Ain't No Fashion," *Z Magazine,* "Sisters of the Yam" (May 1992): 27–29.

8. Beyala underscores the opposition between present and past by using the present tense to describe the children and the imperfect tense, marking a past time, to speak of Mali and the Malinkes.

PART THREE

*Toward a
New Political Novel*

7

Archetypes of
Feminine/Feminist Writing

To write to say that one has loved father and mother? What's new about that! I hope I have been doing a little more than that, that I have gone beyond the taboos of silence that reign over our emotions. (my translation)

[Ecrire pour dire qu'on a aimé père et mère? La bonne nouvelle! J'espère avoir fait un peu plus, avoir été au-delà des tabous du silence qui règne sur nos émotions.]

—Nafissatou Diallo
(*De Tilène au plateau: Une enfance dakaroise,* 132)

As a preamble to this part of the book, I would like to recall Séwanou Dabla's work *Nouvelles écritures Africaines* (1986), in which he analyzes the evolution of Francophone African literature and describes the production of the African novel from its beginning to the second generation of novelists. In particular, he defines stylistic specificities of this new writing. In the same spirit, I want to focus in this last part on some of the narrative strategies used by the female novelists of the new generation.

The question of a feminine/feminist writing has given rise to many debates in the past and remains a topic of discussion in academic circles. At the roundtable "Male versus Female Narrative Theory" at the 1987 African Literatures Association Conference at Cornell University, panelists attempted to identify the specific traits of African feminine writing in relation to the general body of African literature. Critics argued that it is best defined neither by themes (e.g., polygamy, ritual sexual mutilation, infertility) nor by narrative structures such as autobiography or the epistolary form. Also rejected were the immediacy of communication and elements of the oral tradition, although these categories emerged as somewhat less limited and thus more promising for analytical speculation. Only the question of the "sexualization of space"—or the different "spaces" inhabited by women and determined by culture—received serious consideration as a trait specific to African women's literature. A healthy skepticism resulted from this discussion with participants pointing out the limitations of theoretical approaches and even questioning the necessity of defining the specificity of feminine African writing.[1]

Rather than address here whether there are elements specific to African women's writing, I want to focus on themes and narrative strategies that, in combination, aim at breaking a status quo in which the male-authored Francophone African novel of the 1980s seemed to be stuck. The novel of that period is bitterly critical of the postcolonial situation, caustic and violently accusing, yet it neither promises a better tomorrow nor seems to search for alternatives. In contrast, texts of the period by women writers seem to offer a different perspective.

In this regard, Evelyne Accad's analysis of the evolution of Arab women's writing is enlightening, as the approaches adopted by the authors reveal the evolution of their writings (Accad 1993). We can divide their writing into two phases: an initial phase that betrays anxiety about biculturalism and the loss of their own identity, and a second phase that depicts a more explicit sense of the social, sexual, and political issues that confront women today.

The first phase corresponds to an introspective exploration of personal problems; it is a testimonial literature that uses the genre of the autobiography or semiautobiography. Using female protagonists, Arab women writers develop the quest of the person as a subject and try to shake off the yoke of objectification. Accad remarks that if these texts are seemingly too self-reflective, they are nonetheless authentic and, most important, necessary: "One must know a certain number of things about oneself before being able to start writing about one's place in the millennium" (1993, 225).

The second phase appears to depict rebellion more. Accad characterizes this second phase as bearing a more mature vision, as it shows the realization that freedom of the self cannot be separated from social context or, of course, from the resulting political implications.

> Characters discover that they are not rebelling merely against a single custom, a particular oppressor, but are facing the complex and total interrelationship between their own beings and the society that has shaped them. (1993, 250)

In the second phase, society comes to play a role in the global vision, just like any character in the plot, with its "principles of choice and action" and "its flaws" (Accad 1993, 225). Accad concludes that the recent literature by Arab women, without being a literature of propaganda, is in its mere commitment likely to generate forces and conditions that are favorable to creative and positive social and political changes.

I have tried to follow Accad's creative approach in order to better define the new orientation of the African novel by women. I have looked at the thematic and narrative elements that appear in the first generation in order to next examine the ones that the "rebellious women" of the second generation have initiated.

Recurrent Themes and Issues

Using *The Madwoman in the Attic,* Sandra Gilbert and Susan Gubar's (1970) classic work on the representation of madness and the discovery of recurrent literary motifs in women writers' texts from the Victorian era, Florence Stratton, in "The Shallow Grave" (1988), raises the question of similar characteristics in texts by Francophone African women writers. While aware of the differences between the cultures and respective eras, Stratton starts with the hypothesis that there is a similarity of artistic response to what remains a constant fact for female psychology, that is, patriarchy.[2] According to Stratton, the writing of cultural elements such as myths, rituals, and social traditions into texts is the definite mark of a female literary tradition. She also notes the frequent analogy between woman and the state due to the similarity of their respective conditions.[3]

Stratton suggests the existence of a feminine literary tradition that surpasses cultural boundaries. She also proposes a reassessment of women writers' texts in terms of aesthetic and artistic choices, whereas critics have usually reduced them to political tracts.[4]

Following Kathryn Frank (1984), Stratton recommends an approach that looks for archetypes, for they enable us to perceive not only what is specific to the feminine environment but also how writers experience reality and transcribe it in an artistic way, that is, through the use of metaphors, symbols, and other techniques specific to them. Stratton thus comes to identify archetypes that are particular to the African woman's experience:

> Their female characters are enclosed in the restricted spheres of behavior of the stereotypes of a male tradition, their human potential buried in a shallow definition of sex. Silenced, like the slave woman, by blows—either to their bodies or their psyches—they are forced to submit to the necessity of conforming to the externally imposed requirements of their masculine societies. (Stratton 1988, 147)

Most characters are sacrificed, losing all individual personality, to become witnesses to their own inescapable victimization. Hence, we have the recurring textual image of woman's confinement and of her life leading to an impasse. Another implication for the married woman is that of disapproval of infertility by the patrilineal and matrilineal lineages. The only acceptable identity for a woman comes through the laws of marriage and maternity. Because they are incapable of conforming to the law, a number of female characters have no alternative but marginalization and madness. In Chapter 3, I defined the archetypal physical and psychological features of the madwoman. The recurring use of the double allows the juxtaposition of two characters: one who conforms to the norms of society and another who is outside the norms but liberated from the constraints of daily reality.[5] Beyond that, the feminine character illustrates woman's sacrificial death. In particular, Stratton demonstrates in her analysis of *So Long a Letter* that through Ramatoulaye, Mariama Bâ gives an account of the blindness and paralysis woman is reduced to because of her extreme conditioning:

> And by having her heroine tell her story while literally confined to a house of death, Bâ tells the story of the living death of every woman who is unable to break out of that conditioning. In effect, Ramatoulaye mourns her own demise. (Stratton 1988, 166)

Among recurring features in female characters, Stratton notes (1) the writing of the psychosomatic (anorexia, apathy, sudden anger, withdrawal into oneself, insomnia, nightmares, etc.); (2) the inscription of ritual into narration as a dynamic mechanism; (3) the rejection of motherhood as mandatory for validatation and completeness as a woman.

The rejection of ritual is particularly evident in Bâ's *Scarlet Song* and Sow Fall's *L'appel des arènes*. Both protagonists (Mireille and Diattou, respectively) are irritated by the fondness of their relatives for the tam-tam: Mireille cannot stand listening to such music. As for Diatou, she refuses to go to the arena and watch the fights and dances to the sound of drums; in her eyes, they are synonymous with ignorance and backwardness (primitivism). Unlike their counterparts, the characters reject the therapeutic and regenerating aspect of music or of any traditional activity that involves the whole community. Both reject the celebrations based on traditional baptism, as these also oppose their aspirations to modernity and their systematic rejection of African traditions. The same goes for their refusal of motherhood through infanticide. This is merely an extension of their closing up to the social group to which they belong (or into which initially they have tried to integrate, as, for instance, in the case of the foreign spouse). This behavior characterizes almost all female characters of the novels of the first generation. These protagonists are in an urban, middle-class environment, and each voices her suffering and her frustrations without being aware of the more global aspects of her social environment.

Although the same behavior appears in *Fureurs et cris de femmes* by Angèle Rawiri and *Sous la cendre le feu* by Evelyne Mpoudi Ngolle, the reasons for its being there have changed, and the perspective of the narrative voice differs: It no longer constitutes a rejection of traditional culture but of specific elements limiting woman's lot in African society. For Emilienne *(Fureurs et cris)* and Mina *(Sous la cendre),* the child is secondary: A man, a husband, comes first and is the center of focus. Their behavior, therefore, constitutes a rebellion against mandatory motherhood; this rebellion includes demands that woman be acknowledged as a full member of her community and that marital love be defined and shared by both parties without the burden of family pressures. Some recurring themes thus appear in these first texts: a disappointing and unhappy love; a rejection of rituals, of marriage, and of motherhood; infanticide; depression, neurosis, and madness. More recent texts, which still use some of the same motifs, especially that of madness, illustrate a more powerful sense of rebellion than a sense of despair about woman's lot. In this case madness becomes a sign of collective active resistance; it is no longer synonymous with abandonment and self-confinement. Moreover, the narrative tone changes as the protagonist actively resists social pressure, searching not only for a personal solution but also for an alternative way of life that can be valid for her sisters, and beyond that, for the whole society of which she is a part.

In this regard, Werewere Liking, with her *Elle sera de jaspe et de corail,* can be considered a leading voice, for her writing takes on a visionary quality and she attributes a decidedly active role to woman and social changes:

> Starting with the preface, this book will oppose all the prognostications about "Black Africa is drifting, is not doing well" and all the pessimistic judgments, that, for decades, have been condemning this "unlucky continent." . . . Curiously, amusements will not consist in valorizing Africa; the other truths that we have been promised will improve on the first condemnations. And Lunai—a clear metaphor for Africa—will appear in this book like an infernal universe, taxed with all possible evils and miseries, a universe where men live silently, absent and ill. And this cynically clear-sighted game is organized around a "mysovire woman" who reacts against her "devirilized" fellow-citizens and critically follows the aberrations of her people.
>
> The text, however, opens onto an optimistic prophecy announcing a new Race, that of "children of air and fire, of jasper and coral," the children of an elite, correct in finally deciding to control their own destiny, as they have been able to free themselves from their ancestors and the complexes that restrained their fathers.
>
> *[Dès la préface, ce livre veut s'opposer à tous les pronostics concernant "l'Afrique noire mal partie. . . . L'Afrique mal partie" et à tous les jugements pessimistes qui, depuis des décennies, condamnent ce "continent guigné." . . . Curieusement, le divertissement ne consistera pas à valoriser l'Afrique; les autres vérités que l'on nous a promises renchériront évidemment sur les premières condamnations. Et Luna—L'Afrique évidemment—apparaîtra dans tout le livre comme un univers infernal,*

accablé de tares et de misères où les hommes vivent en silence, d'absen-
téisme et de maladie. Et ce jeu, cynique de lucidité, s'organise autour
d'une femme devenue "mysovire" par réaction contre ses concitoyens
"dévirilisés" et qui suit avec une attention critique les égarements de son
milieu.
   Le texte débouche néanmoins sur une prophétie optimiste qui an-
nonce l'avénement de la nouvelle Race, celle des "enfants de souffle et
de feu, de jaspe et de corail," descendance d'élite, précise en somme, car
enfin maîtresse de son destin pour avoir su se libérer des carcans qui im-
mobilisaient ses aînés et pour s'être affranchie des complexes qui em-
barrassaient ses pères.] (Liking 1983, 188)

Undoubtedly, such a path turns out to be difficult and cannot arise unless one passes first through a whole rethinking of the fundamental principles—cultural, religious, social, and political—on which life is based. In
the first place, this reconception requires a collective initiation and the use
of ritual. The mysovire in *Elle sera de jaspe et de corail* accomplishes these
different tasks. She rethinks language and even each word, thereby recreating the philosophical connotations of these words. She thinks of new
bases for history, religion, art, culture, desire, and the meaning of life.[6]

> And there cannot be a real life without desire
>   And there cannot be an Art without desire
>   . . . a desire for life
>   a desire for art
>   an art of desire (my translation)

> *[Et il ne peut y avoir une vraie vie sans désir*
>   *Et il ne peut y avoir Art sans désir*
>   *. . . un désir de vie*
>   *un désir d'art*
>   *un art du désir]* (Liking 1983, 65)

Richard Bjornson, in *The African Quest for Freedom and Identity,*
stresses the decisive factor for a new woman who reconnects with the
myth of origins:

> She [the narrative voice] discovers the key to the birth of this new race in
> her own womanhood. In mythological terms, she explains that woman
> first came into contact with the cosmic power of love and consciousness,
> but because she was afraid, she called man, who usurped the power, dis-
> torting its meaning and keeping it from her. Yet because woman experi-
> enced this power first, she retains the ability to enlighten man about its
> true meaning and to guide him out of the corrupt mental state into which
> his desire for dominance precipitated him. The new woman's message
> implies a world based on unselfish love, freedom from false construc-
> tions of reality and the creative urge that wells up in people who allow
> the cosmic force to work through them. (1991, 453)

It is on this very basis of a collective initiation, of the necessity of training the reader, and, most important, of rethinking and recreating woman that the texts of the new generation operate. Thus they are the concrete illustrations of the vision catalyzed by Werewere Liking and of the questions raised by Ken Bugul.

In Rawiri's *G'amàrakano* (1983), Toula invites us to ponder the objectification of woman-beauty within the framework of a consumer society. Ateba, Tanga, and Megri (in Beyala's *C'est le soleil* [1987], *Tanga* [1988], and *Seul le diable* [1990], respectively) point to woman's exploitation, to the artificiality and commodification of family and love relationships, and to the uncertain future of children in such a world. Finally, these characters demonstrate the need to create a new woman, and thus also a new man, who together will be able to lead tomorrow's world.

Emilienne, in *Fureurs et cris de femmes* (Rawiri 1989), broadens the debate about infertility and mandatory motherhood for African women and the difficulties for women of having professional lives. *La tache de sang* (Bassek 1990) deals with the generation gap by way of the different perspectives of mother and daughter.

A vol d'oiseau (Tadjo 1986) introduces fundamental questions about the meaning of life for women and the responsibility of each one for the emptiness and lack of vision that erode African societies. *Le royaume aveugle* (Tadjo 1990) indicates the steps leading to a radical change of life in a corrupt Africa. Both works offer concrete examples of what Africa is and will be as long as women do not play a more active part in political life.

We cannot fail to notice that the texts of the second generation of women writers display a more overt engagement with the social environment; it is no longer simply in the background but has come to play an active part in the story, just like any character in the novel. Echoing Evelyne Accad's analysis, I want to underline the African female authors' rise to political and social consciousness, a rise that parallels that of Arab women writers in their ways of rendering different examples of oppression in society. This development is also, I believe, the sign of an overt rebellion by female characters searching for themselves—even if the negative charge of the social context seems multiplied and the scope of the struggle considerably enlarged.

> And as the nature—and magnitude—of the obstacles becomes clearer, there is an increase in poignancy, anger, and at times, other-directed, even symbolic, rebellion. Even the negative responses of the characters in the later fiction—withdrawal, refusal to make the leap, suicide—appear to follow logically from an appreciation of the sweeping role of the social context in shaping individual behavior. What the characters discover is that they are not rebelling merely against a single custom, a particular

oppressor, but are facing the complex and total interrelationship between their own beings and the society that has shaped them. (Accad 1993, 250)

The novels of the 1990s are not limited to pointing an accusative finger at the aftermath of colonialism or simply to bearing testimony; they do, however, offer a new gaze turned to the future, actively reflecting on the elements necessary for a transformation of African society and a reevaluation of woman's status within that society. As a symbol of this creative approach, the narrative structure is tightly connected to this search for alternatives through the creation of polyphonic effects.

In this regard, in *Nouvelles écritures africaines,* Dabla identifies a number of textual principles that he sees as characteristic of the changes in the novel written by the second generation of male authors. In particular, he describes orality rendered by a multiplicity of dialogues, thus substituting the single dialogue and the palaver for the pure diegesis, mostly using the "narration of the griot."[7] Dabla also remarks that the daily chaotic universe in these works can be attributed to the propensity of African literature to cultivate "the monstrous, the savage," (in this respect, he quotes Thomas Melone and his theory of "teratology"), and to link it with "both artistic and magic practices" (1986, 211). The insertion of folk tales and myths that have been somewhat modified also creates an effect of circularity, of a well-rounded writing taking inspiration from its roots. In addition, Dabla sees narrative strategies in these novels that are similar to those in the "nouveau roman," especially the replacement of a single chronological and linear plot-story with "multiplicity and discontinuity" (220), that is, with a fragmentation of places; descriptions that are rarely subjective; a time frame that is vaguely accurate; and a "profusion of *flash-backs*, of dreams, oneiric times and daydreams" (221; my translation). Moreover, writers have introduced a new gaze in and on African literature, in particular through the new presence of the writer as a character, and a narrative voice that is identified and official, thus creating a constant interaction between writer/sender and receiver.

A number of these narrative techniques can be found in the African novel by women, particularly in those by Beyala, Liking, and Tadjo. There one can also find strong narrative voices and narratees, a focus on the dialogue with the readers, the creation of new myths and legends, the use of climactic effects through semantic and syntactic emphasis, all leading to the creation of a chaotic universe that is opposed by a visionary narrative.

Recurring Narrative Strategies: Multiplicity of Narrative Voices and Insertion of One or More Narratees

All the novels selected for this analysis have a complex narrative structure. Women writers have refined the basic tools of the genre of autobiography or semiautobiography by making the narration polyphonic—that is, by using multiple voices that echo and reply to each other and thus create an effect of mirroring and countermirroring for readers. This interplay of multiple narrative voices (for example, a diary or letter by one of the narrative voices may run through the main narration in fragments) combines with the multiple narratees and readers to add to the complexity of the form and reinforce the possibilities of communication between the sender and the receiver of the message.

With *Loukoum,* Beyala sets the narration in Paris, in the African community of Belleville immigrants. No longer do we have the usual theme of the uprooted African student in contact with the Western world, as found in novels from the time of independence. Instead, Beyala's subject is the African immigrant and his family who have come to settle in a country that seems promising. The writer gives an account of the disillusions of the husband, of his problems with adjustment, and of the changes for his wives and children as they discover a new way of thinking and living.

Beyond the geographic change, *Loukoum* makes an innovation on the narrative level: The novel is structured around the alternation of two male narrative voices—that of Loukoum, a seven-year-old boy who is the protagonist and homodiagetic narrator, and that of Abdou Traoré, "the honored father of Loukoum," [père vénéré de Loukoum] the intradiagetic narrator. The register of the father's voice as narrator contrasts sharply with both the child's voice and the father as a character in his interaction with his wives and Loukoum. There is a contrast in (social) style and register between his spoken language, as given through the child's account, and his poetic letters. Like the son, the father addresses a given reader. Like him, he uses a number of narrative strategies to maintain contact with his reader, using the tone of the griot to keep in touch with the past and the country of origin. Loukoum represents the new version of a griot, the modern griot of his family, the one whose gaze is directed at the current moment and the future.

The father, Abdou, openly addresses a white reader: Through his interjections and questions, he interrogates the other, the one who presides over his life against his will and without understanding him. The recipient of the letters, surnamed "L'ami" (my friend) and addressed as "toi" (you), is accused but also is asked about his way of being and of treating his own wife. Abdou attempts to establish a male-to-male closeness beyond the separations of race. As for Loukoum, he addresses a novice (white) reader and so offers didactic comments on African cultural specificities. The two gazes are simultaneously directed at the same scenes or situations. Loukoum gives a straightforward account of the facts of daily reality within the frame of a child's world. The father's gaze, in contrast, forms a screen through which matters sift. Only the essential remains when he analyzes an event as a global phenomenon, thus drawing conclusions for the future of the community and of Africa. The father's narrative voice contrasts with his professional status (streetsweeper, currently unemployed), thus offering two linguistic levels of address, one in his interaction with friends, wives, and children and another in his letters.

Loukoum is a modern version of Saint-Exupéry's Little Prince. Loukoum is the little prince of Belleville; he looks around and, like the Little Prince before him, comes to conclusions about the gratuitous nature of adults' actions. Writing plays a therapeutic role for the child, as for his father. He writes to kill time but also to forget and to flee his surroundings, and also, paradoxically, to have a better grasp of things:

> I watch television but I don't see nothing, I hear nothing. You'd think there were too many things inside my eyes clogging up my sight. So, to pass the time I started writing. I am writing a real book. About my life and one day, I tell myself, they'll make a movie out of it. (Beyala 1995, 167)

Loukoum's narrative voice also offers a humorous presentation of certain aspects of African life that are often misunderstood, particularly polygamy. In a family where there are two mothers, one is illegal in the eyes of French law. La Soumana's children are officially declared as the children of the other wife (M'am), who in this case is barren. The theme takes on an official quality as polygamy becomes a juridical question— Abdou is arrested for what is considered a fraudulent misappropriation of funds from the French welfare system; his children have been declared under one woman, which enables him to receive more child support.[8] As for the plot itself, the shock of the discovery that Loukoum is the child of neither of the two women justifies the child's narration; he directs it toward finding the identity of a mother that he does not know and thus reopens the chapter on mother-son relationships.[9]

By giving man a textual voice, Beyala enables the reader to explore the male perspective and the way the "other" sex functions. His behavior and ways of thinking are meticulously analyzed and deconstructed. In particular, the author examines the masculine concept of woman, of what she means for him, for his system of life. The father's voice, which is a poetic voice, reminds us of the legend about woman in *C'est le soleil*. The male child's voice shows women in their weaknesses, for the gaze of the child is straightforward, crudely honest, and without guile.[10]

Every woman whose life revolves around the child has a sad or tragic story. As with Beyala's previous novels, the story is anchored in the grayness of daily reality. It is still, as usual, a world of women within which a man and a child revolve. The only difference is that the viewpoint comes precisely from these two sources. The child offers a male gaze in his understanding of women, and also in his refusal to participate in house chores that he cannot do because of his status as a man.[11] Under the cover of a pseudo-child's voice, Beyala presents raw observations, apparently without drawing her own conclusions.[12] The child thus directs another type of gaze at women, noting their activities, emotions, and troubles within the daily routine.[13] The gaze that the child casts on adults and on the relationships between man and woman brings out the incongruity and paradoxes of what they say and do. The pseudo-child's voice draws the reader's attention to a given problem as unresolvable or incomprehensible. Hence, the reader is encouraged to interact and participate in considering the matter (and to consider it as an adult thought to be in a position to explain). The voice of the child also functions to report the official discourse; for instance, Loukoum takes down the media's report on his father's arrest. He writes in capital letters:

A FAMILY OF IMMIGRANTS REGISTERS FALSE BIRTHS AND DI-
VERTS SEVERAL MILLION CENTIMES FROM FAMILY BENEFITS.
(Beyala 1995, 167)

In contrast, the father recounts a situation and the evolution of the situation. Through his voice, a number of questions are raised about the status of immigrants and the role of women in their adjusting to life in a foreign country. The opening discourse gives an account of his discouragement, his bitterness, his malaise in facing life in France. The second letter in particular introduces the motif of twenty years of exile and the resulting disappointment. With this in mind, he recalls the situation in his country and the discourse that was held on France as the promised land of fortune and success:

Mouths would whisper hope: Money! Money! It is there in that transparent country across the seas, amidst the cars, the candelabras and the cracked walls. . . . Mouths would say: There's money, millions to be gathered everywhere, with your head, with your heart, with your behind. (Beyala 1995, 10)

The metaphors and ellipses at the end of the sentence clearly refer to making money by selling one's body, literally and figuratively. In effect, Beyala introduces a change of theme here: Africans (men and women) leaving for Paris not to study but to earn a living. This change of focus also indicates an evolution in the African novel itself in that she alters the almost fixed thematic about the intellectual African elite.

The third letter directly addresses a white and French interlocutor. For this interlocutor (reader), Abdou underlines bits of truth about his life as an immigrant. In particular, he recounts the instant contempt to which he is exposed because of his status as an immigrant:

> At the border patrol you registered my body and wrapped it in contempt, in hatred. In your wide-open eyes I was already suspected of rape or of murder. Obsessed with sex. A pile of mud charged with obstructing memories and propagating AIDS. (Beyala 1995, 20)

We see his marginalization, entrapped as he is between two types of attitudes and two cultures. The interjections to his interlocutor indicate a certain responsibility in his self-denigration, recalling the times of colonization and what the interlocutor's ancestors did to Abdou's country. But these observations are also a ground for dialogue, for trying to explain the reasons for polygamy. In this way, the male narrative voice introduces the leading theme of his observations—woman and her ambiguity as a contact point with this foreign culture. Woman is also looked at in terms of her vital importance for man. As his savior, she is the only solid mooring he has in this foreign world where he is wandering:

> A heavy sob sits on the edge of my eye. I clasp on to her breast, her belly, the warm fleece of her sex, as if on to a new land, a new dawn. And for me these images reinvent the legends of yore in a mystical farandole. (Beyala 1995, 35)

Because of his status as an immigrant, man reveals his position of extreme vulnerability and fragility, as if he were a crying child. It is through woman and in her that man can exist; woman creates man and she is the reason why he can continue to live: "Woman is my drug. I never get tired of it" (Beyala 1995, 65).

Thus, sexuality and love find all their justifications through man's voice; they are vital elements both in maintaining his sanity and in keeping his identity. Outside of love and sexuality, man feels that he is excluded from society. In explaining the meaning of woman, the immigrant man tries to engage in a dialogue where he extends his hand to bridge the gap between him and his interlocutor. Behind this attempt lies his desire to be understood and acknowledged as a complete being.

His recurring evocation of woman introduces another important narrative thread that shows the discrepancy between man and woman in facing their exile. Woman is searching for a new freedom; she discovers other ways of being and of doing things as a woman and as a spouse (hence undergoes some physical changes that man does not understand). In contrast, man resists changes and displays nostalgia in this new society. Because he feels lost in this world, he prefers to look to the past, and he becomes unable to communicate his suffering to women—who no longer listen to him.

The exchange with his interlocutor takes on a new twist: The rhetorical questions cease and give way to real questions. These are man-to-man questions (as they echo the ones that men ask each other throughout the story—Kouam and Abdou, Ndongala and Kouam). In particular, Abdou asks the white man about his marital relationship:

> I wonder how you mask your jealousy. Your understanding escapes me.
> . . . Enveloped in madness I imagine your jealousy and your grudges,
> which you must swallow in order not to seem reactionary. (Beyala 1995,
> 117)

Man is trying to establish an atmosphere of complicity and closeness through a solidarity of the sexes. Power between narrator and narratee also changes to become a warning from the former to the latter. The African narrator describes what will happen if the white man does not pay attention to the situation. He proceeds to underline the dangers of woman's emancipation. Through this speech, he hopes to gain the white man's support and put pressure on the white woman, who in turn will speak to the African woman. This is his last resort in trying to see "things return to normal." He makes a new distinction in his relations with the white woman as opposed to the African woman. Even Pigalle women make him feel his difference. Their gazes overlook him, for he is transparent and does not exist. He thereby discovers a need to create a woman according to his own imagination, a woman who would meet his needs not only sexually but also affectively.

> And then Star came. She came out of my imagination so that the dream
> would survive. . . . And so Star came. A small brunette with sunshine hair
> in the black forest of time. . . . She wouldn't speak. Out of decency and
> because of a proper education. Submissive. Never triumphant. Nor rebel-
> lious. (Beyala 1995, 127)

This image disappears with the arrival of a real woman of flesh and blood who can fulfill his needs: "The M'am arrived. The image disappeared" (127). Then, because M'am evolves and no longer fits his idealized representation, the need for an image reappears.

This need has become all the more important because the West is infiltrating his house, not only through his wives but, more immediately, through his son. The generation gap opens between immigrants and their children, who assimilate more deeply into the other culture. In the end, the narrative male voice of the father becomes silent, as he has admitted his vulnerability and the dangers of madness threatening him. His narrative voice is then replaced by direct dialogues between M'am and Abdou. The time of the narration corresponds to a time of apprenticeship, of man's apprenticeship to love, of his effort to listen to woman's voice.

Maman a un amant plays on the alternation of two narrative voices. The difference between this novel and *Loukoum* lies in the fact that in

Maman a un amant the voices alternate between Loukoum's and his mother's, M'am. Abdou's voice is now perceived and filtered through the child's and the mother's/the spouse's. Another difference worth noting concerns the gender difference of the voices. M'am's letters are not hers directly, as she cannot write, but are the result of Loukoum's translation. M'am's letters are more pragmatic and to the point. They revolve strictly around her personal situation. Unlike Abdou, she does not extrapolate or draw conclusions about the African woman's general situation and status. It is only indirectly, almost retrospectively, that some conclusions can be drawn. In rendering both woman's and man's writing and discourse according to commonly perceived stereotypical differences, Beyala invites us to ponder these common perceptions: Male writing and discourse are represented as clear, analytical, synthetic, whereas female thoughts appear more pragmatic, less refined and elaborate, yet more convoluted.[14]

Each of M'am's interventions constitutes a stage in her life: how she met Abdou, why she decided to follow him, her ensuing disappointment regarding France, her suffering from being barren, and the deterioration of their relationship. The same events are evoked, but from M'am's viewpoint: La Soumana's arrival, what she first represented (a rival), then the children that, indirectly, she brought her. She then recounts her change in spirit, her lack of feelings for Abdou, and in the end, her emptiness. We knew her emotional state in *Loukoum,* but here it is cast in a new light, presented from the perspective of the dominated person. This perspective does not change the general structure, for, like Abdou, M'am addresses an identified interlocutor, the equivalent of Abdou's: a white woman, the spouse/partner of Abdou's interlocutor, whom M'am calls, similarly to Abdou, "L'Amie" (My [female] friend).

The novel is in all senses a sequel to *Loukoum:* The first few pages are a summary of the preceding novel with a reminder about the characters. Through M'am's voice, Beyala goes back to some of Abdou's comments, his thoughts, even his questions addressed to his interlocutor. This time, woman speaks out and gives her own version of the same facts. Again, Loukoum serves as an intermediary, giving caustic comments about adults' behavior through his translations and inside jokes addressed to his own reader. However, he shows a higher degree of subjectivity toward M'am then he did previously toward Abdou. The gaze is definitely male and judgmental. When the woman aspires to a certain freedom, Loukoum's reprobation betrays the general feeling of the entire community of Malian immigrants, thereby expressing gender solidarity among men. In addition, there is a striking difference between the two novels that must be stressed. The ending of *Loukoum* illustrates an evolution of the couple Abdou and M'am in reaching happiness (and, by extrapolation, we are led to believe in the construction of a new ethics between man and woman); the later

Maman a un amant demonstrates that the paths to happiness are more than complex and, most important, that they respond to one definition of happiness, and that is a male one.

Finally, man is shown again with his two faces—the *soft* man and the *tough* man—but in the later novel these are fused into the same mold, that of the mutilated, weak, and vulnerable man who uses his weakness as affective bribery, trying to force his woman to abandon her aspirations for the benefit of the community (woman's own benefit is, of course, excluded from the discussion). Through the interplay of the two systems of narrative voices, Beyala reformulates the question of a new sexual ethics within the couple, raising doubts about man's sincerity in his desire to change. In fact, M'am's letters and Loukoum's commentary on her behavior reveal her disorientation and dissatisfaction, her frustrations and her need for love. The legend about woman that was introduced in *The Sun* reappears here in order to be revised: Man did not merely ask woman to stay on earth, he kept her in slavery without caring for her well-being, simulating an absolute need for her, pretending, by some act of attention, that he had responded to her needs and fulfilled his duties as a man.

I am tracing here a double transitive discourse: one on the microtext, that is, on *Loukoum* and *Maman a un amant,* the other on the macrotext, that is, Beyala's entire works. Through the constant interplay between narrative voices (male voice/child voice; female voice/child voice) the same reality is revisited and revised; in that process we are pointed back through a series of indirect references to the previous texts. The legend introduced in *The Sun* is reproduced in the fifth novel, but it is no longer the same.

The grandmother's words to Abdou convey a different meaning than what was initially said in the legend: The atavistic comparison between woman and child reappears; like the child, woman must be forgiven and comforted. But she must also set an example.

> My daughter, you are the light of this house. You are its life. Whatever suffering your husband may inflict on you, you shouldn't stoop to imitate him. You should maintain your dignity. Don't ever forget. You are the superior spirit that should guide the man.
>
> [*Ma fille, tu es la lumière dans cette maison. Tu es la vie. Quelles que soient tes souffrances que te fait endurer ton mari, tu ne dois pas t'abaisser à l'imiter. Tu dois rester digne. N'oublie jamais. Tu es l'esprit supérieur qui doit guider l'homme.*] (Beyala 1993, 296)

Advised by the traditional female voice of the grandmother, reconciliation takes place in front of the entire African community. M'am and Abdou fall into each other's arms while everyone else cheers and claps: All is well that ends well. Woman returns to her home and the position that is hers.[15]

Happiness has a price: The price in this case is nothing less than M'am's sacrifice, a sacrifice born of love for her children as she resigns herself to returning, empty-hearted, to her husband. The final pages show the whole community's exultation as they see her back on the "right track."

> Only the spirit of the tribe counts.
> I baked a pie for my parents. What would our lives be without women, children and trees? They are our guides. I repeat it to you verbatim, having heard it straight from the intellectual N'dongala. It's true. . . . My Dad is feeling his oats again and M'am shivers in front of him like some Scarlett and everything around them goes soft and fuzzy like an illusion. They're happy, those Belleville negroes with their love that bloodies them like a setting sun.

> *[Seul l'esprit de la tribu compte.*
> *J'ai cuisiné une tarte en l'honneur de mes parents. Que seraient nos vies sans les femmes, les enfants et les arbres? Ils sont nos balises. je te le dis texto, vu que l'intellectuel Ndongala me l'a dit. C'est vrai, mon papa reprend du poil de la bête et M'am frissonne devant lui comme une Scarlett, et tout est limpide autour d'eux comme une illusion. Ils sont heureux ces Nègres de Belleville, avec leur amour qui les ensanglante comme un coucher de soleil.]* (Beyala 1993, 298)

The end leaves us with a bitter aftertaste: The *happy ending* is to be read ironically, for the happiness of some is achieved with the sacrifice of another; and since the beginning of time, the sacrifice has always been woman's.

The last word is taken away from her in an important symbolic gesture; woman loses her narrative voice and her authority. She is reduced to an indirect intervention of Loukoum's. If the conclusion is expressed by a pseudo-child's voice, it is nonetheless overtly male. Woman's history is no longer her story but spoken only under man's supervision. Consequently, the narration assumes a new dimension within the whole body of Beyala's work. The interplay of narrative voices, the novelty of a male textual voice, and then the disappearance of the female narrative voice indicate the difficulties of equal sharing of power and speaking. The question of power, and of a possible new ethics between the sexes, thus reappears, having been directly inscribed in the narration in order to be questioned. Beyala therefore produces two discourses, one on the microtext (*Loukoum and Maman a un amant*), the other on her own corpus. She thus forces us to a new reassessment of man-woman relationships and leads us to anticipate any possible clues about sexual ethics in her next text.

In Beyala's *Loukoum* and *Maman a un amant,* I have examined an elaborate narrative structure based on multiple narrators. Multiple narratees constitute another equally complex system. *Juletane* and *Tanga* are especially representative of the complex interaction between multiple narrative voices and narratees. Besides the therapeutic value that writing represents for Juletane,[16] the entire narrative benefits from the combination of an inserted diary with two given narratees. One of these narratees, Mamadou, is identified, official, and named. The other, Hélène, is unofficial and unknown to the narrator. The reading of Juletane's personal diary, not by the intended narratee but by the unidentified one, produces a dual effect. On the one hand, it illustrates the vain effort of Juletane, who hopes that through her husband's reading of her diary, he will be forced to confront his responsibility for her suffering; she looks for revenge through his reading, hoping that he will grasp Juletane's responsibility in the death of Awa's children. The irony is that Mamadou dies before he can read the diary, thus depriving her of this satisfaction. On the other hand, the reading of Juletane's diary by fragments forces Hélène to think about her own life and confront it.

In the presence of a reader, Hélène creates a space of identification and a possible way to avoid madness. This mad woman is not us; if there is empathy and identification, it is with the other, the reader in the text. As such, Hélène constitutes a safeguard because of her paramedical status and also because she is the proof for the possibility of a positive experience for an Antillean or foreign woman in Africa. Juletane's diary, however, has a therapeutic effect on Hélène, who is finally able to break the barriers constraining her. Thus if the diary did not play the ultimate role that it was supposed to for its narrator, it nevertheless does have a salutary effect on its reader, thereby signaling the same possibility for us readers. Thus the novel reveals a complex multilayered narrative text.

Warner-Vieyra (1988) further explores the potentials of such narrative combinations in *Femmes échouées,* particularly in "Les naufragés," which shows a diary that takes on a different value depending on the identity of the reader. There too, as in her previous novels, Warner-Vieyra plays with her characters' madness and thus also with the possibility of multiple voices. This twofold aspect of the diary as escape and testimony can also be found in Gad Ami's *Etrange héritage* (1985); the letter there is to be understood both as a heritage left to Déla's son and as her obsessive recalling of the past.

As for Calixthe Beyala, she excels in the elaboration of a polyphonic narrative structure. Her texts take on certain narrative forms, themselves symbolic of the impossibility of being and of the protagonist's "jouissance" (in the Barthesian sense). For instance, this jouissance is in the multiplicity of female narrative voices ("the voice,"[17] Ateba) in *The Sun,* to which a multiplicity of female narratees responds (woman/women, God, Irène, Betty). Jouissance is also manifested through the constant interaction between the two voices—Tanga's and Anna-Claude's—in *Tanga,* where the borders between the two roles blur; they are both the locutor and the interlocutor, the teacher and the learner. These different strategies act as buffers with the purpose of attenuating the spectacle of suffering and horror. At the same time, the relay of voices creates an echoing effect in the text. As in an ancient tragic Greek drama, a lamenting chorus is present.

Like writing, the dialogue becomes a refuge and acts as therapy. Writing becomes an erotic process, a special space for exchanges and contacts between narrator(s) and narratee(s), between author and reader. In the very process of Tanga's narrating and transmitting her story to Anna-Claude, the two women succeed in forgetting about the surrounding physical and psychological violence. Tanga and Anna-Claude forge new ties that make up for the missing family structure: Anna-Claude is both the mother and the daughter of Tanga. She is the one who comforts; she is also the one who listens. However, their discourse also bears the mark of desire, each discovering in the other the lover that she could never find. To transmit one's story to the other is for them an expression of radical rebellion against human violence, against man and patriarchy. Deprived of love, the two women manage to leave the vicious circle in which they have been imprisoned by creating a new discourse of their own. The presence of a narratee in constant interaction with the narrator breaks with the usual norms of discourse; the limits between active writer and passive receiver become blurred and dissolve through the narrative process. Beyond the principle of total empathy that acts as therapy, the discourse takes on a new dimension: The personal becomes political. Here, the denunciation of patriarchal norms in society is written between the lines.

The use of these different narrative techniques, such as the multiplication of narrators and narratees, enables the authors to build a system of polyphonic voices intended to create two real dialogues: an interactive listening process between women and a dialogue between man and woman. These are both premises for elaborating a new sexual ethics and new behaviors between the sexes, between one and the other.

Notes

1. The foregoing paragraph is part of the article by Christiane Makward, with Odile Cazenave on Francophone women's writing: "The Others' Others:'Francophone' Women and Writing" *Yale French Studies* 75 (1988): 190–206.

2. Stratton quotes Millet (Kate Millet, *Sexual Politics* [London: Hart-Davies, 1971]) in defining the patriarchal archetype: "A social institution, patriarchy functions according to the two principles that 'male shall dominate female' and 'elder male shall dominate younger' (Millet 25), its purpose being to regulate the sexual life of the dominated to the advantage of the dominator."

3. See Eileen Julien's article (1991); see also Rhonda Cobham ("Misengendering the Nation: African Nationalist Fictions and Nuruddin Farah's *Maps, in Na-*

tionalisms and Sexualities, ed. Andrew Parker, Mary Russo, Doris Sommer, and Patricia Yaeger [New York: Routledge, 1992], 42–59) on the relationship between nationalism and sexuality and its narrative and thematic consequences.

4. In this regard, Stratton refers to Katherine Frank's (1984) discussion of the Western feminist critical apparatus and its relevance to African texts: "Judgment is passed in accordance with sociological and moral rather than aesthetic criteria" (Stratton 1988, 36). She also quotes Lloyd Brown for an assessment of stereotypical criticism toward women writers: "The critics have treated the [women] writers as if the novels, plays, short stories and poems are simply political tracts, or anthropological studies. In so doing they ignore the extent to which such works should be approached as committed works of art in which theme or social vision is integrated with an effective sense of design and language" (Stratton 1988, 12).

5. Stratton refers in this respect to Claire Rosenfeld (via Gilbert and Gubar's 1970 analysis): "The novelist who consciously or unconsciously exploits psychological Doubles' frequently juxtaposes two characters, the one representing the socially acceptable or conventional personality, the other externalizing the free, uninhibited, often criminal self" (Gubar 1970, 314).

6. Liking has tried in her own life to apply these new principles: She believes in the primordial force of art and ritual in the process of regenerating a society that has been slipping away. She has to that end created a village community of African artists from all parts of the African continent. Through their work, these artists enable the community to thrive, some of them acting in ritual theater, others sewing and preparing the costumes, and others making artifacts that will be used during the performance and/or that will be sold after the performance.

7. He uses as an example Liking's 1983 *Elle sera de jaspe et de corail* with its combination of four voices plus that of the mysovire, which "calls for the reader's attention, organizes the discourse and how it will be received" (Dabla 1986, 220).

8. With this case Beyala is alluding to an incident that occurred in summer 1991: Right-wing politicians called into question the right of immigrant families to family allocations of welfare benefits. Their argument was that these families received more money in allocations than French families because of their large number of children from different spouses, whereas the French judicial system does not allow polygamy.

9. To accomplish this, Beyala explores the relationship between parents and children from a new viewpoint. The family structure is the focus of the story, but she stresses both its aberration and its internal force. The polygamous family illustrates the extreme case: The family unit grows as the narration progresses (Mam'zelle Esther becomes pregnant and assumes a new status, that of mother; then Aminata, Loukoum's real mother, arrives on the scene). In addition, that the children are declared under M'am's name but are really Soumana's creates a power struggle between the two. Each one uses it to her advantage at different times. Besides, Mam'zelle Esther, and Aminata even more, belong to the world of prostitution. The family revolves at the periphery of this world, for which the café and Monsieur Kaba are the patent signs. Hence the numerous descriptions of and discussions on the prostitute, approached by Beyala with two different male perspectives.

10. For example, as Loukoum develops affection for Aminata, his narrative voice admits this new feeling and acknowledges his new happiness to be with her. The voice also recognizes M'am's love for him, all her courage, strength, and determination.

11. The child's voice gives an account of the distribution of roles, of his nascent feeling of being a man; for instance, he would not overdo it in helping M'am, since he is a man.

12. For instance, the following scene presents a case of parataxis, that is, an absence of logical articulation. But the juxtaposition of sentences induces readers to draw their own conclusions: "Father has gone for several days. He doesn't come back home and Miss Esther has disappeared as well. She no longer comes swimming with me. The women are talking among themselves. M'am prays, that's all she does, pray. And Soumana is angry. Sometimes she says: 'I won't calm down till I've killed him'" (*Loukoum,* Beyala 1995, 55).

13. "At home the women are talking. They get up, they're chattering. They wash the floor, they're chattering, they cook, they're chattering" (Beyala 1995, 60).

14. See the analysis by Elaine Hoffman Baruch, "He Speaks/She Speaks: Language in Some Medieval Literature," in *Women, Love and Power: Literary and Psychoanalytic Perspectives* (New York: New York University Press, 1991), 31–51.

15. The fact that it is a woman who is traditionally respected because of her old age is symbolic and shows that the tradition has been maintained, that certain rituals regarding woman are administered by other women, and that they participate in the patriarchal system (e.g., genital operations).

16. In this regard, see Béatrice Didier's analysis, *Le journal intime* (Paris: PUF, 1976).

17. "The voice" continually gives the reader feedback on Ateba's actions. At times, she (definitely a female voice) comments; at times she gives a subjective interpretation of Ateba's motivations; at times, she can be interpreted as Ateba's conscience; at times, she appears more like our own conscience.

8

Writing's Political Role: Shock Therapy

I am not writing to you today in order to speak of our miseries, but of several means to escape them. . . . I am not speaking of despair. I am speaking life. I am writing this book for an Africa that is being forgotten, for Africa in its long slumber.

[Aujourd'hui, je n'écris pas pour vous parler de nos misères, mais de quelques moyens pour y échapper. . . . Je ne parle pas de désespoir. Je parle vie. J'écris ce livre pour une Afrique qu'on oublie, pour l'Afrique au long sommeil.]

—Calixthe Beyala (*Assèze l'Africaine*, 20)

Portraying a corrupt African world seems to be the subject par excellence of male writers of the 1980s. Bernard Nanga's *Les chauves-souris* (1980); Valentin Nga Ngondo's *Les puces* (1984); Mongo Beti's *Les deux mères de Guillaume Ismaël Dzewatama, futur camionneur* (1983) and its sequel, *La revanche de Guillaume Ismaël Dzewatama* (1984); and Firmin Bekombo's *J'attends toujours* (1989) are exemplars of the bitter critique of contemporary Africa that stresses the continent's malaise. They all denounce the pettiness and corruption of the bourgeois elite, the hypocrisy and distortion of traditions, the burden of the family, and the readaptation and reintegration of Africans who return after studying abroad. These novels have typically been written in a caustic, if not vitriolic, style.

Female writers have taken a different approach in their social criticism. True, they offer examples of women's oppression at different levels of African society, but women, unlike their male colleagues, search for possible alternatives to and a way out of a desperately static and pessimistic mode of thinking. Writing about this approach in "Les femmes et l'écriture-parole," Borgomano underscores the power in the tone and direction of the new novels by women.

Recent women's novels often preserve traces of the engagement that has long been a force in African literature. Their works are still novels of

215

protest and contestation. However, they do not give in to the monological temptation. Instead, these novels are characterized by their dialogical writing and integration of multiple heterogeneous voices. There is no omnipotent narrator with its fictional authority used to impose a single reading with only one meaning. (1994, 88; my translation)

These novelists move beyond the world of corruption and violence in order to reflect on the foundations of a more promising world. This move engenders the visionary conception of social relations that appears, for instance, in Tadjo's (1990) *Le royaume aveugle* or in the development of the new sexual ethic that we have seen in Beyala's work. These works present a political program in the guise of strategies and techniques that are fundamentally unorthodox. As we have seen in previous chapters, marginal characters and the exploration of taboos are essential components.

More important, this writing gains new strength from its depiction of an atmosphere tinged with anguish, horror, and passion. Dabla stresses the frequency of images and semantic networks associated with violence. He relates this device to the "thematic and esthetic 'obligation of violence' that takes shape in the corpus" (1986, 240). He explains how these leitmotifs of excess function on two levels at the same time, for the readers and for the writer.

> . . . this "narrative tumult" that charms the reader and provokes disgust or fear in him. At the same time it is the writer who furiously frees herself from the grief and malaise arising from her sensitivity to deplorable situations. These liberating excesses are meant once and for all to attain some matter of redemption and thus seem like acts of contrition. . . . It is now a matter of "leaving the swamps and the filth" and undertaking "the cure . . . and the immersion in the sacred speech" of purification. (240; my translation)

I will now take up how women writers actually portray violence in all its varying nuances, as laden with physical and psychological suffering—anguish, extreme horror, and pain.

The Anguish of Emptiness

Bugul's The Abandoned Baobab

The first part of Ken Bugul's *The Abandoned Baobab*, "Ken's Pre-History," begins as a reflection on life through the figure of the father.

> You have to ask yourself how the world worked without expecting any answers. Events inevitably follow upon events every day of your life. You can dream your life, but you can't dream your reality. Daily life only takes shape gradually through individual moments.

The formulas fail to coincide. Lost, being runs wild in reflection, meditation. Notions are formed, ideas abound, projections spread, comparisons compare. Each one frays an empty path, but their flight inspires creation, and to create is to fill the void, man's only real enemy. (Bugul [1983] 1991, 22)

"Ken's History" becomes an illustration of the second passage. Ken's wanderings in Belgium, her attempts to flee from her history, and her identity quest translate into the protagonist's need to realize a dream that she thinks will be able to fill an indefinable void. Her dearest dream, that of being like white people, is the very thing that causes the disintegration of her identity. Irène d'Almeida (1994b) admirably illustrates that Ken's general detachment results from the departure of her mother when she was a child. She appears to lack basic points of reference, when in fact she continues to think of her native village and several moments spent with her mother and her grandmother, using them as basic points that anchor her identity. The identity crisis she experiences in Belgium is just an extension of this emotional emptiness that she feels in the absence of maternal and familial love. As d'Almeida points out, Bugul is attracted to the most negative and pathological aspects of the West. Her dreams have been fabricated in accordance with these distortions.

Ken's entire experience in Europe is actually characterized by the dispersal and fragmentation of her identity. She makes a series of discoveries that are signs of her tutelage in "Toubab" life but that are also stages of growing awareness. The first stage in this development occurs when she discovers the great similarities between each woman's lived experience; like her, Leonora had to have an abortion.

Ken's feminine and feminist identity has been awakened. This awareness anticipates the experience of Beyala's protagonists, even if Ken's new awareness is "a conclusion she reaches only by way of a nearly total alienation from self, from family and from society" (d'Almeida 1994b, 47). The second stage begins when Ken discovers her constant dissatisfaction and a feeling of emptiness that she cannot explain. From this point, she lives in the mode of the "apparently happy" until she begins to ask herself some basic questions, including those she would rather avoid: who she is, why she is doing what she is doing, why she is feeling so lonely, in what ways she is missing the reassuring presence of her mother.

Ken believes that organizing parties and meeting new people—the same ones who will later introduce her to the world of drug dealers and prostitution—are ways to escape this growing void, but they are merely attempts to escape her loneliness. A temporary return to Africa for her father's funeral brings no comfort and instead only confirms her desire to continue in the process of estrangement: "I spent two weeks of gloom telling myself that it wasn't here either that I would find the eternal dream.

I had to turn around and let eternal torment begin again instead" (Bugul [1983] 1991, 79). In *Elle sera de jaspe et de corail,* Werewere Liking also identifies a lack of passion and overall lack of interest as the source of the sickness that is devouring modern African and Western society. This illness is characterized by the belief that consumption and its objects have been able to replace life's meaning and the need to define oneself.[1]

The story leads up to the climactic point of Ken's nervous breakdown. As the plot advances, the artificial nature of her life and the aspirations she has invented for herself become more and more obvious and finally lead to her inability even to dream. At this point, Bugul refuses to continue to fool herself. She interrupts the process of self-destruction in order to return to Africa.

We have come full circle with Ken's return to her point of departure. In the meantime, Ken has been able to realize that what she was desperately seeking somewhere else, the key to this empty feeling that afflicted her, could be found within herself and was closely related to her traumatic separation from her mother. In *Journeys Through the French African Novel,* Mildred Mortimer examines this point by taking up the meaning of Ken's return to Africa and by asking if it amounts to a victory or a failure. She considers it a victory: By transcribing her experiences and going back over the course she followed, Ken has succeeded in confronting her trauma and anxieties.

> The final chapter not only confirms her victory but attests to the power of the word. Throughout her narrative, Ken uses the process of writing as therapy. She focuses on loss—the loss of maternal love in Africa, the broken dream of assimilation in Europe—as her life spirals downward. . . . The journey and its written record come together at the same point. The protagonist attains lucidity and conquers solitude by concluding the written record of her spiritual and physical journey. (Mortimer 1990, 176)

Ken Bugul was the first African female novelist to ask direct questions about biculturism and about integration and assimilation in Western society, both as a woman and as a black person. (She repeatedly refers to herself as a black woman.) With her, we can see the African woman's growing awareness of her identity in terms of race and gender. In fact, Ken Bugul's work ushers in a new kind of African writing. It is new in the dimensions of its voice and in the language that she uses. In her latest novel, Beyala continues this exploration of feminine identity in relation to dreams and aspirations but also in relation to this feeling of emotional emptiness.

Beyala's Assèze l'Africaine

Assèze displays an even sharper awareness of the emptiness and the lack of direction in her life. From the beginning, she defines herself negatively; she has no occupation or passion and, once again, is dependent on man.

During the day, I don't practice any pastime like music or painting. I am not interested in makeup or dressing up either. I live in Paris and I don't have a garden. When my husband eats, I am hungry. When he goes to bed, I am sleepy. When people visit us, they only talk to my husband and that's fine with me.

[Dans la journée, je ne m'adonne à aucun passe-temps comme la musique ou la peinture. Je ne m'intéresse pas plus aux toilettes et aux fards. J'habite à Paris et je n'ai pas de jardin. Quand mon mari mange, j'ai faim. Quand il se couche, j'ai sommeil. Lorsque les gens nous rendent visite, ils ne parlent qu'à mon époux et ça m'arrange.] (Préface, Beyala 1994)

Assèze's experience and reflections give way to a critical assessment of the situation in Africa.

All of these weaknesses must have influenced my personality. I don't think that they justify my behavior. I am not looking for any extenuating circumstances for my actions. I am not writing to you today to speak of our miseries, but of some means to escape them.

[Toutes ces infirmités on dû avoir une influence sur ma personnalité. Je ne crois pas qu'elles justifient mon comportement. Je ne cherche pas des circonstances atténuantes à mes actes. Aujourd'hui, je n'écris pas pour vous parler de nos misères mais de quelques moyens pour y échapper.] (Beyala 1994, 19)

The change in the possessive adjective, from the first-person singular to the first-person plural, marks the tie between the personal and the collective and between Assèze's destiny and that of Africa in general. The narration actually becomes an excuse to introduce a series of portraits of contemporary African men and women who represent many different facets of society.

I had acted in the midst of chaos, imitating the various possibilities for success and other vanities of that nature. I was like Africa as it makes its decisions. I would act on the spur of the moment, without any mature reflection. I was up shit creek more than ever before and I could see all the shit.

[J'avais agi dans le flou, miroitant des possibilités de réussite et autres vanités du même genre. J'étais comme l'Afrique dans ses décisions, j'agissais au coup par coup, sans mûre réflexion. . . . Plus que jamais, j'étais dans la merde, et je voyais cette merde.] (Beyala 1994, 315)

These tableaux and portraits illustrate a state of crisis in which, once more, women are the ones who see the reality of the situation while men continue to cradle themselves in illusions. As in Beyala's first three novels, the protagonist has no known father and comes from the remnants of a family; it includes her grandmother and her mother, who later gives birth to "a fibroma of the male sex" [un fibrome de sexe masculin] (Beyala 1994, 154) whose father is also unknown. In this survival-based world that links Africa to France and rural space to the urban milieu, the narrative voice trumpets its dissatisfaction and desire for success. Each time Assèze examines herself, her experiences, her sisters, the behavior of men (Awono, Paul, Océan, Ousmane, Alexander), Beyala reassesses relations between men and women, their dreams for success, and the threatening difficulties of the contemporary world. Sorraya, the countess, Amina, and Assèze each illustrates her respective strategy for confronting emptiness. The countess represents the young prostitute who has managed to acquire a certain respectability. As the mistress to the rich businessman, Awono, she has figured out how to exploit the system.

> The Countess liked to talk money. . . . The Countess didn't believe in feelings. . . . She had a heart somewhere, but life isn't about the heart.
>
> *[La Comtesse aimait parler sous. . . . La Comtesse ne croyait pas aux sentiments. . . . Elle avait du coeur, au fond. Mais la vie n'est pas une question de coeur.]* (Beyala 1994, 82-83)

Amina illustrates a different kind of determination. She displays a certain resignation as she faces a life of daily humiliations inscribed upon her body. With her stunted arms, spindly legs, and flattened hips, she has aged beyond her years and failed to obtain the same benefits as Sorraya in doing so, that is, "money, happiness, men, clothes and food." [l'argent, le bonheur, les hommes, les vêtements et la nourriture] (Beyala 1994, 98). Nevertheless, she displays great lucidity in judging the country's political situation and difficult economic conditions. She proleptically announces a social and political upheaval along with a hope for revenge on the profiteers.

Sorraya presents, one after the other, a number of different questions. With her narrative voice she uses her changes to introduce the questions of education and the proper milieu for raising a daughter. Sorraya's character allows us to examine some young African girls' dreams, such as finding success by resembling a white woman or becoming a classical ballet dancer. Sorraya's accumulated imitative expressions, gestures, speaking habits, and tastes in reading and music are a more emphatic version of Diattou's preoccupations in *L'appel des arènes* and Ken's in *The Abandoned Baobab*. Like Ken, her character evolves toward self-alienation and the growing awareness of an emptiness that she is powerless to fill.

> I have lived all my life, my ass between two seats. I tried to ape the White man. It's not my fault! In Africa, they made us believe that we were backward and, me, I believed it. I wanted to gallicize myself and shed any traces of blackness within me, because blackness is dirt. Blackness is

misery. Black is a curse. I was upset with myself for being African. I wanted to be like Dupont or Durant. It was ridiculous.

[Toute ma vie, j'ai vécu le cul entre deux chaises. J'ai essayé de singer le Blanc. C'est pas de ma faute! En Afrique, on nous faisait croire que nous étions des arriérés et moi, j'y ai cru. Je voulais me franciser, désincruster toute trace de noir en moi. Parce que le noir, c'est la saleté. Le noir c'est la misère. Le noir c'est la malédiction. Je m'en voulais d'être africaine. Je voulais ressembler à Dupont, à Durant. C'était ridicule.] (Beyala 1994, 333)

You thought that I felt superior to you because I didn't feel inferior to any men. I would have wanted so much to be one of you. You would not consider me as one of your own. . . . In France, I still belong to a minority. I will never be considered as a White woman. I don't belong to anything. A hybrid! A non-meaning!

[Vous pensiez que je me sentais supérieure à vous parce que je ne me sentais nullement inférieure aux hommes. J'aurais tellement voulu être des vôtres. Vous ne me considériez pas comme une des vôtres. . . . En France, j'appartiens encore à une minorité. Jamais je ne serai considérée comme une Blanche. Je n'appartiens à rien. Une hybride! Un non-sens!] (339)

Like Ken, Sorraya suffers from a cultural and geographical estrangement. Also like Ken, she eloquently formulates and confronts the fundamental questions that relate to her identity and development:

Where is Africa in these frenzies of ambitions and corruption? Where are you? Where am I? You thought that I was mean in Africa. You thought that I was nice here. I am nothing like any of that. I don't even know where I am anymore. I have failed in life. I have failed in life as a girl and I have failed today as a woman, do you understand?

[Où est l'Afrique dans ces déchaînements d'ambitions et de corruption? Où es-tu? Où suis-je? Tu m'as crue méchante en Afrique. Tu m'as crue gentille ici. Je ne suis rien de tout cela. Je ne sais même plus où je suis. Je n'ai pas réussi ma vie. J'ai raté ma vie en tant que jeune fille et aujourd'hui en tant que femme, tu comprends?] (Beyala 1994, 341)

The only solution that she finds for her extreme "depression" is suicide. Faced with this situation, Assèze in turn is forced to reassess her own objectives and direction in life. In the course of her adolescence, she imitated Sorraya, blindly seeing her as a symbol of beauty and success, whereas Assèze felt miserable, ugly, ignorant, and deprived of everything. In the final account, the record Assèze establishes is hardly positive, and it amounts to a step backward compared to the protagonists of the previous novels. If Assèze represents the new woman, she also sadly illustrates the impossibility of charting a new path outside those already cleared by man.

And I asked myself if some day Africa would emerge from its ill-fated instincts and criminal dispositions. I had no answer. I was too tired and had too many emotions inside me.

[Et je me demandais si un jour l'Afrique sortirait de ses néfastes instincts, de ses dispositions bagnardes. Je n'avais pas de réponse. J'avais au fond de moi trop de fatigue et d'émotions.] (Beyala 1994, 341)

In fact, I realized that I had it all wrong from start to finish. My calculations for success were ultra-false. I finally understood that happiness was not in my purse and that I had to look somewhere else. Where? All they had to do was tell us where happiness was, and we believed them. What bothered me more than anything else was my own condition as a woman. I was no longer sure that I really was one! Oh, sure, you will say that I was acting, that I was doing different things. Was this a given or was it through my own efforts? Let's suppose that the keepers of my happiness and my status as a woman wake up one day and decide that I am not a woman anymore. What will I become? I was full of doubts and torn by my choices. And besides, just thinking that I had to find work and lodging somewhere literally exhausted me.

[En fait, je me rendis compte que j'avais tout faux, du départ à l'arrivée. Archifaux, mes calculs pour réussir. Je comprenais enfin que le bonheur n'était pas du côté de la bourse, qu'il fallait chercher ailleurs. Où? Il avait suffi qu'on nous dise, le bonheur c'est où. Et nous y avions cru. Ce qui me perturbait par-dessus tout, c'était mon propre état de femme. Je n'étais plus sûre en réalité, d'en être une! Oh bien sûr, vous me direz que j'agissais, que je faisais des choses. Etait-ce par don ou par volonté? A supposer que ceux qui étaient détenteurs de mon bonheur et de mon titre de femme se réveillent un matin et décident que je n'en étais pas une, que deviendrais-je? J'étais en plein doute, tiraillée par mes choix. D'ailleurs rien que d'envisager de trouver un travail ailleurs, et de me loger, m'épuisait littéralement.] (343)

When Assèze finds Sorraya nearly dead from an overdose of barbiturates, she cannot even decide what to do and, in her indecision, lets Sorraya die: "Maybe choosing one of the two courses of action would have saved her, but I was exhausted by all of these past episodes and just lay down at her side" [Prendre l'un ou l'autre parti l'eût peut-être sauvée, mais exténuée par toutes ces histoires du passé, je m'allongeais à ses côtés] (Beyala 1994, 345). Assèze later suffers from the same sickness. She feels emptied of any feeling, "absent from reality" [absente de la réalité] (345). Assèze carries her sickness of living around with her from France to Africa and back again.

I represent a continent whose survival has been compromised. I was born on the path of development. I am living on the path of extinction. I have no neuroses. My torture screams out to another place, to Africa as it lives its disgusting depression and can only see itself in the shadow of its ruins. I don't blacken reality. I green it in the fashion of a rotting Africa.

I understand better than anyone why I let Sorraya live her death. I was completely justified, and with this action I touched today's Africa in its deleterious structures and ancestral rites. I scratched my own soul a bit. The danger wasn't that I could lose myself, but that I would find myself.

[Je représente un continent dont la survie est bien compromise. Je suis née en voie de développement. Je vis en voie de disparition. Je n'ai aucune névrose. Ma torture hurle ailleurs, vers l'Afrique qui vit un blues dégueulasse et qui ne se voit qu'à l'ombre de ses propres ruines. Je ne noircis pas la réalité. Je la verdis, à la façon de l'Afrique qui faisande. Je comprends mieux que quiconque pourquoi j'ai laissé Sorraya vivre sa mort. En tout état de cause, par cet acte, j'ai touché à l'Afrique d'aujourd'hui, à ses structures malsaines, à ses rites ancestraux. J'ai égratigné un peu de mon âme. Ce n'était pas risquer de me perdre, mais de me retrouver.] (348)

After letting Sorraya die, Assèze plunges into confusion and an immense lethargy. Nevertheless, the novel ends with Assèze's hope of finding herself again, reminding us of the beginning when she declared her intention of leaving the conjugal home, which she found empty of meaning and love, in order to open an African restaurant and finally be independent. Beyala uses the narration to examine a new aspect of the depths of the feminine soul. She depicts the setbacks caused by envy and jealousy and the misguided dreams of success in the evolution of individual women and, therefore, also of society as a whole. She again offers a portrait of an "Africa torn apart" [Afrique déchirée], exhausted and full of cries of suffering.

The Weight of Violence and Horror

Visions of a Corrupt World in Tadjo's
Le Royaume Aveugle *and* Boni's Une Vie de Crabe

In *A vol d'oiseau*, Véronique Tadjo (1986) introduced the idea that love is necessary in order to confront a world that is falling apart. Two vignettes (on pages 39–41 and 69–72) develop this point in the context of a legend. The first of these vignettes depicts a reciprocal love:

> For days and days now she would twist and torture herself with pain. . . .
> He looked at her and he knew that he loved her more than ever. . . .
> Today, he would have liked to have lived through the same suffering—to feel the same pain in his flesh that was replacing pleasure on this day.
>
> *[Cela faisait des jours et des jours qu'elle se tordait et se torturait de douleur. . . . Il la regardait et il savait qu'il l'aimait plus que jamais. . . . Il aurait voulu aujourd'hui vivre la même souffrance—dans sa chair, la douleur qui aujourd'hui remplaçait le plaisir.]* (Tadjo 1986, 39)

Faced with the impending death of his companion, the man carries her across deserts and seas, wanting to be with her to the end. Though he does not triumph over death, he demonstrates the unequaled strength of his love. The second vignette develops this notion of a strong love that is nourished by the promise of a better future attainable through the child they have conceived. This child is a new messiah who will bring the strength and hope needed for the construction of a new society:

> Love has triumphed! We have created life! Our son will be our messenger. . . . Rebuild the cities destroyed by violence and oppression. Let the mad weeds grow and do not crush the clouds. . . . And especially, most of all, believe in yourself.
>
> *[L'amour a triomphé! Nous avons créé la vie! Notre fils sera notre messager. . . . Reconstruis les cités détruites par la violence et l'oppression. Laisse pousser l'herbe folle et n'écrase pas les nuages. . . . Et surtout, surtout, crois en toi-même.]* (Tadjo 1986, 69–70)

As Irène d'Almeida emphasizes in her analysis,[2] "This is a message of justice, creativity, hope and self-reliance, all positive values, but difficult to [en]act in a world whose social fabric has been badly damaged" (1994b, 157).

The child grows up, travels, and meets a young girl whom he desires. He gets her drunk, seduces her, and she wakes up in the morning expecting a child: "I am dying, she murmurs. This child is not mine. He will bring misfortune" [Je me meurs, murmura-t-elle. Cet enfant n'est pas de moi. Il amènera le malheur] (Tadjo 1986, 72). And in fact, the universe collapses in an apocalyptic vision:

> A violent breath of air burnt everything and swept away buildings. Skin fell off in patches. Eyes evaporated in their sockets. Everyone died violently. . . . An enormous mushroom cloud sculpted the burnt out horizon.
>
> *[Un souffle d'air violent brûla les êtres et renversa les buildings. La peau se détacha en plaques. Les yeux s'asséchèrent. . . . Tous moururent violemment. . . . Un énorme nuage-champignon sculpta l'horizon incendié.]* (72)

The moral of this legend, as Irène d'Almeida says so well, is that (1) love and education alone do not necessarily create a better world; (2) as long as he refuses to treat woman as an equal, man will cause the destruction and misfortune of those around him. "The story implies that to betray a woman, even in the name of love, is to risk total destruction, and Tadjo's surreal vision of the world's end emphasizes how the unhindered presence of women is vital to the survival of the cosmos itself" (d'Almeida 1994b, 159). The second vignette portrays a different man who knows how to respond to the needs of an equally new woman.

Le royaume aveugle adopts some of these same elements (a man, a woman, the name Akissi, a passionate but forbidden love, a corrupt world) in order to further explore the conditions for the successful creation of a better world. The novel portrays an anonymous place marred by corruption and inertia in which only Akissi, the king's daughter, seems, like Cassandra the Greek prophet, to see things clearly. She is warned by repeated nightmares:

> She knew exactly what this nightmare meant: the end was near. So, why didn't he want to understand? Didn't he know that now he was supposed to yield his place? Greed, corruption, and waste all ate at the kingdom.
>
> His rule was falling apart, but the courtesans continued to sing their flattery. The praise multiplied, glorifying the present and abolishing the future.
>
> [*Elle savait très bien ce que ce cauchemar voulait dire: la fin était proche. Pourquoi ne voulait-il donc pas comprendre? Ne savait-il pas qu'il devait maintenant laisser la place? La corruption, l'avidité, le gaspillage, tout rongeait le royaume.*
>
> *Le règne se décomposait et pourtant, les courtisans continuaient de chanter leurs flatteries. Les éloges se multipliaient, glorifiant le présent et abolissant l'avenir.*] (Tadjo 1990, 23)

In this country "without hope," a "country that is falling apart," (62), the only alternative is to leave:

> Akissi couldn't take it anymore. Where could she go to escape this machine and keep her head clean? . . . Where would she go to escape the lies and the madness of the entire horde of blind men?
>
> [*Akissi n'en pouvait plus. Où aller pour échapper à cet engrenage, pour garder la tête propre? . . . Où aller pour échapper aux mensonges et à la folie de toute une horde d'aveugles?*] (24)

The text consists of an elaborate metaphor for the direction Africa has taken, highlighting the ills of nepotism, the abuse of power, corruption, and venality. The story focuses on a search for possible solutions.

Like Megri in *Seul le diable,* Akissi thinks that she can fill the void and "become" from the beginning. Again like Megri, her maturation and new awareness are formed as a result of the experience of total love with the other, the stranger, who by definition dwells in the margin. In contact with Karim, and then with the old woman who becomes her teacher, Akissi will see through the veil and recover the sight that she has metaphorically lost.

> She wanted to say how much she already needed him and his difference and truth. She wanted to approach this passion that she could feel shivering inside him and which proved that he really existed.

She knew the kingdom's decadence and she knew that with the courage needed to confront life she would be able to discover the colors of existence and reality.

[Elle voulait lui dire combien déjà elle avait besoin de lui et de sa différence et de sa vérité. Elle voulait se rapprocher de cette passion qu'elle sentait frémir en lui et qui prouvait qu'il existait vraiment.

Elle connaissait la décadence du royaume et elle savait qu'avec le courage d'affronter la vie, elle serait capable de découvrir les couleurs de l'existence et de la réalité.] (Tadjo 1990, 35)

Akissi is compelled by Karim to stay in the village instead of returning to the city. The village represents her return to traditional origins. The heartless "stifling big city of stone" [grande ville de pierre . . . étouffante] (Tadjo 1990, 26) embodies emptiness and deshumanization. The image was already sketched out in *A vol d'oiseau* (Tadjo 1986).

Akissi's discourse is marked by the change from the interrogative to the imperative mode—"Give me awareness," "Give me the courage to combat my fear," "Let my expressions be changes" ["Donnez-moi la conscience," "Tendez-moi le courage pour combattre la peur," "Que mes gestes soient changements] (89). Through the development of Akissi's discourse and the resolution that she makes ("I want to get rid of this inaction. . . . Inertia erases my presence. Enough of this retreat made by a frozen people" [Je ne veux plus de cette inaction. . . . L'inertie efface ma présence. Assez de cette déroute d'un peuple figé] (89). Véronique Tadjo marks the stages in the protagonist's growing awareness and decision to take action. She thus creates a vision of a new world where things would be different,[3] where the city would be fertile rather than destructive.

The city will also be cured of its afflictions. It will be purified and become beautiful and even more maternal.
It will open its arms and will be:
A Haven-City
A Lover-City
A Loved-City
A Fecund-City.

[La Ville aussi guérira de ses maux. Elle se purifiera, deviendra plus belle et même plus maternelle.
Elle ouvrira ses bras et sera:
Ville-refuge
Ville-amante
Ville-aimée
Ville-féconde.] (Tadjo 1990, 99)

Strengthened by her initiation, Akissi is ready upon her return to confront the corruption, the stench, and the disorder of the kingdom: "Reality appeared that day in all its horror. The filth and the stench of those places made her turn her head away. She had to keep moving forward. On the inside, everything was a great disorder of colors, forms and materials" [La réalité apparut, ce jour-là, dans toute son horreur. La saleté, la puanteur des lieux lui firent tourner la tête. Elle dut continuer à avancer. A l'intérieur, tout n'était que désordre de couleurs, de formes, de matériaux] (Tadjo 1990, 121). Her actions reach their limit, however. Here, unlike the character with the same name in *A vol d'oiseau* (vignette 63) who shows a great resolve to reject a birth that was imposed on her, Akissi is exposed in all her indecision. A wall rises up between her and Karim. She admits her weakness and her fear of choosing his path. At this point, however, she emerges with a different perspective on the future. Unlike Karim, who has stopped believing in life and who is prepared to die for his convictions, Akissi expresses hope for a better tomorrow: "She wanted to give this man back his desire to live—to find some solution—to release him once and for all from a torture he did not deserve." [Elle voulait redonner à cet homme l'envie de vivre—trouver une solution—le sortir une fois pour toutes d'un calvaire qu'il ne méritait pas] (122). In order to accomplish this, Akissi compromises and accepts a pardon from the king so that peace may return to the kingdom. In other words, she is ready to return to the original conditions of status quo at the beginning of the story as well as give up her and Karim's dream for a better world.

Should we speak here of procrastination or of the wisdom of believing in the possibility of future success? Is there wisdom in clarifying and drawing conclusions from past errors while showing patience and renewed hope?

> We must not despair. We will start again from ground zero. With more experience and insight. We will take the strangeness and complexity of the world into account. We will know how to avoid simplistic symbols and erroneous simplifications. We will know how to live reality. But for the time being, we have to accept failure and survive.
>
> *[Il ne faut pas désespérer. Nous recommencerons à zéro. Avec plus d'expérience et de vision. Nous tiendrons compte de l'étrangeté du monde et de sa complexité. Nous saurons défaire des symboles faciles et des simplifications erronées. Nous saurons vivre la réalité. Mais pour le moment, il nous faut accepter l'échec et survivre.]* (Tadjo 1990, 25)

There are as many questions as possible courses to take and aborted attempts to succeed, and then there is the constant return to the inevitable question, What future is there for the Africa of tomorrow? when today is filled with so many commonplace disasters such as civil wars, dictatorial coups, internal power struggles, and all the ills that result from them: pain and suffering, loss of human life. *Le royaume aveugle* ends with a voice that cries out, overflowing with Akissi's horrendous despair and suffering.

She is alone, face-to-face with her solitude, a prisoner of her gilded environment.

> Akissi's loneliness had no end. Each day she would descend deeper into the void. She drowned herself in the muddy waters of her nightmares and she would have wanted to end her life, except her belly was as large as a ripe fruit . . . the protector of a birth to come.
>
> *[La solitude d'Akissi était sans fond. Chaque jour, elle descendait un peu plus dans le vide. Elle se noyait dans l'eau boueuse de ses cauchemars et elle aurait voulu en finir avec la vie mais son ventre était gros comme un fruit mûr . . . protecteur d'une naissance prochaine.]* (Tadjo 1990, 136)

Like Beyala's first three novels, Tadjo's depicts an outbreak of horror and abjection, visions of haggard characters wandering around the abandoned palace. The stench of rot and mildew fills the air. And there is the shocking pain of the punishment that the blind inflict on themselves as they put out their own eyes: "And the world became a night without morning, a deep cave where the senses were lost, a nightmare in which time had no bearing" [Et le monde devint une nuit sans matin, une grotte profonde où les sens se perdaient, un cauchemar dans lequel le temps n'avait nul repère] (Tadjo 1990, 135).

Because the inhabitants of the kingdom did not believe in change, have refused to listen to Karim, and have sacrificed him, they have reached this point of no return:

> Those who bet everything on the present and the present alone, without ever thinking even once about tomorrow, those who let themselves be carried away by an ocean of lies, who refused to see in spite of their open eyes, who chose to sit down and sup with injustice, all of those people now felt that their existence was being shattered.
>
> *[Ceux qui ont misé sur tout le présent et le présent seulement, sans jamais avoir une pensée pour demain, qui s'étaient laissé emporter par un océan de mensonges, qui avaient refusé de voir malgré leurs yeux ouverts, qui avaient choisi de s'asseoir avec l'injustice, ceux-là sentaient maintenant que leur existence était brisée.]* (Tadjo 1990, 134)

This is a terrible vision, a vision of a society that prefers the lie to possible radical change. Tadjo forces her readers to take stock of their own world. Considering Karim's death and Akissi's imprisonment, the question of this project's success remains open. Unlike Ateba, Tanga, and Megri (in Beyala's *The Sun, Tanga,* and *Seul le diable,* respectively), Akissi actually remains a prisoner of her environment and, even more, of her remorse, as she is faced with the dilemma of the tragic eternal choice between duty and love: "How will I survive, knowing that I could not find the words to make you renounce death and that I could not find the strength to kill my father?" [Comment vais-je survivre, sachant que je n'ai pas su trouver les mots pour te faire renoncer à la mort, que je n'ai pas su trouver la force de tuer mon père?] (Tadjo 1990, 131).

Karim's death, nonetheless, has made Akissi stronger. She has found the resolve to change her condition of "being chained to the role of the king's daughter" [enchaînement de fille de roi] and to plunge "into the crowd of Others" [dans la foule des Autres] (Tadjo 1990, 130). The birth to come especially carries the promise of hope. Where the parents have failed, the child may perhaps succeed. Akissi's pain gives way to a smile. The birth of twins, a son and a daughter, seems to anticipate a brighter future. This final note of optimism suggests that where the leaders have failed by plunging themselves and their citizens into the deepest horrors, their successors will perhaps manage to avoid the eternal dangers of violence and corruption in order to build a livable world.

In *Une vie de crabe,* Tanella Boni also depicts the status quo of corruption and repression in which so many African countries and their citizens have been imprisoned. However, she anchors her story in boredom and in banal incidents of daily life. Behind Léti's memories, behind the fragmented story of her loves and records of daily life, behind the development of her relationship with Niyous, his experiences in the strike, his arrest and detention in a prison camp, we find a vivid portrayal of a West African city and its inhabitants, from the most humble to the most wealthy. Once again, we can draw up a list of the societal ills that exist in Tadjo's texts: corruption, bribery, beggars and unemployed and homeless people, lost youth like Niyous, censorship of radio and the press, difficult living conditions, student strikes, military repression, and so on.

> She grabbed the newspaper as she passed in front of the stand: "Massahacre is dead," they announced on page one. There was also an account of the debates about the new school year. It was a calming, syrupy, soporific discourse. "There are no problems. Students are returning to school as ordered," they wrote. . . . Curiously enough, everyone who read this page didn't speak a word. There was total silence. It was as if they saw nothing and understood nothing of what was written. The people seemed tired and had somber faces that afternoon.
>
> *[Elle prit le journal en passant devant le kiosque: "Massahacre est mort," annonçait-on à la une. Il y avait aussi un compte rendu des débats sur la rentrée scolaire, un discours mielleux, calmant, soporifique. "Il n'y a pas de problèmes, la rentrée se faisait sous le signe de l'ordre," y écrivait-on. . . . Curieusement, tous ceux qui lisaient cette page ne disaient mot. Silence. C'était comme s'ils ne voyaient rien, n'entendaient rien à ce qui était écrit. Les gens avaient le visage sombre, l'air fatigué ce midi-là.]* (Boni 1990, 70–71)

She had escaped the death that runs in the streets one more time. She had crossed the bitterness of hell. She no longer had a job. She had feet, hands, a head, senses. She no longer had a thing to lose. From now on, she would melt into the anonymous crowd of people who have no work and no papers. She looked like them. They had the same blood. They were made of the same mud and had been plunged into the same stench. Together, they would all be stronger than the mud. They would conquer the stench of the sewers that were falling apart everywhere.

[Elle avait échappé une fois de plus, à la mort qui court les rues. Traversé l'amertume de l'enfer. Elle n'avait plus de travail. Elle avait des pieds, des mains, une tête, des sens. Elle n'avait plus rien à perdre. Désormais, elle se fondrait dans la foule anonyme, des sans-travail, des sans-papiers. Elle leur ressemblait. Ils étaient du même sang. Faits de la même boue, plongés dans la même puanteur. Tous ensemble, ils seront plus forts que la boue. Ils vaincront la puanteur des égouts qui craquent de partout.] (73)

Another difference between Tadjo's *Le royaume aveugle* and Boni's *Un vie de crabe* is that Boni uses a humorous tone.[4] She combines expressions from the street and from soccer to treat "the most serious subjects," as Borgomano puts it. She further comments, "This lightness makes the spectacle of the small world of the cities seem even more ferocious with its general dishonesty and the smiling corruption of the police, the insignificant division of energies (even feminine energies!) around national football teams, the disintegration of families, the multiplication of lost and marginal characters, the general pollution . . . " (1989, 94; my translation).

In a final surreal vision, *Une vie de crabe* returns to its point of departure without offering any solutions or hopes for a better world: "The past was dying and there was no future . . . no future because we were in the midst of the flood and watching our backs. Watching our backs forever" [Le passé mourait et il n'y avait pas d'avenir. Car l'on était, dans le déluge, sur le qui-vive. Sur le qui-vive à l'infini] (Boni 1990, 107). This is Léti's last disillusioned glance as she finds herself alone, lost in the crowd: "Happiness only lasted as long as a nightingale. It has flown away" [Le bonheur n'avait duré que le temps d'une hirondelle. Envolé] (107).

Beyala begins with a world much closer to that of Tadjo and Liking, a world of violence and misery where the organizational value is chaos. Beyala, however, goes one step further by examining the conditions for this better future in more detail and by depicting woman as the active instrument for change. She explores suffering in all its fullness, examining woman's suffering as well as that of the child and, therefore, of man. To this element, she adds an extraordinary dose of violence.

Abjection, Suffering, and Catharsis in Beyala's Texts

The failure of love for female characters in Beyala's first three novels foreshadows the presence of abjection, violence, and horror in a symbiosis with love and life. All of the corporeal elements of decay figure here: vomit, pus, rot, nauseating smells, mould, mildew, mud, and anything that has to do with scatology and coprophagy.[5] Natural elements, water and earth in particular, appear in the most repulsive combinations: "All night long, torrents of water poured down and the glutted earth discharged the surplus in a flow of muddy vomit" (*The Sun,* Beyala 1996, 32). Mud becomes a symbol of the stagnation of African society.

In fact, images of corruption, rot, and invading mud proliferate in recent women's novels. For example, we can find a similar image of mud and stench from the sewers and filth in *Une vie de crabe.*

> The children would play beneath the rain in muddy pools. Streams rusted with time had emerged under the pressure of the water and the mass of garbage. People lived amidst the foul odors of the sewers and subterranean life. They waited with their feet in the mud, where they had lived for time immemorial. They still kept watch for the arrival of the saving hand that would purify them, that would finally raise them up out of their crab holes!

> *[Les enfants jouaient sous la pluie, dans les mares boueuses. Des canalisations rouillées par le temps avaient sauté sous la pression de l'eau et la masse de déchets. Les gens vivaient dans les odeurs fortes, celles des égouts, celles de la vie souterraine. Ils attendaient les pieds dans la boue où ils vivaient depuis des temps immémoriaux. Ils guettaient toujours l'arrivée de la main salvatrice. Qui les purifierait. Qui les sortirait enfin de leur trou de crabes!]* (Boni 1990, 69)

Similarly, in Werewere Liking's *L'amour-cent-vies,* Lem realizes his agony in a world of abjection where horror and ugliness are combined with sickness and decomposition.

> When I ran away, when I pulled my legs up to my neck, it was always out of fear, this deaf fear of the void that knotted my belly, the fear of ugliness. . . . In my nightmares, the stumps of lepers poisoned me. I was eaten by maggots. Slugs and reptiles crept over my skin drooling! I screamed and lost consciousness in order to escape my disgust.

> *[Quand je fuyais, quand je prenais mes jambes à mon cou, c'était toujours de peur, cette peur sourde du vide qui me nouait le nombril, la peur de la laideur. . . . Dans des cauchemars, des moignons de lépreux m'empoisonnaient, des asticots me mangaient, des limaces et des reptiles rampaient sur moi en bavant! Je hurlais et perdais conscience pour fuir le dégoût.]* (Liking 1988, 109)

One important difference between Liking's world and those of Beyala, Boni, and Tadjo is that Liking's offers a possible refuge and an alternative to violence and corruption in beauty: "In order to get away from the disgust, I would wake up with a beautiful image of beauty in my head. I no longer hated myself, and you were my queen" [Pour fuir le dégoût, et je me réveillais dans une belle image de beauté: je n'avais plus de haine de moi et tu étais ma reine] (Liking 1988, 109). If the love between Lem and Madjo, like Megri's love for the Foreigner, is forbidden, in this case by the taboo against incest, it blooms differently, through a song of renewal for the coming day.

> What I would like, what I would love, is just to restore our hope and courage, to all of us, to the young in general and to Africans in particular, to all of us who lose hope over the rot, the corruption and the injustice, and who wait for the apocalyptic salvation to fall from the sky. I think that we evoke them so as to keep a good conscience in our renunciation and our irresponsibility.
>
> There have always been ends of the world. That is why there have always been and will always be rebirths. . . .
>
> But renaissances have to be prepared!
>
> Why not by us?
>
> [Ce que je voudrais, ce que j'aimerais, c'est tout simplement nous re-donner espoir et courage, à nous tous, aux jeunes en général et aux Africains en particulier, à nous tous qui nous déséspérons de la pourrit-ure, de la corruption, de l'injustice, et attendons du ciel l'apocalypse sal-vatrice. Je crois que nous les évoquons, pour avoir bonne conscience dans notre renoncement, dans notre irresponsabilité. . . .
>
> Il y a toujours eu des fins de monde. C'est pourquoi il y a eu, et il y aura toujours, des renaissances. . . .
>
> Mais les renaissances, ça se prépare!
>
> Pourquoi pas par nous?] (Liking 1988, 157)

In "Les femmes et l'écriture-parole," Borgomano notes that Liking gets to the bottom of some taboos but that she transgresses them with art and poetic speech. Madjo saves Lem from suicide with her song. "The story of *L'amour-cent-vies* thus becomes a 'story for survival.' As it is rooted in art, music, and legend, it has no use for taboos; isn't art trans-gressive by nature?" (1994, 92; my translation). Borgomano demonstrates that by mixing epic and love with the portrayal of contemporary Africa's extreme despair, the work "assumes a complicated and ambitious political dimension" and "bears witness while taking a position" (94).

Beyala's protagonists must go through a process of exorcism to over-come the violence and horror. First, they plunge into hell in order to attain a catharsis by confronting the abject.

In *Seul le diable,* abjection reaches new depths with the Pygmy's ca-daver. That the Pygmy succumbs to death in the middle of a sex act is symbolic. Megri stays alone with the cadaver. Later, the mother is tied to the cadaver during a purification rite ordered by the village. As Kristeva describes the scene in her study of horror in literature, "The cadaver rep-resents fundamental pollution. A body with no soul, a non-body" [Le cadavre représente la pollution fondamentale. Un corps sans âme, un non-corps] (1980, 24). Thus death reassumes its therapeutic and sacrificial value. By their deaths, the guard named "666," the Pygmy, and the Foreigner bring the community face-to-face with abjection in all its force. Their deaths necessitate the community's participation in a rite of exorcism by which the collective group will be regenerated and purged of all its ills including corruption, venality, inertia, indifference, and irresponsibility.

In *Tanga,* the prison and the guards' violence create a world of horror and despair from the very beginning. The child Pieds-Gâtés best illustrates this world; in order to survive in it he has cut himself off from the love of others. Because love is unknown to him, Tanga's attempt to build a bridge between them fails. As Bjornson remarks in *The Quest for Freedom and Identity,* "The meaning of Tanga's life is crucial to Beyala because it reflects the living death to which African children are born" (1991, 419).

Through horror, violence, and death, Beyala achieves what Kristeva calls "the cleaning of our contemporary universe" [le ménage de notre univers] (1980, 24). Suffering is in fact at the heart of every one of Beyala's novels, especially *The Sun* and *Tanga.* More important, suffering itself becomes the subject. In their suffering and their contemplation of abjection, Ateba, Tanga, and Megri undergo a series of psychological transformations. Each becomes a wandering soul, "a traveler fleeing to the end of the night" [un voyageur dans une nuit à bout fuyant] (16), someone who by definition exists in the margin, at the frontier. The abjection of motion is embodied by Ateba, for she is always in motion, moving from her house to the bar, from the bar to a room where she will meet a man, from the room to the street to Irène's house, and so on. Megri does the same thing, writing from Paris to her mother in Africa, traveling between her village and the Foreigner's, traveling around the world in her dreams for a night; she wakes up somewhere in between, in search of her own space. It is, nevertheless, this situation of estrangement that ultimately produces pleasure and desire for the protagonist, because as Kristeva describes, "It is this roaming on unknown grounds that gets her off" (16).

In this structural framework, the distinction between subject and object is lost and gives way to a long "cry of suffering" [cri de souffrance] in which crude words, violence, and abjection combine to render a powerful stylistic intensity. The protagonist in turn undergoes a kind of purification that builds to a crescendo, ending with first the shattering of the personality and then a complete catharsis. The catharsis functions on two levels: One level is the protagonist's and the other is the reader's.

In the first case, the author utilizes peripheral characters as reflections or projections of the protagonist's character. In *The Sun,* Betty, Ada, and Irène are each mirror images of Ateba's life and future. These characters act as catalysts, forcing Ateba to become aware of the emptiness that holds

234 --- Toward a New Political Novel

her mother, her aunt, and her friend captive. In *Seul le diable*, Bertha serves as an alter ego to Megri as she matures and grows. The mother represents everything that Megri rejects. The process of maturation followed by Ateba and Megri is based on the observation of people who are close to them. This process falls within the category of theatrical techniques used in psychodrama, particularly role reversal. In his study on catharsis in literature, Kenan Abdulla (1985) explains that the character can actually benefit from the observation of auxiliary selves who reproduce or imitate on stage certain actions that he or she is likely to accomplish.

If we reexamine the first three novels in this perspective, we find a number of narrative strategies for therapeutic effects. One primary example is the confrontation between Tanga and Anna-Claude in *Tanga*. As prisoners, they live side by side. That one listens to the other with the purpose of adopting her personality and assuming her identity creates two new women and suggests a way out. This self-reproduction enables them to expel violence from their surrounding world and to create a new space for love.

Psychodrama also plays an important role in *Seul le diable,* functioning primarily through group therapy. For example, the village is used as a stage for a psychodrama directed by the Foreigner, whose arrival has caused numerous difficulties. By his very presence, the Foreigner acts as a stimulus for negative tensions. Like a stage director, he is simultaneously passive, offstage, and the main catalyst for the events. His indifference and then his disappearance are decisive factors in Megri's maturation and growth from an adolescent into a young woman. Catharsis intervenes here not only as a release for emotions but, more important, as an element that facilitates the character's social transformation. In Megri's case, the loss of her lover gives her new strength.

The psychodrama affects not only Megri but the two fathers and her mother. Papa bon Blanc and the Pygmy become aware of the dominating power that Bertha (Dame maman) wields over them, and they leave. The first one leaves of his own free will, literally. The second leaves figuratively, by dying. After the shock of these two departures, Bertha finds new strength, shedding her passivity and becoming more self-confident. She hauls the cadaver back to his own house so that no one will suspect her in his death. She attempts to protect Megri against the anger of the village, proving her ability to love as a mother. The series of public confrontations in the form of trial, gathering, meeting, and theatrical game all play out as collective encounters that allow each character to become aware of her potential. In a similar fashion, the initial chaos of the community's corruption, venality, and sexual desire, presented as the community's sole centers of interest, appears as a necessary phase in the maturation of Megri her mother, her fathers, and the entire community.

The text acts as a catalyst for its readers, leading them to confront their own inertia and the ills suffered by the African collectivity. The novel is a portrait of an Africa that has been torn apart. The flirtations of the African woman become metaphors for Africa's indecisiveness about the European model. The emptiness that Megri feels—brought on by the impossible situation of having two absent fathers and a femme fatale for a mother—is symbolic of African intellectuals who have returned to their country and, having to coordinate two cultural systems, remain incapable of determining what direction to take.

Thus through writing with cathartic force and a bold exploration of women's interactions with others, Beyala raises a number of crucial points that reflect on the current African situation. She emphasizes the deterioration of relationships not only between men and women but also between parents and children. Moreover, she deals with the disintegration of the family structure in its traditional configuration, along with the exploitation of children by their parents and, in particular, of daughters by their mothers. Beyala also stresses the dangers of dreams of success based on Western standards. *Assèze l'Africaine* is especially representative of these different dreams. This critique of African society and Africans themselves proves to be just as bold as the recurrence of erotic scenes, of scenes of violence, and of the use of vernacular language. In fact, the representation of sex and degradation and of woman's needs and aspirations in Beyala's texts should not be taken as a new form of exoticism for the interests of Western readers. On the contrary, it is to be understood as an active component of a socially engaged writing.

Beyala sharply provokes her readers in order to illustrate a new ethic for behavior between the sexes that will allow a new woman to be born. The author employs a radical analysis of relations between mother and daughter, man and woman, articulated in terms of sexuality and abjection. Beyala's radical approach to the feminine condition raises the question of women's responsibility in a number of situations. She thus communicates directly with her readers and implicates them in her exploration of taboos.

The birth of a new woman is not an end in itself but the prelude to the formation of a new Africa. The predominance of the abject, even in sexual relations, leads us to the following conclusion: An alternative form of a modus vivendi should develop through a complete change in behaviors, but first, through a transformation in ways of thinking. Modifying political and social structures is secondary to a transformation of ideas and behaviors that form the basis of interactions between individuals, between men and women.

These feminine writings suggest that if Africa is doing so poorly, it is in part due to the fact that women have practically no political power. Women must therefore take it upon themselves to break the mold in which society has confined them. They must reject the dreams of success bound up with social appearances and the Western model. The solution must come from a radical reform in women's ways of thinking and acting. Women must shed their stultified behavior in such a way that men, in turn, can learn a new way of being in their interactions with them and, therefore, also with their fellow men.

Through the interaction between the protagonist and her sister, Sorraya, the novel also illustrates the limitations of relations between women who are jealous and competitive. Women are responsible for this fact and for their own difficulties in *becoming*.

Through the description of the tensions between men and women, female writers tackle relations between social and ethnic groups, their impact on the struggle for and participation in power, and, especially, the notion of crisis in contemporary Africa. By writing texts that either have mythical overtones or are rooted in daily life, these authors reveal important social and economic changes that account for the directions the continent has taken.

They resort to systematic provocation in the form of shock therapy, hoping to thereby incite the radicalization of their African readers. The violence and horror they render in their works constitutes a chaotic universe and a prelude to redemption. Dabla notes that the recurrence of the apocalyptic world is a sign of literary innovation. This innovation is "first of all, due to its esthetic founding of the destruction of the world . . . of letters, . . . but we must also read in it an ambition for mythical renewal, the renewal of a 'recreation of a new universe.' And these bold writers become prophets who anticipate what will happen, sometimes one or two generations later, in other sectors of social and cultural life" (Dabla 1986, 241; my translation). This shock therapy also gives rise to the movement for a cultural renaissance and the narrative technique of the griot/griotte who confronts his or her readers and wants to "move" them. This aspect of provocation characterizes this new generation of writers. The African novel in the feminine mode responds to this principle of creation. It is not simply limited to the vision of a chaotic world that one wishes to accuse or flee. Instead, it evokes the possibility of a better world, and in this evocation is its force.

Notes

1. Hence the misovire declares: "And I think that the lack of desire in Lunaï is a serious problem, because here no one ever goes crazy about anything anymore, not about love and not about hate. People don't even love money. They are caught up in it and would kill for it, but not with any passion! People don't even despise poverty anymore, but they would sell themselves to get out of it, with no aspirations

and with no other goals." [Et je crois que c'est un problème sérieux le manque de désir à Lunaï. Car ici on n'est jamais plus fou de quoi que ce soit: ni d'amour ni de haine. On n'aime même pas l'argent: on est pris dans son engrenage et l'on tuerait pour lui mais sans passion!!! On ne déteste même plus la misère mais on se vendrait pour en sortir sans aspiration sans autre but] (Liking, 1983, 64).

2. See d'Almeida 1994b, 154–168.

3. A similar approach is used in Werewere Liking's *Elle sera de jaspe et de corail*. Both novels search for the conditions required to build a new world. The main difference is that Liking delegates this commanding task to the woman, whereas Akissi acts only under the impulse of her love and, therefore, remains dependent on an initial movement that tells her which impulse to follow—if she is not captive to passivity.

4. Beyala also uses spontaneous, caustic humor, especially in *Loukoum* and *Maman a un amant*. The use of humor and irony represents a change in women's writing because, again, women are appropriating a strategy that typically has been considered part of the masculine domain.

5. Rawiri's *Fureurs et cris de femmes* (1989) depicts the same elements of the abject applied to the feminine body. (See Chapter 5 in this volume.)

Conclusion

The past fifteen years have ushered in a new generation of female writers. These writers have made innovations in conventional themes and in literary form. Like Dabla, we can now conclude that the Francophone African novel in the feminine mode has freed itself from the forms of simple testimony and been able to "report experiences and present the current state of African societies" (Dabla 1986, 244). Writers such as Beyala, Liking, and Tadjo "have produced 'novels of rebirth' suggesting the path to a cultural renewal" (244).[1]

In this book I have attempted to explain how these writers' strategies—selecting female characters at the margins of society and addressing taboos and what have been thought of as insignificant issues—have produced a mechanism of rebellion. With their decision to take on powerful questions, they have introduced a new, subversive form of writing.

In the first part of my analysis, I considered the various types of marginal feminine characters selected as part of a transitional strategy. This strategy allowed the authors to move from a literature of testimony to one of revolt. We saw how each one of the characters introduced and problematized a different aspect of the modern African woman's life. Through this presentation, semi-autobiographical narratives evolve into narratives of the construction of the self. In returning to the themes of the interracial couple and the foreign wife (as part of another culture or ethnic group), Mariama Bâ and Myriam Warner-Vieyra refocused our attention on the character of the outsider, using her to point to problems faced by the modern African woman.

The character of the prostitute offers a more complex treatment of women's exploitation by the familial and social system. This trope illustrates certain social phenomena, in particular, the subscription to appearance and semiprostitution as a normalized means of financial support. According to this system, the woman is supposed to maintain the family by marketing her own body.

239

The character of the mad woman was previously used by European and Caribbean women writers, but in Africa it has been used as an act of resistance against the social constraints imposed on women. As mentioned earlier, Gilbert and Gubar (1970) remarked that madness thus becomes an assertive force that is inextricably tied to the concept of power. The writer takes greater liberties as a direct consequence of the greater freedom of speech granted to her character. By making this choice, the author highlights the different conditions that limit women's freedom of action.

Through these variously marginal characters, African women writers have reviewed and challenged certain traditional ideas that have locked women into fixed social and familial roles. The texts we have studied share one common point: They all introduce the possibility of a different life for woman beyond her role as wife and mother. In this context, these authors have struck a blow against the familial pressures to which African women who choose a different lifestyle have been subjected, particularly those women who choose to pursue studies or a career. If the marginalization of these feminine characters reveals the difficulty for the African woman of choosing a direction in life that is different from the one prescribed, this type of character also marks a stage within a process; it is a transitional phase that contributes to shape what I have designated the birth of a new feminine African novel. It was first necessary to speak out and to do so through these marginal characters in order to then be able to take a sharper look at certain forbidden areas that these same characters allowed the author to approach.

The novels of the second generation of writers explore areas that until recently were either taboo or dismissed as uninteresting. At the same time, these authors have returned to more traditional themes. Although they return to the theme of parent-child relations, they treat them in an entirely new way. On the one hand, they demystified the complicity between mother and son, emphasizing the mother's castrating power, particularly in her control over the son's conjugal relationships. On the other hand, they have begun to explore the mother-daughter relationship, stressing its ambiguities, its tensions, and the malaise arising as a result of the mother's exploitation of her daughter. They have examined various forms of exploitation of woman within society, marriage, and the family.

Along the same lines as Antillean women writers, the Africans question the notion that maternal love and motherhood are woman's defining qualities. *La voie du salut suivi de le miroir de la vie* (Maïga Ka 1985), *La tache de sang* (Bassek 1990), *Fureurs et cris de femmes* (Rawiri 1989), and *Sous la cendre, le feu* (Mpoudi Ngolle 1990) all explore the familial resistance that woman has to face in this matter. They cast doubt on the idea that a woman necessarily wants to have children. If the narrative retains the form of testimony, as in the texts I have just mentioned, it assumes a much broader significance through the perspective in which these issues are approached. Emilienne *(Fureurs et cris de femmes)* does much more than complain about the problem of being sterile and having to struggle against marital and familial pressures. She offers a complete account of the life of a couple, the implications of being barren, and her reading of masculine behavior. The discussion exceeds the limitations of any particular individual case and builds up to the question of the fate of children born in an Africa that is not prepared to receive them.

In addition, we note a change in the type of milieu within the framework of the familial and conjugal relation. Although the novel remains set within an urban environment, the scene has shifted from the middle and lower-middle classes to the poorer and underprivileged social strata, including street people and slum-dwellers. In other cases, an anonymous milieu functions as a metaphoric image of an aimless Africa. This is especially true in the works of Beyala and Tadjo, who have followed Liking's example. The nature of the problems treated has clearly changed. The narrative moves away from self-introspection. Instead, it turns to questions of woman's existence, coexistence, and survival in a system that exploits her and in which she winds up being deprived of moral and financial support in the face of familial disintegration.

Generally, Francophone and Anglophone early writing by women showed different characterizations of women: rural and from a humble background in the Anglophone women's writers' works; urban, middle-class, educated in the Francophone works. There was also a difference in tone. Anglophone writers gave their characters a more determined outlook on life, whereas female characters in the Francophone novel often reflected on their experiences as women and their suffering or ordeals. Beyala's works seem closer to those of the Anglophone writers because of the type of milieu she chose for her early novels and because of the determination of the protagonists.

If they deal with conservative resistance to change and bourgeois materialism, it is to deconstruct these phenomena in their diverse manifestations by denouncing the race for its focus on appearances and dreams of success based on the Western model. Through Toula in *G'amàrakano*, Rawiri in particular illustrates how the rush for a certain image results in corruption, bribery, the commodification of relationships, and prostitution or semiprostitution. Chapter 5, on the body and sexuality, emphasizes above all the dictatorship of appearance and beauty that reduces woman's body to merchandise. In *La tache de sang* and *Fureurs et cris de femmes*, respectively, Bassek and Rawiri explore the body in its suffering and pain. The writers examined in this book suggest replacing this suffering body with one that is positively transformed through self-control and an attentiveness to one's own sexuality.[2] Rawiri's *G'amàrakano* and Beyala's *The*

Sun Hath Looked upon Me, Your Name Shall Be Tanga, Seul le diable le savait, Loukoum, and *Maman a un amant* respectively emphasize the importance of sexuality as an active agent in the construction of society. Both of these authors depict sexual behavior in a political manner. In other words, a new sexual ethic is a precondition for a new order of conduct among individuals within the family, in the community, and in the larger context of society.

We have discovered a new representation of woman in her being and social functions, but we also end with an entirely innovative reflection on man. The authors have established his profile and analyzed his ways of thinking and acting, especially in the love relationship. Moreover, they have given him a voice of his own. The presence of a masculine narrative voice allows the writer to alternate between male and female perspectives and present the possibility of an open exchange between the sexes. This search for a new sexual ethic and a harmonious dialogue is particularly evident in the works of Beyala and Tadjo. Beyala's *Assèze l'Africaine,* nevertheless, sums up the limitations of the dialogue between men and women in the pursuit of their misguided dreams of success.

The second generation of writers reach new dimensions with their narrative tools. These tools testify to the writers' search for a new society and define a new political novel in the feminine mode. The concluding remarks in *Nouvelles écritures africaines* are appropriate to our own corpus of texts:

> This act of rebirth, through which our [female] novelists propose an understanding of both present conditions . . . and the "primacy of action," [has been] illustrated logically by the renewal of a form whose principles (authenticity of description, the use of orality, a violent message, a flexible approach to textual devices) correspond to the elements of the proposition. (Dabla 1986, 244; my translation)

The multiplication of masculine and feminine narrative voices and the presence of multiple narratees situate the story within the discourse, conferring new power on the act of telling. At the same time, particularly in the case of Beyala and Tadjo, the integration of invented or traditional myths into the story expands the narrative fabric. These evocations of myth do more than reinforce the image of a lost past; they allow a focus on contemporary problems that repeat themselves and that maintain an unstable and unequal world. With these works, our eyes turn to the future. This new writing is truly visionary, as it offers us an alternative vision, one of a better Africa.

In their *prise de parole,* these women strive to establish a more active interaction between writer and readers in order to call on them directly and bring them into the quest for a new social and political balance. Sexual representations and the depiction of violence and horror act as catalysts for the purpose of provoking and "moving" readers. Both men and women are forced to conduct their own individual reassessments of their participation in the construction of the African continent.

The novel in the feminine mode thus reveals a significant transformation occurring in the form of subversion. As d'Almeida states in her article "Femme? Féministe? Misovire?," "their *prise d'écriture* . . . far from being innocent" is "rather an act of subversion."

> The subversion is in the choice and the manner of approaching these themes. Subversion again in the judicious use of "orality," for example, by Beyala, Liking or Tadjo, who recreate ancient myths and invent new ones in which women occupy the main position. Subversion, finally, in the very structure of these novels. Subversion above all in the use of language in which women break all taboos. . . .
>
> Thus, when these women take on writing, they engender a multi-formed and polysemic form of speech. It is suggestive, spellbinding, prophetic or rebellious. Women's voices will be raised from this point on in order to decry abuses against women, but also those committed against children and society in general. (1994a, 50–51; my translation)

Behind their creation of marginal characters and their exploration of taboo subjects, women writers take up questions concerning the relations between different social groups and their participation in the struggle for power. Without these more probing questions, the description of marginal characters and taboo subject matter could pass for a simple spectacle meant only to entertain.

The question of ethnicity and nationality appears through the filter of the story, in particular in Beyala's *Seul le diable le savait* and Tadjo's *Le royaume aveugle*. On a metaphorical level, these two texts examine questions about the form of government and the diversion of power for the benefit of the few. In addition, these two novels explain the political, social, and economic changes taking place on the African continent at the end of the twentieth century. They speak directly to the current crisis in Africa.

African writers of the second generation do not, however, limit themselves to making accusations or to simply recreating a piece of collective memory. They each strive to think of and portray an Africa that is different from the one that exists today. Writing on this subject in his study of African feminine novelistic writings, Romuald Blaise Fonkua (1994) conducts a synthesis of the differences between men's and women's perspectives on the political reality. He states that male authors tend to carry out the critique of the political order "by relying on a critique of the men in power to create myths of hope that are sometimes based on the people, sometimes on the writer, and sometimes on the charismatic leader." In contrast, female writers are primarily interested in "reflecting on the ways in which modern and traditional societies conceive order; they want to identify the realities concealed by this will to institutionalize a patriarchal order on top of a matriarchal order; to ask what, at the very foundation of African societies, determines attitudes, behaviors and forms of social discrimination; or, more precisely, to ask what the social order contains, transports and distributes at all levels of culture, politics and ideology" (122; my translation). I wholeheartedly agree with him on this point but disagree with his view that "this position . . . is indicative of these novelists's desire to understand how these realities are constructed, rather than to construct modalities for the resolution of social and political problems" (122). Women writers actually engage in a profound reflection on society's operating mechanisms, from the smallest to the largest unit and from the level of individual interactions to the structures of power. In addition, their reflection is essentially different in that they analyze elements that until now were considered insignificant or worthless.

I believe the second generation of women writers participate in the construction of a possible society. More specifically, they participate in this construction through their vision of new political, social, and personal relations. And they do so "neither as 'pistolographers' nor as legitimate or obligated spokespersons for their respective peoples" [ni comme des 'pistoléographes,' ni comme des hérauts légitimes ou obligés, de leurs peuples respectifs] (Fonkua 1994, 122). It is no less true that they wish to at least suggest, if not demonstrate, that man has failed in his exercise of power and that the vast majority of women's nonparticipation in political power is a major factor in the vices and abuses of power that consume any given country on the African continent. Confronted with the failure and social and political decline of various powers, women have come together to reflect and to take man's hand in order to guide him in what could be an alternative way of life.

Their dynamic writing marks the birth of a new African novel, written this time in the feminine mode. It is characterized by the strength of their visionary outlook on African societies. In a burst of poetry and vision, strengthened by the oral traditions of their female ancestors who preserved the stories and poems of traditional Africa, *they see and tell us of the Africa of tomorrow.* Let's listen to them.

Notes

1. I have slightly modified the first quote from Dabla and eliminated the terms "simple" and "facile," which seemed to me to translate into more of a value judgment on testimonial literatures. Dabla was speaking about the male-authored African novel.

2. Béatrice Rangira Gallimore (1994) reaches similar conclusions in her study of the body in African literature.

Bibliography

Primary Sources

Ami, Gad. *Etrange héritage*. Lomé: Nouvelles Editions Africaines (NEA), 1985.

Bâ, Mariama. *Un chant écarlate*. Dakar: NEA, 1981. *Scarlet Song*. Translated by Dorothy Blair. London: Longman, 1986.

Bassek, Philomène. *La tache de sang*. Paris: L'Harmattan, 1990.

Beyala, Calixthe. *C'est le soleil qui m'a brûlée*. Paris: Stock, 1987. *The Sun Hath Looked Upon Me*. Trans. Marjolijn de Jager. Oxford and Portsmouth, NH: Heinemann, 1996.

———. *Tu t'appelleras Tanga*. Paris: Stock, 1988. *Your Name Shall be Tanga*. Trans. Marjolijn de Jager. Oxford and Portsmouth, NH: Heinemann, 1996.

———. *Seul le diable le savait*. Paris: L'Harmattan, 1990.

———. *Le petit prince de Belleville*. Paris: Albin Michel, 1992. *Loukoum, the Little Prince of Belleville*. Trans. Marjolijn de Jager. Oxford and Portsmouth, NH: Heinemann, 1995.

———. *Maman a un amant*. Paris: Albin Michel, 1993.

———. *Assèze l'Africaine*. Paris: Albin Michel, 1994.

Boni, Tanella. *Une vie de crabe*. Dakar: NEA, 1990.

Bugul, Ken. *Le Baobab fou*. Dakar: NEA, 1983. *The Abandoned Baobab: The Autobiography of a Senegalese Woman*. Trans. Marjolijn de Jager. New York: Lawrence Hill Books, 1991.

Liking, Werewere. *Elle sera de jaspe et de corail: Journal d'une misovire*. Paris: L'Harmattan, 1983.

Maïga Ka, Aminata. *La voie du salut suivi de le miroir de la vie*. Paris: Présence Africaine, 1985.

Mpoudi Ngolle, Evelyne. *Sous la cendre le feu*. Paris: L'Harmattan, 1990.

Rawiri, Ntyugwatondo. *G'amàrakano, au carrefour*. Paris: ABC, 1983.

———. *Fureurs et cris de femmes*. Paris: L'Harmattan, 1989.

Sow Fall, Aminata. *L'appel des arènes*. Dakar: NEA, 1982.

Tadjo, Véronique. *A vol d'oiseau*. Paris: Nathan, 1986.

———. *Le royaume aveugle*. Paris: L'Harmattan, 1990.

Warner-Vieyra, Myriam. *Juletane*. Paris: Présence Africaine, 1982. *Juletane*. Trans. Betty Wilson. London: Heinemann, 1987.

Secondary and Critical Sources

Abdulla, Adnan K. *Catharsis in Literature*. Bloomington: Indiana University Press, 1985.

Accad, Evelyne. "The Prostitute in Arab and North-African Fiction." In *The Image of the Prostitute in Modern Literature*. Ed. Pierre L. Horn and Mary Beth Pringle. New York: Frederick Ungar, 1984, 63–75.

———. "Rebellion, Maturity and the Social Context: Arab Women's Special Contribution to Literature." In *Arab Women, Old Boundaries New Frontiers*. Bloomington: Indiana University Press, 1993, 224–253.

Adiaffi, Anne-Marie. *Une vie hypothéquée*. Abidjan: NEA, 1984.

———. *La ligne brisée*. Abidjan: NEA, 1989.

Aries, Philippe. *L'enfant et la vie familiale sous l'Ancien Regime*. Paris: Plon, 1960.

Augustin, Barbara. *Mariages sans frontières*. Paris: Centurion, 1985.

Bâ, Mariama. *Une si longue lettre*. Dakar: NEA, 1980.

Badinter, Elisabeth. *L'amour en plus*. Paris: Flammarion, 1980.

———. *XY: De l'identité masculine*. Paris: Editions Odile Jacob, 1992.

Barthes, Roland. *Sade, Fourier, Loyola*. Paris: Editions du Seuil, 1971.

Bebey, Francis. *Le fils d'Agatha Moudio*. Yaoundé: Editions CLE, 1967.

Bekombo, Firmin. *J'attends toujours*. Paris: L'Harmattan, 1989.

Berrian, Brenda, and Art Broek. *Bibliography of African Women Writers and Journalists: Ancient Egypt–1984*. Washington, DC: Three Continents Press, 1985.

Beti, Mongo. *Les deux mères de Guillaume Ismaël Dzewatama, futur camionneur*. Paris: Buchet/Chastel, 1983.

———. *La revanche de Guillaume Ismaël Dzewatama*. Paris: Buchet/Chastel, 1984.

Bodé-Thomas, Modupé, trans. *So Long a Letter*. Oxford: Heinemann, 1989.

Bjornson, Richard. *The African Quest for Freedom and Identity: Cameroonian Writing and the National Experience*. Bloomington: Indiana University Press, 1991.

Borgomano, Madeleine. *Voix et visages de femmes dans les livres écrits par les femmes en Afrique francophone*. Abidjan: CEDA, 1989.

———. "Les femmes et l'écriture-parole." *Nouvelles Ecritures Féminines*, special issue, *Notre Librairie* 117 (1994): 87–94.

Boucoulon, Denis. *Mon mari est capable*. Paris: Flammarion, 1988.

Boyce Davies, Carole, and Anne Adams Graves, eds. *Ngambika: Studies of Women in African Literature*. Trenton, NJ: Africa World Press, 1986.

———. "Private Selves and Public Spaces: Autobiography and the African Woman Writer." In *Crisscrossing Boundaries*. Ed. Kenneth Harrow, Jonathan Ngate, and Clarisse Zimra. Washington, DC: Three Continents Press, 1991, 109–127.

Brière, Héloïse. "Le retour des mères dévorantes." *Nouvelles Ecritures Féminines*, special issue, *Notre Librairie* 117 (1994): 66–71.

Brown, Lloyd Wellesley. *Women Writers in Black Africa*. Westport, CT: Greenwood Press, 1981.

Butler, Judith. *Gender Trouble, Feminism and the Subversion of Identity*. New York: Routledge, 1990.

Chabal, Patrick. *Power in Africa*. New York: St. Martin's Press, 1992, 1994.

Chemain-Degrange, Arlette. *Emancipation féminine et roman africain*. Dakar: NEA, 1980.

Chesler, Phyllis. *Women and Madness*. Garden City, NY: Doubleday. 1972.

Chevrier, Jacques. *Littérature nègre*. Paris: Armand Colin, 1984.

Cixous, Hélène. "Le rire de la Méduse." *L'Arc* 61 (1975): 39–54.

Condé, Maryse. *Hérémakhonon*. Paris: Union Generale d'Editions, 1976.

Cornaton, Michel. *Pouvoir et sexualité dans le roman africain*. Paris: L'Harmattan, 1990.

Dabla, Séwanou. *Nouvelles écritures africaines: Romanciers de la seconde génération*. Paris: L'Harmattan, 1986.

d'Almeida, Irène Assiba. "The Concept of Choice in Mariama Bâ's Fiction." In *Ngambika: Studies of Women in African Literature*. Ed. Carole Boyce Davies and Anne Adams Graves. Trenton, NJ: Africa World Press, 1986, 161–171.

———. "Femme? Féministe? Misovire? Les romancières africaines." *Nouvelles Ecritures Féminines, 1. La Parole aux Femmes,* special issue, *Notre Librairie* 117 (1994a): 48–51.

———. *Francophone African Women Writers: Destroying the Emptiness of Silence*. Gainesville: University Press of Florida, 1994b.

Dadié, Bernard. *Un Nègre à Paris*. Paris: Présence Africaine, 1957.

de Beauvoir, Simone. *Le deuxième sexe*. 2 vols. Paris: Gallimard, 1949.

Dehon, Claire. *Le roman camerounais d'expression française*. Birmingham, AL: SUMMA, 1989.

Delaygue, Elisabeth. *Mestizo*. Paris: Présence Africaine, 1986.

Diallo, Nafissatou. *De Tilène au plateau: Une enfance dakaroise*. Dakar: NEA, 1975. *A Dakar Childhood*. Trans. Dorothy S. Blair. Harlow, Essex: Longman, 1982.

———. *Awa, la petite marchande*. Paris: EDICEF, 1981.

Dooh-Bunya, Lydie. *La brise du jour*. Yaoundé: CLE, 1977.

Douglas, Mary. *Purity and Danger*. Boston: Routledge and Kegan Paul, 1969.

Ekwensi, Cyprian. *Jagua Nana*. Trans. Françoise Balogun. London: Heinemann, 1961.

Fakoli, Oumbi. "Review of *Tu t'appelleras Tanga* by Calixthe Beyala." *Présence Africaine* 148 (1988): 147–148.

Fanon, Frantz. *Peau noire, masques blancs*. Paris: Editions de Seuil, 1952.

Farooq, Ghazi M., Ita I. Ekanem, and Sina Ojelade. "Family Size Preferences and Fertility in South-Western Nigeria." In *Sex Roles, Population, and Development in West Africa: Policy-Related Studies on Work and Demographic Issues*. Ed. Christine Oppong. Portsmouth, NH: Heinemann; London: J. Currey, 1987.

Felman, Shoshana. *La folie et la chose littéraire*. Paris: Seuil, 1978.

Felski, Rita. *Beyond Feminist Aesthetics*. Cambridge: Harvard University Press, 1989.

Fonkua, Romuald Blaise. "Ecritures romanesques féminines: L'art et la loi des pères." *Nouvelles Ecritures Féminines,* special issue, *Notre Librairie* 117 (April–June 1994): 112–125.

Frank, Katherine. "Feminist Criticism and the African Novel." *African Literature Today* 14 (1984): 34–48.

Gilbert, Sandra, and Susan Gubar. *The Madwoman in the Attic: The Woman Writer and the Nineteenth Century Literary Imagination*. New Haven: Yale University Press, 1970.

Groult, Benoite. *Ainsi soit-elle*. Paris: Grasset, 1975.

Gunew, Sneja. "Framing Marginality, Distinguishing the Textual Politics of the Marginal Voice." *Southern Review* 18 (July 1985): 143–155.

Guyonneau, Christine. "Francophone Women Writers from Subsaharan Africa." *Callaloo* 24 (1985): 453–478.

Hamon, Phillippe. "Pour un statut sémiologique depersonage." In *Poétique de récit*. Paris: Seuil, 1977, 114–180.

Hansen, Joseph, and Evelyn Reed, eds. *Cosmetics, Fashions, and the Exploitation of Women.* New York: Pathfinder Press, 1986.

Harrel-Bond, Barbara. "Interview with Mariama Bâ, Winner of the First Noma Award for Publishing in Africa." *African Publishing Record* 6 (1980): 209–214.

Harrow, Kenneth. *Thresholds of Change in African Literature: The Emergence of a Tradition.* Portsmouth, NH: Heinemann, 1994.

Horn, Pierre L., and Mary Beth Pringle. "Introduction." In *The Image of the Prostitute in Modern Literature.* Ed. Pierre L. Horn and Mary Beth Pringle. New York: Frederick Ungar, 1984, 1–7.

hooks, bell. *Feminist Theory from Margin to Center.* Boston: South End Press, 1984.

Hutcheon, Linda. "Colonialism and the Postcolonial Condition: Complexities Abounding." *PMLA* 110, no. 1 (January 1995): 7–16.

Irigaray, Luce. *Speculum de l'autre femme.* Paris: Livre de Poche, 1974.

———. *Ce sexe qui n'en est pas un.* Paris: Livre de Poche, 1977.

———. *Sexes et parentés.* Paris: Editions de Minuit, 1987.

———. *Je, tu, nous: Pour une culture de la différence.* Paris: Editions Grasset & Fasquelle, 1990.

Julien, Eileen. "Rape, Repression, and Narrative Form in *Le devoir de violence* and *La vie et demie.*" In *Rape and Representation.* Ed. Lynn A. Higgins and Brenda R. Silver. New York: Columbia University Press, 1991, 160–181.

Kane, Cheikh Hamidou. *L'aventure ambigüe.* Paris: Julliard, 1961.

Katz Kaminsky, Amy. "Women Writing About Prostitutes: Amalia Jamilis and Luisa Valenzuela." In *The Image of the Prostitute in Modern Literature.* Ed. Pierre L. Horn and Mary Beth Pringle. New York: Frederick Ungar, 1984, 119–131.

Kauffman, Linda. *Discourses of Desire.* Ithaca: Cornell University Press, 1986.

———. ed. *Gender and Theory.* New York: Basil Blackwell, 1989.

Krich, Aron. *The Prostitute in Literature.* New York: Ballantine, 1960.

Krishtain, Khalid. *The Prostitute in Progressive Literature.* London: Allison & Busby, 1982.

Kristeva, Julia. *Pouvoirs de l'horreur: Essai sur l'abjection.* Paris: Seuil, 1980. *Powers of Horror: An Essay on Abjection.* Trans. Leon S. Roudiez. New York: Columbia University Press, 1982.

Kuoh-Moukouri, Thérèse. *Rencontres essentielles.* Paris: Imprimerie Edgar, 1969; L'Harmattan, 1981.

———. *Les couples dominos (les noirs et les blancs face à l'amour).* Paris: Julliard, 1977; L'Harmattan, 1983.

Labou Tansi, Sony. *La vie et demie.* Paris: Seuil, 1979.

Lacrosil, Michèle. *Sapotille ou le serin d'argile.* Paris: Gallimard, 1960.

Lallemand, Suzanne. *L'apprentisage de la sexualité dans les contes d'Afrique de l'Ouest.* Paris: L'Harmattan, 1985.

Lambrech, Régine. "Three Black Women, Three Autobiographers." *Présence Africaine* 123 (Spring 1975): 136–143.

Laye, Camara. *L'enfant noir.* Paris: Plon, 1953.

———. *Le regard du roi.* Paris: Plon, 1954.

Lee, Sonia. *Les romancières du continent noir.* Paris: Hattier, 1994.

Liking, Werewere. *L'amour-cent-vies.* Paris: Editions Publisud, 1988.

Lionnet, Françoise. *Autobiographical Voices: Race, Gender, Self-Portraiture.* Ithaca, NY: Cornell University Press, 1989.

————. "Inscriptions of Exile: The Body's Knowledge and the Myth of Authenticity." *Callaloo* 15, no. 1 (Winter 1992): 30–40.

————. Postcolonial Representations: Women, Literature, Identity. Ithaca, NY: Cornell University Press, 1995.

Loba, Ake. *Kocoumbo, l'étudiant noir.* Paris: Flammarion, 1960.

Maïga Ka, Aminata. "Ramatoulaye, Aïssatou, Mireille, et . . . Mariama Bâ." *Notre Librairie* 81 (1985): 129–134.

————. *En votre nom et au mien.* Abidjan: NEA, 1989.

Makward, Edris. "Marriage, Tradition and Woman's Pursuit of Happiness in the Novels of Mariama Bâ." In *Ngambika.* Ed. Carole Boyce Davies and Anne Adams Graves. Trenton, NJ: Africa World Press, 1986, 271–281.

Medou Mvomo, Rémy. *Mon amour en noir et blanc.* Yaoundé: CLE, 1971.

Midiohouan, Thécla. "Des Antilles à l'Afrique: Myriam Warner-Vieyra." *Notre Librairie* 74 (1984): 39–43.

Miller, Nancy K., ed. *The Poetics of Gender.* New York: Columbia University Press, 1986.

————. *Subject to Change: Reading Feminist Writing.* New York: Columbia University Press, 1988.

Minh-ha, Trinh T. *Woman, Native, Other: Writing Postcoloniality and Feminism.* Bloomington: Indiana University Press, 1989.

Mohanty, Chandra Talpade, et al. *Third World Women and the Politics of Feminism.* Bloomington: Indiana University Press, 1991.

Mortimer, Mildred. *Journeys Through the French African Novel.* Portsmouth, NH: Heinemann, 1990.

Mouralis, Bernard. "Une parole autre: Aoua Keita, Mariama Bâ et Awa Thiam." *Nouvelles Ecritures Féminines,* special issue, *Notre Librairie* 117 (1994): 21–27.

Mudimbe, Valentin. *The Invention of Africa.* Bloomington: Indiana University Press, 1986.

Mudimbe-Boyi, Elisabeth. "The Poetics of Exile and Errancy: Ken Bugul's *Le baobab fou* and Simone Schwarz-Bart's *Ti-Jean l'Horizon.*" *Yale French Studies* 82, no. 2 (1993a): 196–212.

Mudimbe-Boyi, Elisabeth, ed. *Post-colonial Women's Writing,* special issue, *L'Esprit Créateur* 33, no . 2 (Summer 1993b).

Mudimbe-Boyi, Elisabeth. *Anglophone and Francophone Women's Writing,* special issue, *Callaloo* 16, no. 1 (Winter 1993c).

Nanga, Bernard. *Les chauves-souris.* Paris: Présence Africaine, 1980.

Ndao, Aliou. *Un bouquet d'épines pour elle.* Paris: Présence Africaine, 1988.

Nga Ngondo, Valentin. *Les puces.* Paris: ABC, 1984.

Ngandu Nkashama, Pius. "L'autobiographie chez les femmes africaines." *Notre Librairie* 117 (1994): 129–137.

Ngate, Jonathan. "Reading Warner-Vieyra's *Juletane.*" *Callaloo* 9, no. 4 (Fall 1986): 553–564.

Ngcobo, Lauretta. "African Motherhood—Myth and Reality." In *Criticism and Ideology: Second African Writers' Conference 1986.* Ed. Kirsten Holst Peterson. Uddevalla: Nordiska Africainstitutet, 1988.

Nwapa, Flora. *Women Are Different.* Trenton, NJ: Africa World Press, 1986.

————. *One Is Enough.* Engugu, Nigeria: Tana Press, 1981; Trenton, NJ: Africa World Press, 1992.

O' Callaghan, Evelyn. "Interior Schisms Dramatized: The Treatment of the 'Mad' Woman in the Work of Some Female Novelists." In *Out of the Kumbla.* Ed.

Carole Boyce Davies and Elaine Fido Savory. Trenton, NJ: Africa World Press, 1990, 89–109.

Ogundipe-Leslie, Molara. "Not Spinning on the Axis of Maleness." In *Sisterhood Is Global: The International Women's Movement Anthology.* Ed. Robin Morgan. New York: Anchor Books, 1984, 498–504.

———. "The Female Writer and Her Commitment." In *Women in African Literature Today.* Ed. Eldred D. Jones, Eustace Palmer, and Marjorie Jones. London: James Currey, 1987, 5–13.

Ombolo, Jean-Pierre. *Sexe et société en Afrique noire: L'anthropologie sexuelle: Essai analytique, critique et comparatif.* Paris: L'Harmattan, 1990.

Ouloguem, Yambo. *Le devoir de violence.* Paris: Seuil, 1968.

Oyono, Ferdinand. *Une vie de boy.* Paris: Julliard, 1956, 1970.

Pascoe, Peggy. "Race, Gender, and Intercultural Relations: The Case of Interracial Marriage." *Frontiers: A Journal of Women's Studies* 12, no. 1 (1991): 5–18.

p'Bitek, Okot. *Song of Lawino: A Lament.* Nairobi: East African Publishing, 1966.

Pinto, Jean-Marie. *Mémoires de' Emilienne.* Paris: L'Harmattan, 1991.

Pratt, Annis. *Archetypal Patterns in Women's Fiction.* Bloomington: Indiana University Press, 1981.

Propp, Vladimir. *La morphologie du conte.* Paris: Seuil, 1970.

Rabuzzi, Kathryn Allen. *Mother with Child: Transformations Through Childbirth.* Bloomington: Indiana University Press, 1994.

Rangira Gallimore, Béatrice. "Le corps: De l'aliénation à la réappropriation: Afrique noire francophone." *Nouvelles Ecritures Féminines, 1. La Parole aux Femmes,* special issue, *Notre Librairie* 117 (April–June 1994): 54–60.

Rawiri, Angèle. *Elonga.* Paris: Editions Africaines, 1980.

Sabbah, Fatna Aït. *La femme dans l'inconscient musulman.* Paris: Sycomore, 1981; rev. ed., Albin Michel, 1986.

Sahel, André-Patrick. "L'Afrique aux Africaines." *Actuel Développement* no. 40 (1981).

Schipper de Leeuw, Mineke. *Un blanc vu d'Afrique.* Yaoundé: CLE, 1973.

Schipper de Leeuw, Mineke, ed. *Unheard Words: Women and Literature in Africa, the Arab World, Asia, the Caribbean, and Latin America.* Trans. Barbara Potter Fasting. New York: Allison & Busby, 1985.

Schor, Naomi. *Breaking the Chain.* New York: Columbia University Press, 1986.

Schwarz-Bart, Simone. *Ti-Jean l'Horizon.* Paris: Seuil, 1979.

Sembène, Ousmane. *O pays, mon beau peuple!* Paris: Presses Pocket, 1957.

Smith, Sidonie. *A Poetics of Women's Autobiography: Marginality and the Fictions of Self-Representation.* Bloomington: Indiana University Press, 1987.

Smith, Sidonie, and Julia Watson, eds. *De/Colonizing the Subject.* Minneapolis: University of Minnesota Press, 1992.

Songue, Paulette. *Prostitution en Afrique; L'exemple de Yaoundé.* Paris: L'Harmattan, 1986.

Steady, Filomina Chioma. "African Feminism: A World View Perspective." In *Women in Africa and the Diaspora.* Ed. Rosalyn Terborg-Penn, Sharon Harley, and Andrea Benton Rushing. Washington, DC: Howard University Press, 1987, 3–24.

Stratton, Florence. "The Shallow Grave: Archetypes of Female Experience in African Fiction." *RAL* (Summer 1988): 142–169.

———. *Contemporary African Literature and the Politics of Gender.* New York: Routledge, 1994.

Tachi Ndagne, David. "Review of Calixthe Beyala's *C'est le soleil qui m'a brûlée.*" *Littérature Camerounaise 2,* special issue, *Notre Librairie* 100 (1990): 96–97.

Thiam, Awa. *La parole aux Négresses.* Paris: Denoël, 1978.

Ulmer, Gregory L. "The Discourse of the Imaginary." *Diacritics* 10 (1980): 61–75.

Wallace, Karen Smiley. "Woman and Identity: A Black Female Perspective." *Sage* 2, no. 1 (Spring 1985): 19–23.

Warner-Vieyra, Myriam. *Le quimboiseur l'avait dit.* Paris: Présence Africaine, 1979.

⸺. *Femmes échouées.* Paris: Présence Africaine, 1988.

Wilson, Elisabeth. "'Le voyage et l'espace clos': Island and Journey as Metaphor. Aspects of Woman's Experience in the Works of Francophone Women Novelists." In *Out of the Kumbla.* Ed. Carole Boyce Davies and Elaine Fido Savory. Trenton, NJ: Africa World Press, 1990, 49–57.

Wolf, Naomi. *The Beauty Myth: How Images of Beauty Are Used Against Women.* New York: William Morrow, 1991.

Weever, Jacqueline de. "Metaphors of Alienation: Madness, Malaise, and Solitude." In *Mythmaking and Metaphor in Black Women's Fiction.* New York: St. Martin's Press, 1991.

Yaou, Regina. *Lézou Marie ou les écueils de la vie.* Paris: NEA, 1982.

Zanga Tsogo, Delphine. *Vies de femmes.* Yaoundé: CLE, 1983.

Index

About the Book

Writings by Francophone African women have moved to the forefront of the literary stage in the 1990s as they have shifted from a literature of testimony and complaint to one of power. *Rebellious Women* reflects on this change and on its broad significance for African literature and society.

Cazenave examines the mechanisms of rebellion within a new generation of women authors who reject defeatist visions of a postcolonial Africa stricken with unsurmountable burdens and who propose an alternative vision. She details their focus on marginalized characters and their daring exploration of themes hitherto considered either trivial or taboo—mother-daughter relationships, the inscription of female desire, sexual ethics—and also analyzes the provocative language they use to create a new political novel.

Through its rich analysis of new female voices, *Rebellious Women* establishes the innovativeness and central position of women's writing in contemporary African literature.

Odile Cazenave is visiting associate professor at MIT and adjunct associate professor at the University of Tennessee, Knoxville. Most of her recent articles are on the new African diaspora in Paris and on literature of (im)migration.

ADX-7412